Journalism and the Pandemic

ALSO BY TONY SILVIA
AND FROM McFARLAND

Dyslexia and the Journalist: Battling a Silent Disability
(Tony Silvia *and* Suzanne Arena, 2021)

Robert Pierpoint: A Life at CBS News (2014)

*Fathers and Sons in Baseball Broadcasting:
The Carays, Brennamans, Bucks and Kalases* (2009)

*Baseball Over the Air: The National Pastime
on the Radio and in the Imagination* (2007)

Journalism and the Pandemic

Essays on Adaptation and Innovation

Edited by Tony Silvia

Foreword by Bill Whitaker

McFarland & Company, Inc., Publishers
Jefferson, North Carolina

ISBN (print) 978-1-4766-8746-9
ISBN (ebook) 978-1-4766-4677-0

LIBRARY OF CONGRESS AND BRITISH LIBRARY
CATALOGUING DATA ARE AVAILABLE

Library of Congress Control Number 2022035601

© 2022 Tony Silvia. All rights reserved

No part of this book may be reproduced or transmitted in any form or by any means, electronic or mechanical, including photocopying or recording, or by any information storage and retrieval system, without permission in writing from the publisher.

Front cover images: New Africa/metamorworks/Shutterstock

Printed in the United States of America

*McFarland & Company, Inc., Publishers
Box 611, Jefferson, North Carolina 28640
www.mcfarlandpub.com*

Table of Contents

Foreword
    BILL WHITAKER   vii

Introduction: A Collaborative Pandemic Project
    TONY SILVIA   1

Part I. Reporting a Pandemic

The Rapid Pace of Disruptive Change
    TONY SILVIA   7

Personal Perspectives from the Frontlines of News
    JANET K. KEELER   17

Covering Politics During the Pandemic: A Personal Journey
    LACRAI D. MITCHELL   32

Investigative Reporting: Assessing Covid's Lasting Impact
    MARK DOUGLAS IUSI   51

The Future of Collegiate Journalism in the Wake of Covid-19
    JENNIFER FLEMING *and* TERESA PUENTE   76

Community Journalism: The Pandemic as a Catalyst for Change
    BERNARDO H. MOTTA   88

Part II. Gaining Understanding

Coronavirus and the Bermuda Triangle of Public Health Reporting
    MARK JEROME WALTERS   103

Social Media and the Pandemic: Myths and Misinformation
    Tony Silvia *and* Casey Frechette   118

Part III. Charting a Course

Shifting Newsroom Economics: A Lasting Impact
    Elliott Wiser   137

Zooming the Pandemic: Developing New Technologies
    Casey Frechette   148

Diversity: Covid-19, George Floyd and Lessons Learned
    Lillian R. Dunlap   161

Ethical Reporting in the Pandemic and Beyond
    Deni Elliott *and* Andrea Chu   172

Teaching Journalism During (and After) the Pandemic
    Tony Silvia *and* Janet K. Keeler   189

Part IV. Revisiting News Practices Post-Pandemic: A Roundtable Discussion

"Journalism After the Pandemic" Roundtable   201

Suggestions for Further Reading   213
About the Contributors   217
Index   219

Foreword

Bill Whitaker

The second week of March, 2020, my *60 Minutes* colleagues and I were in San Diego shooting a story on the urgent efforts to develop a vaccine for the new coronavirus. Two weeks earlier the first death from Covid-19 had been reported outside Seattle, Washington. The following week a resident of Placer County, California had died of the virus, prompting Governor Gavin Newsom to declare a state of emergency. Dressed from head to toe in cleanroom suits, our team spent a day in a high-tech pharmaceutical lab interviewing scientists who were examining the gene sequencing data released by China in search of novel ways to fight this novel virus. The next day we headed to the University of Nebraska Medical Center's biocontainment unit, a facility for patients with the most dangerous contagious diseases, where doctors were studying treatments that might aid in recovery from Covid-19. We interviewed Carl Goldman, who had contracted the virus on a cruise ship and was now isolated in a room behind an impenetrable window, fed through a locker. We sent in a phone and spoke to him through the thick glass.

As we were about to interview the lead doctor at the unit, I received a call from my boss. He told me there was an outbreak at the *60 Minutes* offices in Manhattan, our home base where my producer and I had been working a week earlier. We were terrified–if the virus wasn't going to get us, the daggers from the eyes of the local freelance crew would. Worse, we'd been breathing for hours on the doctors and medical workers on whose lives all of our lives might depend. After querying us about the dates and length of time of any interactions with colleagues who had fallen ill, the doctor was satisfied we had not been exposed by our fleeting contact and agreed to carry on with the interview. That very day, the World Health Organization declared Covid-19 a pandemic. We raced home to New York, our flight a cacophony of menacing coughs, returning just before the city and soon the country would close down. And so began our years of living distantly and reporting remotely.

The pandemic is just the latest adversity to hit journalism, but our profession has been in crisis for decades. Local newspapers are going extinct, wiped out by digital transformation. Television news audiences have shrunk, and so have news budgets. The first thing cut was global news bureaus. Too often now we swoop into foreign locales to cover wars and disasters, but we provide our audiences far fewer stories of our common humanity. As a result, Americans get a skewed view of the world as a dangerous, dysfunctional place. Additionally, news consumers have turned en masse to social media, which can manipulate beliefs, reinforce biases, and fan fears. The truth is drowned out by a barrage of misinformation.

When honest, factual journalism does break through the din to reach the public, we've seen autocrats around the world come after the journalists themselves. Reporters have been assailed in Mexico, Syria, Iran, Afghanistan, the Philippines, and elsewhere. Many have lost their lives. This past spring the President of Belarus, Alexander Lukashenko, scrambled MiGs to force an Irish commercial jet to land so he could arrest one passenger—a journalist who had reported on the mass demonstrations protesting what truly had been a fraudulent election. Truth is like kryptonite to autocrats and criminals cloaked in power. Attacks on journalists have—like a virus—made it to America's shores and capitals: journalists have been assailed as purveyors of "fake news," as "enemies of the people." Freedom of the press is written into the *First* Amendment of the U.S. Constitution, it is fundamental to our system of government, but we've seen now that it is fragile in the United States, too.

The pandemic has amplified the many challenges facing journalism. The swift adoption of videoconferencing allowed us to keep reporting when travel shut down, but it prevents us from looking people in the eye and responding to a tear—from reading their body language, which can tip us off to follow up questions. Distance is no way to discover where the truth of a story lies. I'm concerned that the reduced cost of remote interviews will make these leaner practices permanent. But the most devastating aspect of the challenges facing journalism in the time of Covid-19 is that they have amplified the pandemic itself. Diminished and discredited, journalists have not been able to get people the facts they need to help save lives and halt the pandemic. During a deadly outbreak, credible information is more important than ever, but our ranks are fewer, and our stories are met with suspicion. It's critical that people understand the science of the vaccines manufactured in the laboratories we visited, but many are as likely to absorb disinformation and doubts manufactured at troll factories. When we are needed most, the journalistic corps is in a weakened state.

But we are *not* on the run. In the midst of a perfect superstorm, we have seen stellar investigative reporting on the pandemic, our politics, corruption in high places, racial reckoning, and the insurrection at the U.S. Capitol. *The Washington Post* and *The New York Times* under siege call to my mind Muhammad Ali on the ropes: heavyweight champions who have come out dealing forceful blows, refusing to succumb. Countless other newsrooms and independent reporters have not been bullied or bowed. Our profession has shone—and shown us the worth of the work the Constitution specifically tasked the press to do.

Photography by Eric Kerchner.

At this writing, my *60 Minutes* colleagues and I have resumed traveling for stories; some weeks I have been tested for the virus all seven days. Two weeks ago I was on a train to Washington, D.C., to conduct interviews on the state of our democracy following the wave of legislation across the country to change election laws and purge election officials. As the train pulled out of Penn Station in New York, I got a call from my wife informing me someone with whom I had been in close contact had tested positive for Covid-19. The interviews had to be called off; the crews were sent home. I have since tested negative, but nearly two years into the pandemic, this virus is still affecting how we work. *Journalism and the Pandemic: Essays on Adaptation and Innovation* puts a spotlight on the challenges to and resilience of our profession in these trying times. Professor Silvia and his fellow authors vibrantly map a way forward for political, investigative, community and collegiate journalism. They have created an essential volume for the moment, advancing this truth about our trade: the health of journalism is crucial to the fate of our public *and* our republic.

–Bill Whitaker, Correspondent
60 Minutes, New York City,
December 22, 2021

Introduction

A Collaborative Pandemic Project

TONY SILVIA

I didn't know it then, but the last time I taught a journalism class *would be* the last time. The course was Media Ethics at the University of South Florida in March 2020. That month brought a series of lasts and firsts: the last face-to-face classrooms for nearly a year and a half, the first time in most of our experiences that we would interact with students, colleagues, family, and friends entirely at a distance and entirely via a screen.

It was a "thing," as one of the contributors to this collection of essays quotes, a "thing" the dimensions of which none of us could fully comprehend. We could date the beginning but had no idea of its end. As of this writing, with the prevalence of new variants of the virus, we still don't.

It was the global pandemic. It had a name: Covid-19, a term so unfamiliar that I, for one, mispronounced it with a short "O" in the beginning: Cah-vid. From talking to friends, I doubt I was alone. Soon, though, it would consume our personal and professional lives. It modified our vocabulary. Terms like "essential workers," "long haulers," "mask mandates," "vaccine reluctance" became part of our everyday conversations.

The gap between those who teach journalism and those who "do" journalism narrowed. We were all just trying to figure it out, coping the best we could, pivoting here and adapting there. Overnight we all grappled with how to deliver our respective "content," as it's now familiarly called, to our "audiences," whether they be students, readers, listeners, or viewers. The changes and challenges we were forced to face as educators were faced by those in all professions. In journalism, however, our closest allies were the reporters, photographers, and editors at newspapers, websites, radio, and television stations. The natural affinity we always had for each other became a brother and sisterhood.

Covid-19 created an opportunity for some of us to sit back, reflect, connect, and contextualize how this deadly virus was impacting both our personal and professional lives. For some of us who are members of the professorate, it also brought offers from the universities to retire; my offer included incentives such as a paid research leave to work on any project I chose. The pandemic created similar incentives for some in newsrooms, although most were probably not as generous (or even as voluntary).

When I began thinking about what I would do with my last semester as professor of journalism and digital communication at USF's St. Petersburg, Florida, campus, there was no better project I could think of than a book about how the pandemic had both immediate and lasting impacts on the practices and processes of journalism in America. I envisioned its biggest impact as causing all of us—journalism educators and practitioners—to re-envision, re-imagine, and, ultimately, reinvent journalism for the first time since the advent of the Internet. Some might find that prospect daunting. I found it exhilarating.

My next thought was that if this book was worth writing, its unique value would result not from one voice—my own—but *many* voices. As you will read in the essays ahead, that theme—many voices—resonates throughout each one. The pandemic taught us, among many other important lessons, that none of us are alone, even when we feel most alone. Colleagues and family become our essential lifelines, even at a distance, maybe especially at a distance.

So this collaboration was born. One constant in the field of journalism is collaboration, made particularly difficult by the pandemic, and that is part of the story being collectively told in the pages before you. So, too, are the creativity, resourcefulness, perseverance, and dedication of so many in this honorable field of journalism—even at a time when journalism itself was often maligned and demeaned by those harboring political motives.

It's a story I couldn't honestly write myself in its entirety, and so I asked some of the finest, smartest people I know—including those from higher education and high up in the profession. They are all individuals I admire and respect—many old, but some new, friends. They each bring a unique perspective, and I believe that between us we have created a portrait of journalism during and (hopefully) after the pandemic.

The range and diversity of the expertise displayed by the authors in these pages is, in itself, a story. The authors include award-winning journalists, a news media manager, a *60 Minutes* staffer, a globally recognized leader in media ethics, and many of the best journalism educators in America. Just a glance at the topics—investigative reporting, political reporting, social media, technology, community journalism, newsroom diversity, student journalism, journalism curricula—reveals the enormity of what we have attempted here.

It would not have been possible without these inspired and inspiring individuals whom I am grateful to know as colleagues and friends. There is no perfect book and, among my others, there certainly is not one. But this one comes close. Our hope is that it is timely and timeless. It is a "collaborative pandemic project" and proceeds from the core value we share: that good journalism is made great by discussing, listening, and, most of all *hearing* others.

Now, as I've transitioned from professor to professor emeritus (something I joke is twice as important because my title has doubled in its number of words), without sentimentality but rightful recognition, I thank all of the contributors to this collection for the gift of their words. We often use the phrase "words matter," and they do. But they really resonate with power when they come from a place where truth, honesty, passion, and care reside—a place called journalism, which was important before, is during, and will be after the pandemic. The goal is that the thoughts and ideas you read here will go beyond these pages to create new conversations that are less about what journalism is than what it *can be*.

PART I
Reporting a Pandemic

The Rapid Pace of Disruptive Change

Tony Silvia

> "The fact that you can do sports from someone's living room, we can do breaking news and press conferences remotely, has just been, 'Wow, we are doing this'"
> —Sally Ramirez, Executive Producer,
> *The News with Shepard Smith*, CNBC

March 11, 2020. While no one has yet done a formal study, that date is burnt into our collective memory and consciousness. For decades into the future, those alive on that date will always remember where they were, whom they were with, and what they were doing. It will become a point of connection, of conversation, of darkness and of light. We will remember it in much the same way past generations recall November 22, 1963, and more recent ones commemorate September 11, 2001. Future students will study it. Scholars will analyze it. Experts from various fields will argue, agree, and disagree on when and where the second global pandemic since 1918 began. It's a moving target that may never be stopped or stilled, making a consensus on Covid-19's origins unlikely, if not impossible. Those are questions for science, but for journalists the questions on March 11, 2020, were much more fundamental: how would we gather, process, and report vital health information during a time when it appeared to us all that the world had stopped?

Journalists, historically, are adept at adapting to change, albeit sometimes with resistance and the skepticism ingrained in our field. It is difficult to comprehend that when Gutenberg invented the printing press, making mass dissemination of knowledge available to a broader audience than ever before in history, there may have been those scribes (and others) who resisted this quantum change in how knowledge would thenceforth be shared. We know there were and still are journalists who celebrate a bygone era of print journalism usurped by the Internet and its digital platforms for news distribution. Change is seldom easy, and it is not something most human beings (and journalists are, after all, human) seek, especially when it is disruptive. And Covid-19 was the ultimate disruption, for society as a whole and for American journalism as an institution. As Jill Geisler, who writes extensively about newsroom processes, leadership, and management, points out, change is uncomfortable because it makes us feel "temporarily incompetent."[1] It is difficult enough when we choose that change, but when it comes without warning or preparation, the intensity and pace of adaptation is necessitated, not chosen.

Stop the Presses

The concept of stopping the presses is a well-worn, overused trope in movies that dramatize the real-life, but rare, occasions when a story was so important that it literally caused newspaper publishers to shut down the printing press, awaiting that story for the paper's morning edition. Without that level of warning or a specific call to action (in this instance, non-action), beginning March 11, 2020, the presses and their contemporary equivalent, digital platforms, didn't stop, but they did face an unprecedented challenge. Journalists had a story of enormous dimensions and consequences to cover. The story was all around us. Ballparks and sports arenas were summarily closed. Concert halls were silent and Broadway was shuttered. The problem wasn't *getting* the story; it was getting *to* the story. The challenges facing journalists and the very institution of American journalism didn't begin that fateful day; however, they did rise to the surface of what was already a simmering pot of change and challenge.

The change involved a slow but steady decline in the number of journalists employed in what we used to refer to as traditional or "legacy" newsrooms. The dissolution of jobs in the field, driven by economics and rapidly evolving technology, began long before the global pandemic. However, it was the *rate* of change that created the challenge. Newsrooms, already depleted of reporters, editors, and photographers, now faced the reality that this space—this physical space where journalists collaborated, researched, and wrote their stories—would no longer be the fulcrum of the news gathering or reporting process. They were sent home, as were most Americans, from their jobs, but the irony became that, unlike news consumers, journalists were expected to *report* the story, not simply *observe* it. The question became how to do that when so many restrictions and limitations were in place, mandated by both health concerns and legal constraints.

Like many Americans, excepting frontline health care providers and public safety personnel, journalists retreated to their homes. Like most of us, they set up camp in the corners and crevices of their houses or apartments and settled in for what we all assumed was—and became—the long haul. It was a new kind of puzzle, the parts hardly carefully molded and refined, one that had to be assembled on the fly, using intuition and experience. It was harder for some journalists than others, just as the pandemic was harder on some Americans than others. But like most Americans who had faced and continue to face challenges in their own jobs, journalists were forced to face the burgeoning challenges that had been facing journalism for decades in a matter of days, if not hours.

Old Challenges, New Responses

One meme circulated early in the pandemic carried the headline "Zooms, Drones, and 'Live from My Closet': How the Pandemic Changed Journalism." It depicted a photographer, at a distance from his subjects (both masked and behind glass doors) attempting to capture their image.[2] In many ways, it's representative of how a Newmark Graduate School of Journalism study summarized the radical changes in newsgathering processes in the beginning and interim times of the pandemic. Its findings represent an early but prescient view of how methodology had to change and adapt in order to retain the ability to interview, report, and disseminate.

Among the findings (some of which will be elaborated upon in subsequent essays presented in this collection) was that longstanding, tried and true journalism traditions like face-to-face interviews, out of necessity, ceased. Knocking on doors and staking out sources was no longer possible, due to health concerns for both journalists and their subjects. That meant witnessing events firsthand, a mainstay of journalism since its inception, was now impossible. Much of journalism, due to lack of physical proximity to a story or newsroom budgetary constraints, has always been done at a distance. However, this was different. There was no longer an option to go to the location of a story, whether a meeting, a news conference, or a major development of an ongoing story. Evaluating sources face-to-face was a thing of the past. The visual element of the in-person interview—a staple of good journalism—was nonexistent.[3]

Instead, the Newmark study points out that reporters were forced to innovate. Across platforms, journalists began working from home, converting their kitchens, dining rooms, even closets, into newsrooms and studios. They either purchased or were given the technology to operate their own cameras, adjust what came to be known as a "ring" or a "zoom" light, and produce their own audio. In some ways, it was reversion to what in one medium, television news, had long been known as the "one-man band" (from the days before there were many women in newsrooms). In the process, the public saw the unfolding of the journalistic process in all its (little) glory and many of its warts. To paraphrase the Upton Sinclair novel *The Jungle*, the audience began to see how "the sausage is made." For better or worse, journalists were seen in their out-of-newsroom habitats. Like the public, reporters were stuck at home, and it might be argued that this created a new kind of bond between news disseminators and news audiences—an occurrence well-timed, given what has been shown by many studies to be a severe deficit in the public's belief in the credibility of legacy news organizations.

One quote, especially, is very revealing of this shift in approach from newsroom presentation to living room accommodation. "The fact that you can do sports from someone's living room, we can do breaking news and press conferences remotely, has just been, 'Wow, we are doing this,'" said Sally Ramirez, who was KHOU news director until the summer of 2020 when she became executive producer for *The News with Shepard Smith* on CNBC. "We've always said, 'Thank you for inviting us into your home through the screen.' For the first time, we're allowing people into our homes."[4]

One label we might apply to these on-the-fly innovations is the "pandemic paradigm response." It's surprising, and somewhat gratifying, to view how journalists not only learned new approaches to the Covid crisis but also had no choice but to enlist the public as a partner in the process. As the Newmark study concluded: "Photojournalists have taught subjects to shoot themselves, while news interviewers regularly grill sources on Zoom. Producers have tapped viewers' smartphone video to document breaking news and subjects' lives. And despite the physical distance that the virus has put between journalists, sources, and audiences, the news and news organizations are connecting with and being challenged by the public as never before."

What strengthened that connection was an online platform few outside of corporate settings had ever heard of pre-pandemic, let alone knew how to access. There is a cogent argument to be made that it became the new town square, the virtual village on the green. What had up until March 2020 been a modest, even diminutive, social media platform existing in the shadow of Skype now became a titan of communication, a lifeline for many in America and around the globe—and an indispensable tool for journalists.

Zoom, Well, Zoomed

Innovation nearly always springs from the desire to fulfill an unfulfilled need. Zoom is the perfect example, though its origins had nothing to do with the pandemic—its creator was simply trying to design a better platform on which to communicate with his long-distance girlfriend. The young man behind perhaps the most utilitarian social platform in history is Eric Yuan, now a billionaire, but a Chinese citizen denied a visa into the U.S. eight times. The confluence of the pandemic with the desire of people across the globe to communicate with family and friends during lockdown drove unprecedented traffic to Zoom. It became the go-to platform for human connection and, in the process, helped journalists who otherwise would have been stymied in their jobs. Overnight, websites arose that catered to journalists' need to learn how to connect with their communities, and articles synthesizing advice on how best to utilize it proliferated.[5]

The scope of Zoom's growth from the period immediately preceding the pandemic to the height of its use at the early stages of Covid isolation is stunning. The peak daily Zoom meeting participants in December of 2019 numbered approximately 10 million. By March 2020, which we generally accept as the start of pandemic recognition and response, that number rose to over 200 million users. By April 2020, it rose again to over 300 million.[6] Zoom's ascension on the global landscape could not have been better timed. The pandemic's spread accelerated one of journalism's biggest pre-pandemic challenges: job cuts and newsroom closings.

The Cuts Are Deep

In early May 2020, the Associated Press distributed a photo that's emblematic of the deep cuts and closures facing journalists. It depicted the statue of a newsboy on a bicycle delivering newspapers. It is not just a throwback to journalism's past; it's a recognition of its present and, at that time, what seemed to be its future. The newsboy wears a mask. The statue is outside the offices of the closed *Edmond Sun*. On Monday, May 4, 2020, the paper, located in Edmond, Oklahoma, published, in its "To Our Readers" column, an announcement that it would merge with *The Norman Transcript*. Subsequently that newspaper would provide its news coverage and the *Sun* was no more. The column cited the economic downturn as a result of the coronavirus.[7]

A study by the Poynter Institute conducted from March 2020 to March 2021 showed that during that period over 60 newsrooms closed nationwide.[8] In its own backyard of Florida, Poynter found the following:

The (Sarasota, Florida) Herald Tribune closed its printing plant, resulting in the loss of 95 jobs, 42 full-time and 53 part-time. *The Tribune* and two other Gannett newspapers will be printing at another Florida Gannett location.

Adams Publishing Group cut pay and hours for employees company-wide, Poynter learned. It owns 13 newsrooms in Florida.

The Tampa Bay Times, which Poynter owns, was eliminating 150 jobs as it closed its printing plant. The work was to be outsourced to the *Lakeland Ledger*, a Gannett newspaper. *The Times* announced that *Times* employees would take temporary pay cuts of 10 percent for up to six months. It's important to recall that this is only a snapshot of a single media market, but it reflects, by scale, the trend throughout America.

Between the reduction in the number of journalists, the increase in need for up-to-the-minute accurate information, and the necessity of reporting at arm's length, the pandemic created the perfect storm for a crisis in the news media's credibility with their audiences. It wasn't a new phenomenon, but Covid put journalists under the public's intense scrutiny day after day, hour by hour. It was, and is still, what a United Nations report called "an unprecedented news story for journalists."[9]

Responsibility and Credibility

The pandemic was a test of the news media's credibility, while at the same time reinforcing its responsibility. One of the earliest studies of public opinion regarding media coverage is revealing. First, a Pew research study showed that Americans early and at the height of the pandemic "followed COVID news very closely and think media are covering it very or somewhat well." Eighty-nine percent of Americans polled said they were following news about Covid-19 closely or very closely, with the majority, 51 percent, saying they watched very closely. Seventy percent of respondents felt the news media covered Covid well, with 30 percent replying "very well" and 40 percent "somewhat well."[10]

The troublesome aspect of this study comes from the finding that the majority (62 percent) believed that the news media exaggerated the risks from Covid-19. Even more troubling, about half of U.S. adults polled said they had seen at least some news about the pandemic that they believed was made up. The study also disclosed a generational divide, with older adults offering slightly more positive views of Covid-19 news coverage than younger adults.

It probably comes as no surprise, given America's political divide, that Pew also disclosed a similar divide in terms of how credible the news media's coverage was perceived to be. Specifically, Republicans gave the news media lower marks in their coverage of the Covid-19 pandemic than did Democrats. Those self-identifying as Republican also were found to be more likely than Democrats to express belief in false claims about Covid-19. The full report, based on research conducted from March 10 to March 16, 2020, is instructive not only in terms of the public's perception of how well journalists were doing their jobs during a crisis, but also of the factors influencing those perceptions—deeply ingrained beliefs that no doubt existed before the pandemic and more than likely will survive in its aftermath.

Left to Their Own Devices

Audiences in select countries overwhelmingly turned to the devices they already had at their fingertips once the pandemic forced them to stay at home. Seventy percent of those Internet users aged 16 to 64 reported that their device of choice was a smartphone or mobile phone. Forty-seven percent reported spending more time on their laptop computers, 33 percent on a desktop computer, 23 percent on a tablet, 32 percent on a smart TV or streaming device, 18 percent on a gaming console, 14 percent on a smart speaker, and 9 percent on a smart watch.[11] What do these statistics suggest?

To start with, not everyone was attuned to news about Covid to the same degree. Rather than looking outward toward information, many turned inward toward distraction. In other words, competing elements like streaming services—Netflix led other streaming services in seeing an incredible increase in its subscription base during the pandemic[12]—as well as digital music and Zoom meetings. At a certain point, it appears that even social media, which began strong at the pandemic's start, began to level off in usage, and the term "pandemic fatigue" came to be used as a descriptor for Americans tiring of hearing about or discussing Covid daily.

There's little wonder that journalism, which occupied such a central role in disseminating information regarding the pandemic initially, began to see a decrease in audience numbers. After an initial surge in news media viewing at the pandemic's start (for one example, the major cable networks CNN, MSNBC, and FOX News Channel saw record viewership[13]), Pew's research showed that all media, including social media, saw a steep drop in usage. During the eight-week period from mid–March to mid–May of 2020, all media experienced a falloff in audience from a high of 62 percent usage to a low of 18 percent.

Pew's research also demonstrated that Americans were overwhelmingly saying they needed a break from Covid-19 coverage. When asked, 71 percent of U.S. adults surveyed replied, "I need to take breaks from COVID-19 news." Only 28 percent stated a need to "stay tuned to COVID-19 news." For journalists on the front lines of Covid coverage, the findings are not encouraging. They reflect the audience's need to escape from the dissonance brought about by news coverage perceived, correctly or incorrectly, as overwhelmingly negative, presenting no solution in sight—or at least not in the immediate future.

Sustaining Effects

The pandemic's impact and lasting effects on journalists and the institution of journalism itself mirror the scars left on society and culture. Like the healthcare workers reporters covered, many journalists experienced severe stress and strain leading to physical and mental fatigue. Like the public at large, the audience for whom they write, journalists in large numbers reported their own mental health challenges. And, like their colleagues in the field and those in many others, at least part of those challenges resulted from the lack of collaboration due to isolation.

Post-pandemic, American journalism will hardly resemble journalism as we knew it, for better or worse, pre-pandemic. If or when we finally emerge from the spread of Covid-19, journalism, like society itself, will never look or be the same. For journalists, the lessons learned present a mandate to change the methodology of storytelling, not only from a technological standpoint but also from an experiential one. The evolution of journalism post-pandemic will require journalists to acquire new levels of specialization and expertise. The trend toward fewer journalists was already in progress, but the pandemic made it clear that those remaining must be versed in areas like medicine, science, and the environment. All are clear markers of priorities long overlooked in our reporting, but now a necessity.

Zoom may have been the salvation of the reporting process during the pandemic, but familiarity with and expertise in other areas of technology—data analysis and visualization, virtual reality, and animation—will be the future of journalism post-pandemic. These newer technologies were already poised to be central to journalism's mission of making important stories understandable and accessible to the public. The pandemic, as with so many disruptive changes in today's world, hastened the speed of that change.

In a field that has relied so heavily on personal connection and interaction, journalists are likely to continue "journalistic distancing" long after "social distancing" is in the past. At the heart of good reporting has always been getting up close and personal with our subjects and our colleagues. The pandemic taught that it might be a better way, but it's not the only way. Budget constraints, in existence decades before the pandemic, became validated when the pandemic proved to news executives that reporting could be accomplished at a distance at a much lower cost.

As a result, the trend toward journalists working alone is likely to continue post-pandemic, with all the value that comes from collaboration being collateral damage. At a time when the public questions journalists' ethics more than perhaps at any other time in our history, the essential role of "gatekeeping," the watchful eye of an editor or a series of editors on reporters' stories, may seem part of a storied past in newsrooms long ago. Beyond accuracy, editors help ensure fairness and balance—essentially the ethics of a story. One sustaining effect of journalists working alone is an increased reliance not on institutional ethics, but on the individual journalist's personal moral and ethical compass. Post-pandemic, journalists will be compelled to leverage the new world left by 2020-2021 with the enduring values of a field that will still demand accuracy, integrity, and credibility.

Enduring Values

Even in these challenging times—and journalists historically have seen few times in history more challenging—retaining the public's trust is an increasingly urgent mandate. Trust doesn't just happen, but—if the early part of the 21st century with its shifting media landscape teaches us anything—must begin with journalists' commitment, sincerity, reliability, consistency and integrity. Facts, while always primary in reporting and editing, take on heightened importance during a global pandemic.

The need to put all the elements of good journalism to work were severely tested during the first phase of the pandemic's roughly fourteen-month duration, beginning in March of 2020 and peaking throughout the summer and fall of that year and into early 2021. The public demanded—and deserved—stories that brought not only information, but context. They sought narratives that helped navigate what had been theretofore an unknown virus—one that killed hundreds of thousands and left many more gravely ill, some with prolonged, even lifetime, afflictions.

Journalism at its best is a delicate balance, a partnership between the journalist and her/his audience. Its fulcrum is credibility. While the news media may have "zoomed the pandemic," using new methods of disseminating information, the delivery system will always matter less than the content.

Now battle tested, journalists who covered this pandemic may one day, somewhat like those who cover war, gather to discuss their common experiences, sharing their stress and trauma. They may stand as a breed apart, similar to those correspondents who reported from the battlefield. They may even become known as "pandemic journalists," a "band of brothers" (and sisters) who were there at the epicenter of a plague. They could serve as a resource for those reporters and editors who were too young to experience what will hopefully go down in history as a once in a lifetime event. The personal journeys of those journalists on the frontline of covering Covid are only now beginning to be told, and they are as much a part of the history of this turbulent time as the pandemic itself.

Notes

1. Jill Geisler, *Work Happy: What Great Bosses Know* (New York, Center Street, 2014).
2. Hiriam Alejandro Duran, photo published in "Zoom, Drones, and 'Live from My Living Room': How the Pandemic Changed Journalism," 2020, http://pandemicreporting.journalism.cuny.edu/.
3. Newmark Graduate School of Journalism, "How the Pandemic Changed Journalism," 2021, http://pandemicreporting.journalism.cuny.edu/.
4. Newmark School, "Broadcasting from Home, Interviewing by Zoom," 2021, http://pandemicreporting.journalism.cuny.edu/broadcasting-from-home-interviewing-by-zoom/.
5. Max Resnick, "A Journalist's Guide to Using Zoom for Community Engagement," May 15, 2020, https://medium.com/cortico/a-journalists-guide-to-using-zoom-for-community-engagement-283c15cd91b7.
6. Natalie Sherman, "Zoom Sees Sales Boom Amid Pandemic," BBC News, June 2, 2020, https://www.bbc.com/news/business-52884782.
7. Sue Ogrocki, May 4, 2020; photograph republished at https://www.poynter.org/business-work/2021/here-are-the-newsroom-layoffs-furloughs-and-closures-caused-by-the-coronavirus/.
8. Kristen Hare, "Newsroom Layoffs, Furloughs, and Closures That Happened During the Coronavirus Epidemic," May 28, 2021, https://www.poynter.org/business-work/2021/here-are-the-newsroom-layoffs-furloughs-and-closures-caused-by-the-coronavirus/.
9. UNRIC Brussels, "COVID-19: An Unprecedented News Story for Journalists," United Nations, 2020, https://www.un.org/en/coronavirus/covid-19-journalists-biggest-story-their-lifetime.
10. Amy Mitchell and J. Baxter Oliphant, "Americans Immersed in COVID-19 News: Most Think Media Are Doing Fairly Well Covering It," March 18, 2020, https://www.journalism.org/2020/03/18/americans-immersed-in-covid-19-news-most-think-media-are-doing-fairly-well-covering-it/. Subsequent references to the Pew research are from this article.
11. Damian Radcliffe, "Covid-19's Impact on the Media," October 14, 2020, https://whatsnewinpublishing.com/covid-19s-impact-on-the-media-in-10-charts/.
12. R.T. Watson, "World-Wide Streaming Subscriptions Pass One Billion During Pandemic," *Wall Street Journal*, March 18, 2021, https://www.wsj.com/articles/worldwide-streaming-subscriptions-pass-one-billion-during-pandemic-11616079600.
13. Ted Johnson, "Cable News Networks See Big Gains in Viewership During Tumultuous 2020," *Deadline*, December 24, 2020, https://deadline.com/2020/12/ratings-cable-news-networks-2020-1234660751/.

Personal Perspectives from the Frontlines of News

Janet K. Keeler

> "Remind yourself that the trauma journalists experience is outweighed by the good work that you do"
> —Al Tompkins, the Poynter Institute for Media Studies

Journalists are used to change. Career reinvention is part of the job description, along with the time-tested ability to pivot from a story about a teenaged Good Samaritan in the morning to coverage of a toxic water spill in the afternoon. In the 1980s, technology transformed the industry dramatically after the first computers made their way into newsrooms. The rise of the Internet and expansion of cable television created the 24/7 news cycle in the 1990s that exploded in the new millennium. That meant more duties for "backpack journalists," who reported, wrote stories, took photos, published their work directly to the web and even marketed it via social media. Industry jobs began to dry up and layoffs started, as digital delivery put pressure on the business model of the legacy media. There were nearly 30,000 fewer newspaper jobs in 2019 than there had been in 2008.[1] Algorithms and search engine optimization (SEO) became part of the journalist's lexicon. The thrill of getting a story "above the fold on 1A" began to lose cachet. A story trending online became the gold standard.

Then along came 2020, and whatever challenges and changes had come before for journalists were dwarfed by the coronavirus pandemic. The fundamental ways of newsgathering were altered as people worldwide, including journalists, sequestered themselves either by choice or by government orders to slow the spread of the virus. Noisy, busy newsrooms were shuttered and journalists were sent home, where they would remain for more than a year, some perhaps forever. Government meetings were held via virtual conferencing platforms like Zoom. Face coverings were as ubiquitous as the skinny reporter's notebook.

Covering the pandemic became a personal story, as journalists worried not only about their own health, but also that of their friends, partners, children, siblings, parents and grandparents. In the early days of the pandemic, several high-profile TV news show hosts cried or teared up during interviews with Covid-19 survivors and sufferers, and medical professionals on the front lines. Some broke down when reporting deaths of colleagues. The days of journalists "sucking it up and moving on" appeared to be over.[2]

In the Moment, Journalists React

Eight journalists from around the country were interviewed, mostly via email, for this essay. They were asked to respond to questions about how the pandemic had affected the way they covered stories, what they did to compensate for that, and the role technology played, as well as to share their feelings about returning to physical newsrooms and their challenges during quarantine. They relayed anecdotes about working from home, along with what they learned about themselves and the craft of journalism. In general, they felt that in the most trying time of their careers, the news was needed more than ever. That is what kept them going amid fears of getting sick, ongoing isolation and continual criticism of the press from the president of the United States, other politicians and citizens.

Their stories are woven with news accounts about other journalists' experiences. Prominent are the reactions of journalists of color who dealt with covering the pandemic while also writing and following news about the racial justice protests following the killing of George Floyd in May 2020. For them, both stories were personal.

Bolstering journalists' perspectives are several 2020 surveys that took the pulse of their attitudes about the profession and their place in it. Among the surveys was one from the International Center for Journalists. It found that nearly three-quarters of respondents were concerned about the psychological toll the pandemic was taking on them. That this was even being talked about was a remarkable sign of progress. Journalism, unlike the medical and public safety professions, has never been a place that attended much to the mental health of the people who produced news reports daily. There were a number of stories in industry publications suggesting the ways in which journalists could take care of themselves.

Al Tompkins, a veteran broadcast journalist and senior fellow at the Poynter Institute in St. Petersburg, Florida, and his wife, the Rev. Sidney Tompkins, a licensed psychologist, co-produced *Managing Newsroom Stress and Trauma*. The video was born in response to the many stressed-out journalists who had contacted him for advice.

One of their suggestions was, "Remind yourself that the trauma journalists experience is outweighed by the good work that you do."[3] The following interviews show that journalists are doing just that, but that still, there's a toll and ongoing worry for the future.

On the Streets of San Francisco

For nearly 20 years, journalist Kevin Fagan has moved among the street people of San Francisco, collecting details of their lives to bring to readers. The *San Francisco Chronicle* enterprise reporter is convinced that he contracted Covid-19 in February 2020 while standing close to his sources in the homeless camps, shaking hands and giving an occasional hug. Without widely available testing, his infection wasn't documented, and yet he is sure he had it. At that time, he was writing stories on a mysterious virus rippling through the city and frightening unhoused people, one of the city's most vulnerable populations.

"I'd been sick several times before from doing such things, including contracting encephalitis and nearly dying a few years ago. And getting mauled by homeless dogs. All part of the job. But not fun," he said.

But in 2020 things were different, and it wasn't just a single West Coast reporter alarmed by the health risks of reporting as usual. The bedrock newsgathering techniques of journalists across the country and the world were about to change, putting the in-person interview mostly on hold. And when interviews were conducted in person, questions were asked through masks and answered the same way, hampering hearing and observation. A cry was muffled and a smile indiscernible. The socially distanced interview was a poor substitute for having a cup of coffee with the police chief or sitting on a curb interviewing a woman whose worldly possessions were piled behind her in a grocery cart. *Personal observation* has been an integral part of reporting since the beginning days of journalism and was always valued as the best way to weave detail into a story. Yet, the journalism show went on, with technology becoming the savior of reporting. There were many reporters who embraced the new reality and expected some of the changes to stick, mostly interviews on video conferencing platforms and continued work from home. Fagan joined a chorus of other big-city reporters who rejoiced at the elimination of lengthy commutes. "I hate what the pandemic has done to my craft, with one exception—the elimination of my usual round-trip commute of two-plus hours. That is a good thing."

Colleen Wright, an education reporter at the *Miami Herald* at the time of these interviews, but who jumped to the *Tampa Bay Times* in summer 2021, joined Fagan's dance on the grave of wasteful commute time. She was in no hurry to get back to rush-hour drives in Miami. Her job was made easier during the pandemic because all Miami-Dade County Public School meetings were live-streamed on the district's website. This made them available not only to media but also to parents and community members who might not otherwise be able to participate in the middle of the day. The pandemic created opportunity for more participation, and she said the virtual platform shielded her from rude comments that officials made to her face about coverage of the schools. She didn't miss the newsroom as a place to report and write, but her life outside work came to a standstill, and that was difficult. Wright's situation exemplified how the concern by journalists *for journalism* spread beyond changes in reporting techniques; some of it was about their own mental health.

Physical Protection and Mental Health

That same 2020 survey of journalists worldwide by the International Center for Journalists (ICFJ) found that more than 70 percent of respondents ranked the psychological toll of the pandemic as their biggest challenge. They were worried not only about the ways in which their jobs had changed, including their beds being transformed into workstations and video conferencing interviews replacing face-to-face interactions, but also about their jobs and their safety while doing their jobs. In the ICFJ survey, 30 percent of respondents said their employers had not supplied any personal protective gear, such as masks, for field reporting.[4] This became apparent in photographs of the detainment of journalists across the country as protests collided with pandemic.

Tampa, Florida, police detained *Tampa Bay Times* reporter Divya Kumar in June 2020 while she was covering a racial justice protest. She was wearing a face covering and her press badge on a lanyard around her neck. By the time a photo of her was taken with the zip ties on her hands being removed, the mask had slipped below her nose, alleviating whatever protection it may have afforded against the virus. She wore no other protective gear, such as a larger face shield, helmet or a vest that would have identified her in a more prominent way as press. After the incident, she tweeted, "I'm ok and grateful the experience was quick. Don't want this to distract from more important story we should be talking about, but reporters need to be able to be there to cover it." Another *Tampa Bay Times* reporter, Jay Cridlin, was detained the same night in St. Petersburg, on the other side of Tampa Bay. The police and sheriff department leaders there apologized. In Tampa, police said *Times* journalists got too close to "problem areas."[5]

The Big Story vs. Economic Pressure

Divya Kumar's tweet is emblematic of the strong belief in journalists' right to cover major news events, especially when they are happening in public places. However, it doesn't address the widespread lack of training in how to cover a potentially dangerous event.

It is typical at most media outlets, save for maybe the nation's largest, and newspapers especially, that all reporters are expected to be able to cover anything, especially when it comes to breaking news. Kumar was the *Tampa Bay Times'* higher education reporter at the time of her detainment covering the protests. Cridlin was the newspaper's music critic.

Across the country, there were more than 130 journalists detained, arrested, even injured, while covering the protests.[6] That the protests happened during the early months of the pandemic made the need for personal protective gear even more crucial, but it also put journalists in an awkward and unwanted position. While they wanted to identify themselves, they didn't want to stick out and perhaps look aggressive in full riot gear. And for photographers already carrying lots of equipment, the additional protection could make it even more difficult to move around.

The pandemic put more pressure on an already teetering industry, and the layoffs that had been part of the media landscape for more than two decades continued through the year. For most outlets, there wasn't money in the budgets for expensive protective gear beyond face coverings. Hundreds of journalism jobs were lost because of falling revenue related to the coronavirus, including positions at BuzzFeed and Huffington Post. That was particularly troublesome because digital publications had been considered immune from the financial problems of legacy media. A whopping 89 percent of respondents in the ICFJ survey said that their news organization had "enacted at least one COVID-19 related austerity measure (including job losses, salary cuts and outlet closures)."[7] At Gannett, the nation's largest newspaper chain, 500 staffers took buyouts, and throughout the country, 55 news outlets ceased publishing during the pandemic.[8] Combine that gloomy scenario with the challenges of going into crowds to cover racial justice protests sparked by the killing of George Floyd, a volatile presidential campaign, and the subsequent ouster of

President Donald Trump—and add widespread misinformation on social media by citizen users and politicians about the virus, and the pressure cooker boiled over for many journalists, the survey revealed.

Focus on Racial Inequities

For journalists of color, the pandemic, paired with protest coverage, ripped the Band-Aid off the wounds of racial inequities in the industry, as discussed in Lillian R. Dunlap's excellent essay later in this collection. While journalists are required to and do put their own beliefs on the shelf while covering stories, the protests became personal for African American journalists who had faced the same discrimination that was the focus of the protests. The code-switching they mastered at work created a false narrative that the newsroom was one for all and all for one. Profiling in stores and unwarranted stops by police were part of their experiences outside of work and even on the job. Journalist Isabel Wilkerson, winner of a Pulitzer Prize and author of the acclaimed book *Caste: The Origins of Our Discontents*, said in several 2020 interviews that she had her press credentials questioned when she was covering a story for the *New York Times*, where she was the Chicago bureau chief. She was accused of masquerading as a reporter.[9] In a June 2020 interview with Judy Woodruff of PBS's *NewsHour*, Dorothy Tucker, president of the National Association of Black Journalists, summed up the reality for African American journalists. Weekends and nights were given over to covering the protests and then falling into bed exhausted physically and emotionally for just a few hours of sleep. "But, on the other side of the brain, I'm thinking of my 28-year-old son, who was traveling from Atlanta to Chicago driving, and praying the entire time that he arrives home safely, that he doesn't get stopped by a police officer, that something doesn't happen to him when he stops at a rest stop," she said.[10]

It is unknown if being in a full-throttle, pre–Covid newsroom with colleagues would have opened up conversations that could have been a salve for the wounds of inequity or filled the gaps in understanding for White journalists. Journalists like to think of themselves as a tolerant bunch, but the experiences of journalists of color don't necessarily support that premise. It is not usually the workhorse journalists themselves that create the culture of a news organization, which is often set by location, history, tradition and upper-level management. Newsrooms in general are not diverse places, despite the professed desire to be just that. According to a 2018 Pew Research Center study, American newsrooms are 77 percent White and 61 percent male.[11] There are indications that the demographics are changing in the younger ranks, but those aren't generally the people making newsroom policy.

In an NPR interview with *All Things Considered* host Ari Shapiro, three African American journalists weighed in on the racial reckoning occurring in U.S. newsrooms. Their comments made clear that what came to light after the protests for racial justice was not new. Racism was a longtime reality for them and their colleagues of color, but a revelation for many White journalists. Tucker of NABJ, along with Astead W. Herndon, national political reporter at the *New York Times,* and Keith Woods, NPR's diversity officer, talked of their experiences being pigeonholed in beats that covered race. This was similar to the 1970s, when more women began to cover sports. Their beats? Women's sports. On *All Things Considered,* the trio discussed the exhaustion of journalists of color mixed with their determination to excel at their jobs while dealing with racism in and out of the newsroom. "Nobody's going to give up because we also recognize that this is a time where our voices are important. You know, we will survive this. But it's difficult," said Tucker.[12] Their comments indicated that being in the newsroom rather than working in isolation would probably not have changed anything on a large scale or even personally.

Technology to the Rescue

While it may not seem like newsroom discrimination—or maybe even worse, colleague and management ignorance and indifference—had a direct effect on pandemic reporting challenges, it did set the stage for the most difficult year to be a journalist in recent memory. Certainly, technology saved the saved the day in a way it couldn't have even 20 years before, but loneliness and alienation took root for some. When newsrooms were shuttered in March 2020, reporters were sent home to carry out their mission of covering the news. Laptops and smartphones were already part of their reporting tools, and those who weren't using video conferencing platforms would soon be adopting them. Zoom became the go-to platform for video interviews. The company's stock value soared to gain more than 800 percent in the first months of the pandemic,[13] and what was a noun quickly became a verb and adjective. Do you want to Zoom? How about a Zoom interview? Besides journalists using Zoom for interviewing, it became the ubiquitous and safe platform for family reunions, weddings, church services, birthday parties and conferences.

Both Laura Reiley of the *Washington Post* and Eric Deggans of National Public Radio gave credit to the rise of computer-assisted video conferencing for their ability to take part in panel discussions or accept speaking engagements anywhere in the world. A veteran newspaper reporter and arts critic, Deggans became NPR's first TV critic in 2013. He said that virtual conferences enabled him to connect with industry sources easier than when someone had to pay to fly him to "Austin or Los Angeles or New York." Those connections were beneficial later on, he noted. Reiley, who is the first "business of food" reporter at the *Post*, also saw virtual engagements as a positive result of the pandemic and as one she expected would continue. "Zoom-ish platforms have allowed people all over the planet to easily be in the same conversation," she said. "That's important when talking about food systems, which are so interconnected." In December 2020, Reiley moderated a discussion for the conference "Resetting the Food System from Farm to Fork" with panelists from Belgium, Uganda and New York. And if a dog was barking in the background? That, she said, was the new normal. So was doing an interview after a run with her hair pulled back. "There are no weekday or weekends, days or nights. I'll get texts from a source on Sunday morning at 10 a.m., so that's when I'll do the reporting." She suspected that video conferencing platforms will save money for media organizations post–Covid because "the bar will be set much higher for when it's 'necessary' to travel for a project."

Getting Access for Sports and More

Press access became an issue during the pandemic in order to maintain social distancing, and perhaps that was nowhere more painful than at the nation's sports venues. Sports journalists have always enjoyed the perks of watching the action live from good seats. The press boxes of stadiums are crowded places, with reporters sometimes sitting so close they can touch elbows. When collegiate and pro sports tentatively returned in summer 2020 with shortened schedules, sports reporters found themselves watching games on TV or via live stream. As some sports corralled their athletes in bubbles, sport journalists were shut out and relegated to broadcasting games from their living rooms, watching the action streamed live on their computers. Print reporters covered the action the same way. While this might continue as a cost-saving measure for their publications, falling broadcast viewership could prevent broadcast media from doing this. According to Sports Media Watch, viewership was down for the Stanley Cup Final (-61 percent), U.S. Open golf finals (-56 percent), NBA Finals (-49 percent), U.S. Open tennis finals (-42 percent) and college football season (-30 percent). Falling viewership may hasten the demise of the globetrotting sports journalist, but what might be more likely, Stefan Hall wrote, is that the sports industry will move more quickly to direct-to-consumer streaming and away from the for-pay cable model.[14]

Sports reporters who were able to attend in person were denied entry into locker rooms, the traditional location to interview athletes after the games. The televised post-game press conferences with coaches and players took on a bizarre atmosphere, as reporters were heard and not seen when their questions were asked via an audio connection. Sometimes that worked and sometimes it didn't, notably when the connection was bad or the questions were unintelligible. Matt Hanifan wrote that the pent-up demand for a return to sporting fun by fans was expected to be the same among sportswriters when some form of normal returned after vaccinations.[15] Hanifan was writing in the Reynolds Sandbox, a digital storytelling platform that showcases the work of journalism students at the University of Nevada, Reno. Sportswriters might be as eager as fans to get back to the stadium, but it is likely that locker room interviews and easy access to players and coaches will be a thing of the past. Virtual interviews fit schedules better and allow sports management to control dissemination of information or decline interviews altogether.

The pandemic created both access and travel issues for veteran journalist Anita Kumar, who was one of the historic cadre of female journalists covering the White House during the Trump administration. She continued as part of the White House press corps through the transition to President Joe Biden, switching from the McClatchy news service to write for Politico. (In August 2021, Kumar was named Politico's first senior editor for standards and ethics.) Pre-pandemic, Kumar regularly traveled with the president on Air Force One or flew separately to cover events, one of her favorite parts of the job. Her last trip before the pandemic was Trump's visit to India in late February 2020. On the eve of the one-year-anniversary of the national lockdowns she said, "It's hard to believe it was only a year ago that I was in the world's largest cricket stadium with Donald Trump, [Indian prime minister] Narendra Modi and 110,000 maskless Indians and we were not worried about coronavirus." It was on the return flight that the reporters got a conference call from the director of the National Center for Immunization and Respiratory Diseases telling them, "Life was soon about to change because of something called coronavirus," she said.

After that trip, Kumar flew a few more times on Air Force One but didn't go to the White House for months. Because some staffers in the White House wore masks and others didn't, Kumar was extra cautious and wore an N95 mask with a cloth face covering over that. She and other masked journalists were encouraged to gather outside the briefing room, but with no chairs or electricity it was difficult to work. Her reporting techniques were different for covering the beginning of Trump's tenure compared to Biden's, which began January 2021. To get to know a president's staff, former aides, outside allies and advocates, she would normally have met people for coffee, lunch or a drink. She did that when Trump won the presidency in 2016 but had to change strategies in 2020, using phone calls and emails as her primary sources of introductory communication. That was not as effective as the in-person meeting, and she was eager to get back to that practice. However, many journalists agreed that while they longed for face-to-face contact with sources, Covid has proven they can "do our jobs from anywhere," she said.

The Beehive Goes Silent

The newsroom has long been the beating heart of journalism and a place of legendary tales of quirky but dedicated journalists. It's a beehive of activity, though much quieter since clickety-clackety typewriters gave way to computers more than 40 years ago. Those four decades are equal to several generations of reporters, and the longing for the creative chaos of the newsroom was not missed as much by millennial journalists who have no clue what a pica pole is. (And for those who don't know, a pica pole—sometimes called a line gauge—is a flexible stainless-steel ruler that was indispensable to anyone who designed newspaper pages prior to computers. A pica is a typographic unit of measure; six picas to an inch.) They've filed stories and photos from their laptops and smartphones since their careers began. Most newsrooms have just a few private offices, and reporters along with editors are jammed together in pods or closely placed desks. The physical design of the newsroom was one reason that publishers and owners were reticent to call people back. Another might have been the realization that the traditional newsroom run by the editor who is counting heads every morning Monday through Friday is as outdated as the landline.

Neal Rubin has been a columnist at the *Detroit News* for 20 years and a journalist for another 15, writing big-hearted opinion pieces backed by his unfailing sense of humor. He was sure that his "micro-manager" editor and publisher was being driven "berserk" by everyone working remotely and still getting the job done. He wanted to return to the newsroom, even the rented quarters that the *News* moved to after its historic building was vacated in 2014. "I miss the conversations and punch lines, and the times I come up with a germ of an idea and ask someone I trust, 'Is this anything?'" It is likely that most journalists would agree with Rubin's assessment, because idea generation in a newsroom is often a team sport. And the democratic nature of the place dictates that the opinion of the person on the right is just as worthy as the person on the left, even if the person on the right is the executive editor and the other is an intern. So journalists like the newsroom in general, but not needing or wanting to go there everyday is a concept that may remain after the pandemic subsides. There are a multitude of places to gather for an idea session, including coffee shops and even parks on good weather days. Virtual meetings will remain an option for those who live miles and hours apart.

Ryan Callihan, the Manatee County reporter for the *Bradenton Herald* in Florida, graduated from college in 2017. While fairly new to the profession, he sounded like a decades-long veteran when discussing how his reporting was hampered during the pandemic, particularly the ways in which he communicated with sources. Changes were coming. Before the pandemic, he was hesitant to give his cell phone number to sources or to connect with them on theirs, opting for office numbers. "Working from home brought me closer to my sources … now I find myself calling or texting my sources at all hours of the day. They're way more accessible than ever before." He expected to maintain the improved communication with key sources after the pandemic. As for internal communication, the journalists at the *Bradenton Herald* (like many news staffs) used Slack, the channel-based messaging platform. Slack was the rebirth of instant messaging but with many more capabilities. It's adequate, Callihan said, but didn't fully replace the in-person communication in the communal newsroom.

Photographers on the Defensive

Another aspect of pre–Covid journalism that Ryan Callihan missed was going on assignments with a photographer. The reporter-photographer team often creates a better report because both journalists know the purpose of the story during newsgathering. If each goes on the story separately, the reporter must create a detailed assignment, which sometimes falls short. Ask any photographer. The pandemic affected the ability of press photographers to cover stories because they didn't want to be exposed to the virus by spending excessive time indoors with subjects. Consequently, there were a lot of photos taken outside with telephoto lenses so that photographers could keep safe distance from subjects. Photojournalists such as Joe Burbank of the *Orlando Sentinel* in Florida had to establish their own parameters with newsroom management about what they would be willing to cover, in order to protect their health. He was okay with photographing at institutions that strictly enforced capacity regulations, mask mandates and other sanitization protocol. "I was not willing to photograph indoors at private residences, apartments or any place where crowds typically congregated (i.e., shopping malls, department stores)," he said. Conversely, many organizations, including schools, hospitals and assisted living facilities, did not allow media inside in order to keep students, patients, residents and staff safe. In the midst of a global medical crisis, writers and photographers were naturally drawn to chronicling the human story. While there were some photographers who had luck getting into medical facilities, many more were shut out, sometimes maliciously.

Unlike reporters, photojournalists were unable to ever work from home. Their camera gear identified them as press to an increasingly disapproving public caught up in the flames of the "fake news" rallying cry fanned by the president, other conservative politicians and even citizens on both sides of the political divide. "The perfect storm scenario of 2020 made it an extraordinarily difficult year to be a newspaper photographer. I have never encountered the amount of aggressive, hostile interactions with authorities and citizens that I experience in the last 12 months," said Burbank, a 40-year veteran who has been a shooter for the *Orlando Sentinel* for more than 30 years. He said he was hassled by private security and public law enforcement officials for taking photos of cars lined up at Covid testing sites; masked ticket agents at Orlando International Airport, and masked crowds at a Walt Disney World shopping complex. At the Disney complex, a private security officer asked to see his images, and when he refused, he was asked to leave the outdoor venue. He had been photographing Disney theme parks and other venues for decades. Most unsettling, he said, was being surrounded by demonstrators at a Black Lives Matter protest who demanded he stop taking photos. "Putting their hands in my face and with one person attempting to grab my press ID, I was shaken by the interaction and feeling lucky that it did not escalate," he said.

Burbank's experience was part of a wider discussion that encompassed the intersection of press freedom and the desire for some protestors to remain anonymous. Photojournalists have the right to photograph events in public spaces, though some protest organizers were asking them to blur the faces of participants to protect them from retaliation or identification by law enforcement that could lead to charges.[16] The core mission of journalism to chronicle both historic and everyday events in unvarnished ways was seemingly misunderstood, as social media continued to blur the lines between journalists and everyone else with a smartphone and a social media account.

Taking Solace in the Need for News

Burbank worried and wondered whether the anti-media bias would continue through a new presidential administration and post-pandemic.

Writers saw that hostility in the online comments on their stories, especially pieces about the pandemic. Those drew comments from conspiracy theorists and others whose outrage about masks and other restrictions were cloaked in First Amendment declarations. But for photographers, aggressive behavior was more personal because it was in person and it hampered both their ability to work and their interactions with people in their community. Burbank's experiences during the pandemic were a stark contrast to those of reporters who said they were still able to do their jobs, with the changes in access and reporting techniques being more inconvenient than dangerous. Still, good journalism is often a product of good access, and that means more than a Zoom interview or an email exchange.

Rubin of the *Detroit News* said he accepted that video conferencing interviews were going to become part of the journalist's reporting toolkit post–Covid, but he didn't see them as much better than a phone call. With the ability to change a background to look like the mythical Tatooine from *Star Wars* or an industrial apartment with a big city view, Rubin said the situation seems "calculated."

Even in the most trying year of many journalists' careers, there was some solace for writers in knowing how much the public needed news, especially as it pertained to Covid-19, the presidential race and elections in general. Wright at the *Miami Herald* said she had more reader engagement with her stories via social media than ever before. "My work had gotten more intense but more rewarding," she said.

Callihan at the *Bradenton Herald* said he had a similar experience, receiving more reader feedback and praise than he had previously. "At a time when journalists have come under fire for just doing their jobs, I'm almost thankful for a pandemic that has kind of rekindled a lot of public trust and appreciation," he said.

Changes, for Good?

The revolutionary changes in newsgathering forced by the pandemic proved at least one thing: journalists can do their jobs without being in a newsroom. This may seem like a small revelation to those in industries that have worked remotely for a while, but it is huge in the world of journalism. The newsroom has always been the locus of the news operation. Accepting that the mission of gathering and disseminating news is more about dedication and expertise than desk placement will revolutionize the business. Posetti, et al., wrote that 61 percent of journalists surveyed reported a renewed commitment to journalism during the pandemic because they believed the public relied on them even more.[17] So, yes, reporters and editors can get the job done without a main gathering place, but they wanted desperately to return to face-to-face time with subjects—and their own friends and family. The desire was strong for the after-work get-together at the local watering hole or an hour of decompression via yoga or spin class. Long commutes to work and endless meetings with editors? Not so much. In fact, a forced return to the newsroom was being seen as punitive, a punishment for a job well done in a dire situation.

Covid, with a serious assist from technology, broke the stranglehold of newsroom tradition. As vaccinations rolled out across the country at a steady clip, journalists were told that newsrooms would reopen in the fall 2021. Guidelines on how that would happen came slowly as fall approached, partially in response to warnings of aggressive new variants of the virus. The pushback against showing up every day was strong. Short of ordering everyone back "or else," newsroom managers wondered how to convince their journalists that working communally was valuable and necessary when they themselves saw the benefits of working from home. This was a challenge when dealing with journalism veterans who learned during the pandemic that even though newsgathering techniques were hampered, their productivity was as good, maybe even better. Mentoring by experienced professionals is vital, but it will also require innovative thinking and thoughtful planning, plus a heavy lean on technology, to develop young journalists and new hires. They have historically benefited from observation of seasoned reporters and editors, but the reality is that newsroom alliances and mentors can be forged over coffee just as well as, or maybe even better than, amid a web of messy desks.

The journalism genie is out of the bottle and stuffing it back into an *All the President's Men* newsroom is not likely. In fall 2020, just six months into the pandemic, executive editor Sherry Chisenhall of the *Charlotte Observer* in North Carolina was already thinking about post-pandemic changes: "I think the time where the office is the home base is probably over. We know that our job is to publish stories that are relevant to the community and to grow an audience that sees enough value in our journalism to pay for it. I think we can actually do that really well without saying that people have to work 40 hours a week in an office."[18]

There are return-to-work details to hammer out, and what works for one newsroom might not work for another. Newsroom executives cannot deny that their remote journalists got the job done. Rather than force them back to the brick-and-mortar office, the smarter move will be to support journalists as they venture from their Covid cocoons back into the field to report and observe. The long-romanticized newsroom may now be dead, but it was already limping long before the pandemic took hold.

Notes

1. Elizabeth Grieco, "U.S. Newspapers Have Shed Half of Their Newsroom Employees Since 2008," Fact-Tank, Pew Research Center, April 20, 2020, https://www.pewresearch.org/fact-tank/2020/04/20/u-s-newsroom-employment-has-dropped-by-a-quarter-since-2008/.
2. R.A. Clay, "Journalists as Vicarious First Responders," APA, April 17, 2020, https://www.apa.org/topics/covid-19/journalists-first-responders.
3. Al Tompkins and Sidney Tompkins, "How Journalists Can Fight Stress from Covering the Coronavirus," Poynter.org, March 15, 2020, https://www.poynter.org/reporting-editing/2020/how-journalists-can-fight-stress-from-covering-the-coronavirus/.
4. Julie Posetti, Emily Bell, and Pete Brown, "Journalism and the Pandemic: A Global Snapshot of Impacts," International Center for Journalists and the Tow Center for Digital Journalism at Columbia University, 2020, https://www.icfj.org/sites/default/files/2020-10/Journalism%20and%20the%20Pandemic%20Project%20Report%201%202020_FINAL.pdf.
5. Dennis Joyce, "Two *Tampa Bay Times* Reporters Placed in Zip Ties While Covering Protests," Tampabay.com June 3, 2020, https://www.tampabay.com/news/tampa/2020/06/03/two-reporters-for-times-placed-in-zip-ties-while-covering-protests/.
6. Aila Slisco, "Florida Reporters Detained with Zip Ties While Covering Tampa-Area Protests," Newsweek, June 3, 2020, https://www.newsweek.com/florida-newspaper-reporters-detained-zip-ties-while-covering-tampa-area-protests-1508566.
7. Posetti, Bell, and Brown, "Journalism and the Pandemic."
8. Lauren Harris, "'I thought you'd go down with the ship': Why One Reporter Chose a Buyout After Twenty Years," *Columbia Journalism Review*, November 25, 2020, https://www.cjr.org/business_of_news/choosing-buyout-after-twenty-years.php.
9. Dax Shepard, interview with Isabel Wilkerson, Armchair Expert, podcast audio, October 16, 2020, https://armchairexpertpod.com/pods/isabel-wilkerson.
10. Judy Woodruff, interview with Dorothy Tucker, PBS NewsHour, PBS, June 9, 2020, https://www.pbs.org/newshour/show/coverage-of-protests-illuminates-journalisms-race-problem.
11. Elizabeth Grieco, "Newsroom Employees Are Less Diverse Than U.S. Workers Overall," Fact-Tank, Pew Research Center, November 2, 2018, https://www.pewresearch.org/fact-tank/2018/11/02/newsroom-employees-are-less-diverse-than-u-s-workers-overall/.
12. Ari Shapiro, interview with Dorothy Tucker, Astead Herndon, Keith Woods, *All Things Considered*, NPR, July 2, 2020, https://www.npr.org/2020/07/02/886845421/black-journalists-weigh-in-on-a-newsroom-reckoning.
13. Matthew Galgani, "IPO Stock with 275% Growth Keeps Zooming in Coronavirus Stock Market," *Investor's Business Daily*, March 21, 2020, https://www.investors.com/research/breakout-stocks-technical-analysis/zoom-stock-ipo-leads-coronavirus-stock-market/.
14. Stefan Hall, "Sports as a Service: Will COVID-19 Change How We Watch Sports?" World Economic Forum, December 20, 2020, https://www.weforum.org/agenda/2020/12/sports-as-a-service-will-covid-19-change-how-we-watch-sports/.
15. Matt Hanifan, "Sports Writers Struggle with Pandemic and Reporting from Far-away," Reynolds Media Lab, February 16, 2020, https://medium.com/the-reynolds-media-lab/sports-writers-struggle-with-pandemic-and-reporting-from-far-away-ff60d51d939e.
16. Eliana Miller and Asbury Nicole, "Photographers Are Being Called On to Stop Showing Protesters' Faces. Should They?" Poynter.org, June 4, 2020, https://www.poynter.org/ethics-trust/2020/should-journalists-show-protesters-faces/.
17. Posetti, Bell, and Brown, "Journalism and the Pandemic."
18. Greg Dool, "The Future of the Newsroom Post Pandemic," Digital Content Next: Advancing the Future of Trusted Content, September 17, 2020, https://digitalcontentnext.org/blog/2020/09/17/the-future-of-the-newsroom-post-pandemic/.

Covering Politics During the Pandemic
A Personal Journey
LaCrai D. Mitchell

> "I remember distinctly that ride in the car from Houston to Austin and us realizing together: this is a thing ... we don't know how long this is going to be a thing for, but how interesting that election officials aren't showing up ... because they're scared of this thing called coronavirus"
> —Nicole Sganga, CBS News Election Embed Reporter

#Covering2020

As we sat in a Charleston bar that was unsurprisingly packed for a Friday night, it still hadn't hit me that the next day was less than two hours away. I'd been counting down to this day for the last eight months and it was almost here. In some ways, it also felt like any other night after a long day of covering a campaign event. The date was February 28, 2020—the eve of the South Carolina Democratic Primary election—and, while I had diverted my attention to tomorrow's logistics, the rough planning in my head was battling the loud clamor of conversations taking place around me.

If I needed to be in Columbia by 9:00, that meant I needed to be on the highway by 6:30, giving myself an extra half hour in case there was traffic (boisterous laughter coming from the left side of the bar). So if I woke up at 5:00, and it was 10:00 now (boisterous laughter coming from behind me) ... if I got 5 hours of sleep that night, it would be better than the 4 hours I'd been averaging each night that week....

My intermittent streams of consciousness were jammed in between conversations with a friend that I'd made on the ground in the Palmetto State and my colleague-turned-good friend Nicole Sganga. After slogging across New Hampshire for most of the primary season, Nicole had come to South Carolina a couple of weeks before to help prepare for the CBS News–hosted Democratic debate in Charleston. She stuck around to help with primary election day coverage and had been with me earlier in the evening when President Trump came to town.

I had spent much of the day trying to ensure that I'd submitted all the information needed to receive press clearance to cover the Trump rally held at the North Charleston Coliseum. This would be the first Trump rally I'd cover, and it was nothing like any of the events I'd covered in South Carolina up to that point. Thousands of people were packed into the 13,000-seat multipurpose center, deafening music blared from the speakers, and there was an electricity that could be felt in the air. Nicole and I began interviewing Trump supporters, some of whom had traveled from as far off as Savannah, Georgia—two hours away—to see him on this night.

"We're prepared for the absolute worst—you have to be prepared for the worst—but hopefully it will all amount to very little," then-president Trump said of the coronavirus. "We are preparing for the worst. My administration has taken the most aggressive action in modern history to prevent the spread of this illness in the United States. We are ready. We are ready. Totally ready."

Our preparedness and how "ready" we were for the coronavirus would be put on full display in the coming weeks. It didn't take long for us to see that speeches like this one would not age well in the coming months.

The rest of the night and most of the next morning are a blur to me, but memories of the South Carolina Primary Election day are clear: scurrying to multiple voting precincts; dozens of interviews with voters who had cast their ballots for Joe Biden; rushing to the ballroom of the Hilton in downtown Columbia for a press conference on how voting was progressing; parking in a garage at the University of South Carolina for what would eventually be Joe Biden's victory party, and racing just as fast to the Tom Steyer event that was void of excitement and instead filled with tears and crushed aspirations.

At the end of a whirlwind of a day, 24 hours had passed, and I found myself at another bar (and despite how it may sound from these first few paragraphs, I did not spend every night at a bar). This time I was with ABC News embed Briana Stewart and a South Carolina–based political strategist, debriefing on what South Carolina's primary election had meant for this historic Democratic presidential primary.

There was nostalgia as we reminisced about the past eight months. We laughed as we remembered trekking camera equipment everywhere, chasing down the 150 Democrats running for president at the "World's Famous Clyburn Fish Fry" in 1,000-degree weather. There was a hint of sadness at what undoubtedly was the end of this first chapter of our campaign trail journey.

However, there was excitement too: excitement that the end of this chapter also meant the beginning of the next. For me, that probably meant splitting time between my home state of Florida and, more immediately, heading to the Tar Heel State for Super Tuesday on March 3. Yes, this was the end of a season, but there was so much more to come—or so we thought.

Even with all of the logistics management I did on a daily basis with my political director, Caitlin Conant, and our supervising producers Katie Ross-Dominick and Keitha Fairhurst-Paleski, there was no way we could have planned for or predicted exactly what was in store for us in the months ahead.

Super Tuesday

There wasn't much time to come off the high of covering the South Carolina primary. Three days later I was in a chilly, rainy Charlotte, where presidential candidate Michael Bloomberg's campaign signs adorned the highways—the most Bloomberg campaign material I'd seen in the past three months since he'd declared his candidacy.

Before leaving the hotel room, I sped through my mental checklist, which had become as routine as brushing my teeth. Phones? Check. Chargers? Check. Backup chargers? Camera kit? Check. Tripod? Check. Extra batteries? Check. (Peeks outside.) Umbrella? Check. Hotel key and car keys? Check. Check.

As I headed to the first of two precincts where I'd spend most of my day, I began running through more mental notes, as I did when heading to cover any event. How many voters did I want to interview? What did they think about the state of the Democratic Presidential Primary?

The night before, Senator Amy Klobuchar and former South Bend mayor Pete Buttigieg had endorsed Joe Biden, in a show of unity, fresh off their own presidential runs. It seemed from a bird's eye view that Biden's blowout win in South Carolina might have been the catalyst he needed for a momentum change—a change that was starting to draw in support from Biden's former Democratic opponents. However, what were North Carolinians feeling? That was the question I hoped to answer that day.

The second precinct I visited was one of the larger ones in the city. As I lugged my camera inside to set up and capture footage of voters casting their ballots, I took stock of my usual reporting metrics: How many voters, how long are the voter lines, how quickly are they moving, more younger voters or older voters ... what time is it? What time do I need to head to my car to begin feeding and logging footage to offer up to the broadcast or CBSN?

After recording some footage and talking to a handful of voters and the precinct administrator, I headed to my car to start compiling notes for an upcoming CBSN live shot and our daily newsletter. (A year earlier our team—led by my boss, who was the CBS News political director Caitlin Conant—had started the newsletter *CBS News Trail Markers* to compile our reporting from the trail.)[1]

As I prepped for the live shot, I received a call from Caitlin, who wanted to make sure everything was going smoothly for Super Tuesday coverage. She'd also called to briefly discuss what was ahead after Super Tuesday. Though we'd previously discussed my heading to Florida next, she said that everyone was going to have a chance to take a break after today. The unit would wait to receive further guidance on how we'd handle travel with the coronavirus pandemic becoming more serious. By this time, some of our *CBS News* colleagues had begun contracting the virus. So the next day, I'd head back to South Carolina, pack up, and move back home to Florida to await our next set of marching orders. A week's reprieve after the South Carolina primary and Super Tuesday sounded just fine to me! I'd get to hang out with my family for a bit before regrouping and potentially moving a few hours away to Central Florida ahead of the election.

For now, though, I'd just focus on getting through the rest of the day. Up next on the schedule was a CBSN report with some of my colleagues. Then–*CBS News* chief congressional correspondent Nancy Cordes, CBSN political reporter Caitlin Huey-Burns, fellow *CBS News* campaign reporter Alex Tin, and I all discussed what we were seeing and hearing from voters across the country.

I rolled my camera equipment to a spot in front of a line of voters. The rain had finally stopped, and the line had grown quite a bit since I had first perched at this precinct four hours earlier. I remember not being cognizant of how many feet apart I was standing from the voters behind me, and I didn't have disinfectant wipes for my equipment, which had been sitting inside the precinct with dozens of voters earlier in the afternoon. The only thing I was thinking about was how to condense dozens of conversations into a coherent recap for CBSN's political show *Red & Blue*, hosted by anchor Elaine Quijano. Here's an excerpt from my dispatch that evening:[2]

> From the dozen of voters that I spoke to today, Elaine, it's evident that ... people who are supporting former Vice President Joe Biden, they always cite his experience.... They say they want to go back to a time that felt more civil, a

time where the country felt a bit more united. And those exit polls also show where 31% of North Carolina voters say that the most important candidate quality for them is someone who can unite the country.

Alex, who had spent much of the primary in Nevada covering the Democratic presidential candidates, was reporting from San Diego. He was following Dr. Jill Biden on the heels of the Biden campaign's monumental win in South Carolina, which had undoubtedly given their team another lifeline[3]: "Coming after these endorsements from multiple former candidates who are no longer in the race, the campaign is excited that they will finally be able to potentially cross the so-called 15% viability threshold in order to pick up some delegates here in the state," said Alex as he described how the Biden campaign had shifted in the past few days. "With the field coalescing—at least *some* of the former field coalescing behind former Vice President Joe Biden—the Biden campaign is openly saying that they feel confident about their chances here in [California] and the excitement was palpable in the room, right here in San Diego."

The team wrapped our conversation and I packed up my gear—again without using any disinfectant wipes—got in my car, and headed to grab a bite to eat before going to evening events.

Across the country, our team's campaign reporters were following candidates and capturing commentary from voters on how they were feeling about their choices. In Texas, my colleague Nicole Sganga had teamed up with another *CBS News* campaign reporter, Adam Brewster. The two took a road trip from Houston to Austin to keep tabs on what was transpiring at the state's Democratic Party headquarters, while also keeping watch on how long lines might play out in the college town. Adam initially covered Iowa during the primary but had put about a thousand miles on his rental car as he covered Texas in the three weeks ahead of Super Tuesday. Both Adam and Nicole remember feeling like coronavirus had started getting more attention, at least on the local level.

"That is actually when I first started even really thinking about the coronavirus in a meaningful way, because as Adam and I were in the car on this road trip, we started seeing local reports about election poll workers who were not showing up in certain counties," recalled Nicole. "I remember distinctly that ride in the car from Houston to Austin and us realizing together: this is a thing ... we don't know how long this is going to be a thing for, but how interesting that election officials aren't showing up ... because they're scared of this thing called coronavirus."

My colleague Tim Perry was in Florida covering Michael Bloomberg on Super Tuesday. Tim had been covering the billionaire's campaign since December, after his other candidates—including then-senator Kamala Harris—had dropped out of the race. Tim said covering Bloomberg was different than covering any of the other candidates because Bloomberg's team had the financial resources to incorporate reporters' transportation into the campaign's infrastructure.

"We would wake up in one state, fly to a different state, do an event with [Bloomberg] there, get on a plane, go to another state, and then finish in the state that we were going to be working or starting in the next day," said Tim.

Covering a presidential candidate versus being embedded in a state came with its own set of unique circumstances. Adam, Nicole, and I were driving across Super Tuesday states with the aim of talking to as many voters as possible and getting a sense of which candidate was doing well in the state. Tim was flying across the Sunshine State and focused on what Bloomberg was doing and saying. Tim remembers kicking off the day in Miami before jet-setting to Orlando and ending the night in West Palm Beach with a large-scale event at a convention center, another sign of pre-pandemic times. Tim said there were cameras everywhere throughout the ballroom and even video performances, all to "make Bloomberg out to be the winner of the night." However, as the evening unfolded, the only victory Bloomberg walked away with was the U.S. territory of American Samoa.[4]

Back in North Carolina, I attended a Super Tuesday election night watch party where dozens crowded into a local brewery. Some sat by the bar, others gathered right in front of the one TV mounted in the corner. Reporters like me scooted in with heavy camera equipment and tried not to get our stick mics into one another's shots as we asked questions of voters. North Carolina congresswoman Alma Adams also stopped by the event, which had been organized by Biden's North Carolina team.

Any real concern for the coronavirus was noticeably absent in the conversations I had with voters. Yet, in a matter of weeks, we'd be covering this election in a setting much different than this night. But for this night, I'd think about how Biden had just swept a handful of states throughout the South on the heels of his victory in South Carolina.[5] I'd archive the sentiments of the attendees that had gathered in this local bar. In between tweets about how voters were feeling, I would relish how blessed I was to be able to cover this election—to have a front row seat to the adrenaline, the excitement, the anxiety, the uncertainty that marked this evening and unbeknownst to me, that would indelibly mark the months to come.

Going Home

After eight months in the Palmetto State, it was time to say goodbye and head home to Florida. With my rental car packed to the rim and a smoothie in hand, I made a quick video log from the apartment parking garage thanking my "home" of the past eight months for such great hospitality. It was bittersweet. I was already missing my favorite restaurants and some of the great people that I'd had a chance to befriend.

Even though we didn't know exactly what was to come after our "break," the severity of the coronavirus hadn't personally registered with me. Not traveling at all didn't even cross my mind as an option for us campaign reporters. Maybe we wouldn't be allowed to travel between states as often as we'd like and, naturally because the primary season was coming to an end, the number of campaign events we'd be covering would decrease. However, I don't think any part of me could have imagined that in just a matter of weeks we'd learn that our traveling assignments would be halted indefinitely due to the coronavirus. And quite frankly, nothing around me would have indicated otherwise. During my 6-hour, 400-mile drive from Charleston to Tallahassee, I don't remember seeing a single person wearing a mask or gloves at the gas stations. And during a quick stop at a coffee shop somewhere in Georgia, no one was sitting six feet apart from their nearest neighbor.

Nearly 1,000 miles away in Ann Arbor, Adam was reporting for CBSN from his home state of Michigan. Voters there also didn't seem to be concerned about the virus, as they came out to cast their votes in the state's presidential primary election on March 10. Hours before the state would announce its first confirmed cases of coronavirus,[6] Adam reported on CBSN that voters he'd spoken with that day said they weren't concerned about it[7]: "People I talked to were still showing up at polling places as a matter of fact. Now there was Purell, wipes, I was at a polling place in Roseville that had gloves for people if they wanted to wear them," reported Adam, as a line of mask-less voters waited to vote behind him. "I spoke to one of the polling officials there and she said she wasn't really even worried about showing up. You know, she was going to be having a lot of contact with a lot of people, touching a lot of things so she was maybe using a little bit more hand sanitizer."

Much like for the voters Adam had spoken with in Michigan, the threat of this virus hadn't yet sunk in for me either. Any second thoughts I may have had about this novel strand of the coronavirus weren't daunting enough to keep me from grabbing a bite at a burger spot when I finally made it home to Tallahassee.

After arriving at my parents' home, I remember leaving most of my luggage and belongings in a corner of the den near the front door. There was no need to carry everything upstairs because I probably wouldn't be staying for more than a couple of weeks. And even if a couple of weeks turned into a few of months, surely, we'd be back on the road by the beginning of summer.

Technical Difficulties

As we now know, weeks did turn into months. Coronavirus cases continued to skyrocket across the country and canceled campaign events naturally followed. Talks of moving to other states were understandably sidelined.

For a lot of us campaign reporters and political embeds, such a change in pace gave us whiplash. We arguably would have had at least a slight change of pace even without the coronavirus due to the transition from the primary election coverage to general election coverage. However, this abrupt halt to our daily schedules was jarring, to say the least.

"I was home and I didn't know what to do with myself.... I went from a hundred miles per hour to maybe like a slow creeping 20 miles per hour," said Nicole Sganga. "I think in the beginning I forced myself to enjoy it.... [I] re-read all seven Harry Potter books. I took walks outside. Eventually those walks turned from walks to walks with my mask on. New York was getting really hit hard by the coronavirus pandemic ... suddenly I went from leading this very chaotic life to everyone around me, leading this very chaotic life. And I sort of felt like the whole, my whole reality switched."

"I felt like I was missing out on ... an experience that I had seen so many people that I looked up to—other embeds from cycles before—go straight through," said Tim Perry. Tim ended up contracting the coronavirus upon returning to New York City after Super Tuesday. "There was just that sadness because ... one, we were stopping but then the unpredictability of everything just made us all a little concerned about what the future would hold for us."

The coronavirus became the central issue of our lives and the most important "voter issue" of the election, which meant that we had to figure out how to cover this pandemic while keeping tabs on campaigns that we couldn't follow in person.

One of the first changes I remember taking place involved our daily Political Unit phone call being replaced by a daily Zoom meeting, so that we could see one another. We were encouraged to "source up" in our states like we usually would. However, instead of scheduling meetings at a local coffee shop or brewery, I found myself scheduling Zoom coffee meetings with the state political party leadership teams. And instead of figuring out which coffee shop in town would be the best meeting spot, now I had to figure out the best room in my parent's house to hold my virtual meeting to avoid competing with dueling conference calls in other rooms.

I was cold-calling voter advocacy groups that I would usually have had the opportunity to casually meet at random campaign or grassroots organizing events throughout the state.

And on the more technical side, the time formerly spent finding decent cell service in the field, so I could transmit my footage back to the bureaus, was now being spent troubleshooting my in-home Wi-Fi during virtual interviews.

And remember how on Super Tuesday, I had to set up my tripod, camera, microphone, etc., for a CBSN live shot? Well, now I was doing CBSN live shots from my parents' dining room via Skype—with a dying orchard and mostly bare off-white colored wall in my background (that is, until I transitioned my workspace to the living room, where a window and more lively plants were able to help spice up my background).

The way we covered campaign events changed too, as candidates moved in-person events to live-streamed virtual rallies. Instead of focusing on how many voters had packed into a space to see the candidate, I was keeping count of how many "views" a virtual event captured on multiple platforms like Facebook Live or a campaign website live stream feed.

Gauging the enthusiasm of attendees at an event was relegated to skimming through posted comments to see if these were excited supporters tuning in or dissatisfied voters who wanted to troll the candidate. I still paid attention to the content of the candidates' speeches, but now I also had to note whether a virtual event was riddled with technical difficulties that distracted from the overall message.

My fellow campaign reporter Tim Perry had done his fair share of traveling across the country as he covered seven different presidential candidates throughout the primary election. He noted that not being able to travel made it harder to get a true pulse of what people were feeling.

"One of the benefits of being on the road and going from state to state covering candidates ... meant that we could spend a lot of time at restaurants. It meant that we were spending a lot of time at airports and spending a lot of time in Ubers," recalled Tim. "Some of the best voices I heard from ... was the waitress or the waiter, the Uber driver, the bartender, the hotel front desk person, or the random person I sat next to at an airport that I could just talk to about the election, get a sense of what they cared about, get a sense of what things people were talking about.... That was always a helpful process for me. When we started working on stories at home, we didn't get that."

In addition to technical workflow changes, the editorial shifted focus in some ways too. My colleague Adam Brewster covered the Wisconsin presidential primary election in April from New Jersey. He remembers having a eureka moment that the election was no longer going to be solely about policy platforms and which candidates some voters were interested in supporting.

"The issue in this election wasn't just going to be *who* people are voting for, but *how* they vote ... that was going to be a huge story of the election cycle and ... that certainly was the case until Election Day rolled around," recalled Adam. "I think Covid, and then the economy, and how the economy would recover, certainly became dominant issues in the election but it was that story of how people were going to vote and what the implications would mean for that. Seeing the expansion of mail voting and early voting too was ... quite remarkable."

As we navigated through the litany of changes that came with this new workflow, we were confronted with another story that would capture the world's attention ahead of this historic election.

In Minnesota, the murder of a Black man who died after a White police officer kneeled on him for nearly nine minutes had sparked international protest. Graphic video of the encounter made the rounds on social media and cable news. And while this wasn't the first time that the killing of an unarmed Black man by police officers had catapulted communities into protest, this killing seemed to weigh differently. Maybe it was because we didn't have work commutes and other pre-pandemic life happenings to distract us. Maybe it was because more people were home and more people were watching the news. Maybe being home forced all of us to really sit and try to process over and over how a man was killed at the hands of an officer who was supposed to protect and serve him. Maybe it was all these reasons and others too.

George Floyd's murder was heavy. And we political reporters were tasked with the important duty of covering the intersections of systemic racial inequity, unfair policing in communities of color, politics, and a global pandemic. We had to inform people who in some cases seemed to just now find themselves exposed to what many have known to be systemic inequities in our country.

George Floyd's murder had thrust longstanding issues into the forefront of the 2020 election with renewed spotlight and there we were, in a pandemic, trying to cover the country's racial reckoning from inside our homes. But how do you cover protests without physically being in the crowds? How could we get an accurate sense of the anger, frustration, fatigue, sorrow, and confusion of the masses without asking people how they felt, in person? There were plenty of reporters who were taking to the streets, wearing protective gear and masks to safeguard themselves from tear gas and the coronavirus. However, some reporters like me and Tim were living at home with parents, and we couldn't put our loved ones in danger of contracting the virus by going out into large crowds and then returning home.

"As a journalist, you always want to be on the ground for those big moments in history but also those big national stories, you want to be there because you don't really get the full sense of what is happening unless you're there. And so to be just miles away from some of the biggest, from some of the worst protests that were happening in the nation ... it was very tough," recalled Tim, who had moved in with his parents in Maryland during the pandemic. "I did not want to even potentially risk getting them sick or carrying the virus back home with me. That was a risk that I was not willing to take."

So, our team had to brainstorm ways to get to the heart of the intersections of race, inequity, community, and a pandemic in a meaningful way without being in crowds. I remember being keenly aware that my life's lens on the subjects of race, inequity, and community in our country were impacted the same way that any reporter's life experiences inform how they view the world. And as a Black woman, I also remember feeling this very personal sense of obligation to write something, anything, that could provide thoughtful context and even additional perspective on a story the whole world was watching unfold.

After some thought, I decided to go to a group of community leaders that have historically had a say in moments like the one we found ourselves in: Black faith leaders,[8] who were historic pillars in their respective communities. I wondered if Black faith leaders across the country thought these marches were different. And with communities across the world marching in mass gatherings larger than any we'd seen since the pandemic began, what did it mean that people were literally willing to risk their health to stand up for George Floyd and all the men and women he represented?

Moreover, after the dust settled, would the Black and brown communities that were already being disproportionately impacted by this virus be worse off? With the support of the entire political unit team, my boss Caitlin Conant and our editor Ellen Uchimiya, I was able to find a way to put some of people's thoughts and feelings into meaningful words. I use the word meaningful because I also remember being especially conscious of my word choice for this story: do I use "protest" or "riot"? Do I say "the death of George Floyd" or "the killing of George Floyd?" Words always matter, but it felt even more so the case with this story. Here's an excerpt of what I had a chance to pen:

> Looters and vandals have at times distracted from what protesters want: a complete overhaul of the criminal justice system and policing. But United Church of Christ Associate General Minister Traci Blackmon argues that the violence is actually the "rage and weariness" of people who have been suppressed for too long.
>
> "Change in this country has never come without the confrontation of power sources ... and that confrontation has always been met with violence," Blackmon told CBS News. "How do you respond to a state-sanctioned murder that is

being shared all over the world ... what is the appropriate response to that level of violence?"

...Calls for racial equality have slammed headlong into a public health crisis that has also illuminated racial inequities in health care. Pew Research data shows that in eight states, the percentage of coronavirus deaths among Black people is at least twice as high as the Black share of the population in those states.

Dr. Marybeth Sexton, an assistant professor of infectious disease at Emory University, says higher rates of Covid-19 cases in minority communities can likely be attributed to factors including housing conditions, health care access, and trust in the health care system. And if there's a surge in Covid-19 cases related to protests, she points out, it could affect already vulnerable communities at disproportionate rates.

"You have people who are out protesting systemic racism, who are potentially at higher risk for COVID—and for complications of COVID—for a multitude of reasons, but some of which are also caused by the legacy of systemic racism," said Sexton.

The coronavirus and this country's historic bout with the virus of racism had collided five months from Election Day. And because the coronavirus pandemic had become the voter issue that overlaid every other story, we had to figure out a way to tell stories about how the pandemic was impacting voters and their decisions ahead of this election. Was the handling of the pandemic swaying voters' choices? Was it strengthening their resolve for their decided candidate? One way that Caitlin decided we could tackle these stories from home was to start a web series. Every week, we campaign reporters would report on how the virus was impacting voters who lived in battleground states and who worked in a variety of industries—fishing, farming,[9] tourism[10] the arts[11]—and in a couple of months we'd follow up to see how or if things had changed for better or worse for these voters.

The series would be called "Covid Chronicles,"[12] and we would conduct virtual interviews with voters that would be used in digital pieces. The first set of digital stories I produced looked at how Black-owned businesses in Florida[13] and North Carolina were faring in June of 2020. I wrote about how two Black business owners in two different industries in North Carolina were facing the same financial struggles as they tried to stay afloat amid the pandemic[14]:

> Patrick Williams, 45, had just become one of four business partners at Pier 34 Seafood & Pub in Goldsboro, North Carolina, when the restaurant was forced to close because of the coronavirus pandemic. Pier 34 had only been open for four months in March and was doing well, Williams said, bringing in roughly $20,000 per month.
>
> Once North Carolina issued a stay-at-home order, the restaurant halted indoor dining. And while Pier 34 continued to offer take-out and delivery

options, in the nearly two months that the restaurant was closed, the team saw its earnings cut in half. Like many small business owners, Williams and his partners dipped into personal savings for expenses like food distributor costs and salaries for their five full-time employees.

"By any means necessary we were going to assure that our staff was paid," said Williams, who also has other jobs. Though the restaurant has reopened, Williams is still using personal funds to help keep the restaurant afloat. The restaurant can stay open for another six months at its current revenue levels by "cutting it hard," Williams said, but his team would have to decide whether it was worth it to keep the business going.

Two-and-a-half hours away in Winston-Salem, Geek in Heels owner Shalisha Morgan said she cried when the stay-home order forced her to shut down her electronic repair kiosk in the Hanes mall. Morgan, who started fixing electronics as a side gig in 2013, had been operating out of the mall for over a year. She told CBS News that she had just begun to recover from a slow period when the pandemic worsened.

"Last summer when sales declined, I lost my apartment and me and my children were homeless. And I had to make a decision, do I keep my home or do I keep my business? And I chose to keep my business," recalled Morgan. "When I had to close at the mall, I had some anxiety because I did not want to lose all that I had regained."

"I knew no Superman was coming in to save me, and everyone felt like I did."

Morgan said longstanding inequities for Black- and minority-owned businesses made it hard for her to succeed before the pandemic. She has found it difficult to access capital and has been turned down for loans....

As the pandemic persisted, Morgan applied for the Small Business Administration Economic Injury Disaster loan (EIDL) and other Paycheck Protection Program loans. She also joined a Facebook group, where small business owners would ask each other questions about the loan application process and share general information. Morgan said members of the group grew increasingly frustrated as delayed responses from the federal government left owners feeling uncertain and undervalued.

Black business owners like Patrick Williams and Shalisha Morgan couldn't seem to find pandemic relief quickly enough as time steadily ticked toward Election Day. The pace of politics, though, felt like it was accelerating and, before we knew it, it was August. Next on deck: the Democratic and Republican national conventions.

There's Still an Election

My colleague Nicole Sganga was one of the first CBS News embeds to cover an in-person event during the pandemic, back in June of 2020. Then-president Trump was hosting in-person rallies, and Nicole reported on one that took place in Tulsa. She describes covering the rally from outside of the event as re-baptism by fire; the rules of engagement for covering campaign events had certainly changed for us.

"Suddenly we were asking questions of this campaign that I never would have imagined asking them, things like ... are you going to require masks? And are there going to be tests available for people? ... Is it going to be inside, outside? How are you going to confirm people are safe? Will there be hand sanitizer there? Will there be temperature checks?" recalled Nicole. "To this day, I don't think I've ever experienced a news event like that Tulsa rally because there were so many intersecting threads and so many important stories that were coinciding at the same time—with the Black Lives Matter movement, with the Covid pandemic and with President Trump's re-emergence ... everything he did had political implications, but it also had larger health implications for the whole country."

On August 22, 2020, I hit the road for the first time in 172 days. The assignment was to cover the Republican National Convention in Charlotte. We'd been covering the play-by-play of how Democrats and Republicans were adjusting their headliner events since April[15]—changing dates, changing formats, changing cities. Would they be able to pull off these massive events in person during a pandemic? Adam Brewster and I even analyzed the local response from the host cities, Milwaukee and Charlotte, in May of 2020.[16]

And as I headed to Charlotte for the Republican National Convention in August, it was evident that a lot had changed. I wore a mask and shield through the airport for extra protection. I used excessive amounts of hand sanitizer, disinfecting everything from the moment I got on the plane—the seat buckles, the arm rest, and after arriving at the airport in Charlotte—the rental car handles, the interior of the rental vehicle—when arriving to the hotel, the hotel room, my camera equipment. All of this was what I had to do just to feel safe enough to sit down in the hotel room.

When leaving the room to meet with colleagues, it was no longer to gather at just any random restaurant or bar. Now we needed to ensure the place had outdoor seating and adequate spacing before considering a sit-down pow wow.

As for covering the actual event, my colleague Eleanor Watson, who covered the event from inside the convention center, had to test negative for Covid-19 to gain clearance. All the media lined up outside where I was posted had to pass temperature checks and received red wrist bands to show we'd received approval to remain in the area. When interviewing voters outside of the barricades surrounding the convention center, we had to keep our distance, using boom mics (microphones at the end of a long pole) instead of our traditional stick (face-to-face, up close) mics.

And after interviewing a person, we made sure to disinfect our equipment before interviewing the next person, per safety rules that we'd agreed to before the trip.

It had been months since I'd done a CBSN live shot from outside my parents' home. And, unlike Super Tuesday, I was now paying *very* close attention to the distance between myself and the people around me. I was also wearing a mask as I reported, hoping that the audio wasn't too muffled.

After the convention, and in the weeks before the election, travel began to resume. With masks, hand sanitizer, disinfectants, lots of Covid tests, and boom mics in tow, we were on the trail again. From trips to Central Florida, the Triangle in North Carolina, and multiple cities in Georgia, my goal was to assess what voters were feeling less than two months away from Election Day. As we did voter survey pieces, we tried to keep our interviews outside so that we didn't have to deal with poor ventilation in enclosed spaces. In the days before November 3, while covering Trump rallies that were packed with thousands of maskless attendees, it became even more important to wear masks, distance as much as possible when conducting interviews, use hand sanitizer whenever possible, and test as often as possible.

Eventually, Election Day was upon us. Pulling up to the Hillsborough County precinct where I spent much of the afternoon, it felt in many ways like the South Carolina primary or like Super Tuesday in Charlotte. Sure, there weren't long voter lines, and we weren't allowed inside the polling location, to minimize the number of people in the precinct. However, some elements had returned.

Supporters for both candidates lined the sidewalk with flags and chanted to support their candidate. Voters with masks stopped and talked to me about who they voted for and what issues were most important to them. The day that had felt so far away in March had finally arrived and, though we didn't know it at the time, we were in for quite the week as we waited for election results to come in across the country.

It felt good to be focused on things that just months ago weren't a thought—preparing for the CBSN live debrief I'd do in a few hours, compiling notes from all the voter conversations during that day, and preparing for what was certain to be an historic election night (*week*) at long last.

Election night felt like a full-circle moment. Here I was, reporting with colleagues with whom I'd first started doing CBSN live shots more than a year ago. On the other hand, the election was far from over, and as the next week unfolded, covering the constantly evolving situation in Georgia—recounts included—brought many lessons and takeaways to process from what we'd all just experienced.

A Final Trail Marker

Earlier in this essay I talked about the daily newsletter that our team of campaign reporters, political correspondents and congressional reporters contributed to during our time on the trail. Trail Markers[17] was another platform where we could share our political reporting, and over time, it had the added benefit of providing a well-documented log that linked to some of our best reporting during 2020. As I looked back at some of my entries for Trail Markers to refresh my memory while writing this essay, I was reminded of the many lessons that stuck with me during this unique experience as a political embed.

Covering politics during the pandemic really stretched the ingenuity of campaign and political reporters across the globe. One of the things I think we did well was navigate how to make connections with people we never had the opportunity to meet in person. Safety measures to protect against Covid-19 forced reporters to master the art of conducting remote interviews in a way that was compelling, even though we were talking with a person through a computer screen in our homes.

As we continue to move into what some would characterize as a post-pandemic era, I think it's important for us to remember that whether we're interacting with an interviewee in person or on the other side of a screen, the value of our reporting isn't defined by the means we use to capture an interview. The value of our reporting is characterized by the *voices* we find to tell a story, the *questions* we ask during a conversation with a person, and the *commitment* that we must maintain to accuracy and fairness, no matter how or from where we're reporting.

Additionally, I hope that the pandemic also reminded us to, when possible, not allow physical location to be a deterrent to pursuing an important story. During the early days of the pandemic, we focused less on whether we could physically get to a place to tell a story, because we all had to find workarounds because everyone was confined to their homes. To be clear, I'm fully aware that some stories simply can't be told without going to a place—especially when the setting is an essential piece of the story. However, before the pandemic, I think it was easier for us to write off pitching a story to our bosses if we couldn't physically travel to a location. Now we know that location doesn't have to always be a hurdle in bringing an important story to light.

Another pandemic-related change that I hope we continue to see integrated into our post-pandemic workflow is a hybrid environment, where we can still work from home when needed. One of the things that I discussed with former political embeds was that when we had to stay home during the pandemic, we were able to write and produce more stories than we ever would have been able to when we had to travel from city to city. While reporting from home isn't exactly what we'd signed up for, I won't say that I didn't enjoy having the extra time to find unique voices for a story—time that otherwise might have been spent driving from one city to the next. Similarly, I'm sure some reporters would agree that the time spent commuting from home to a newsroom or office could sometimes be better spent making source calls or arranging logistics for an upcoming shoot.

For all the ways that working remotely full-time was effective, there is certainly value in being able to interact in person with the colleagues that we work with daily, the politicians we study and track, and the people whose lives are impacted by the policy decisions and political actions about which we report. I look forward to more days like the one when I covered the Trump rally in North Charleston so many months ago—days when I can attend large gatherings without lingering coronavirus-related concerns, interview a person without still feeling like I need to use a boom mic to maintain distance, and then head to a local bar with colleagues as we get ready for the next adventure or story to come.

Notes

1. Caitlin Conant, "Trail Markers," CBS News, November 20, 2020, https://www.cbsnews.com/feature/trail-markers/.

2. LaCrai Mitchell, "Red and Blue Watch Live: Super Tuesday Results and Analysis," CBSN, March 3, 2020, https://www.youtube.com/watch?v=SDkTYnjE0z0.

3. Alex Tin, "Red and Blue Watch Live: Super Tuesday Results and Analysis," CBSN, March 3, 2020, https://www.youtube.com/watch?v=SDkTYnjE0z0.

4. Tim Perry, "Bloomberg Ends Presidential Run and Endorses Biden After Super Tuesday Rejection," CBS News, March 4, 2020, https://www.cbsnews.com/news/bloomberg-ends-presidential-bid-biden-endorsement-super-tuesday/.

5. Grace Segers, Kathryn Watson, Caroline Linton, Stefan Becket, and Melissa Quinn, "Super Tuesday: Biden Sweeps South, Wins Texas, but California Leans Toward Sanders," CBS News, March 8, 2020, https://www.cbsnews.com/live-updates/super-tuesday-14-states-democratic-primary-election-live-updates-stream-2020-03-03/.

6. "Michigan Announces First Presumptive Positive Cases of COVID-19: Governor Whitmer Declares a State of Emergency to Maximize Efforts to Slow the Spread," Michigan.gov, https://www.michigan.gov/coronavirus/0,9753,7-406-98158-521341--,00.html, retrieved August 10, 2021.

7. @CBSNews, "@adam_brew says Michigan primary voters have not seemed concerned about coronavirus, and polling places are prepared with hand sanitizer," Twitter, March 10, 2020, https://twitter.com/CBSNews/status/1237491221536411649.

8. LaCrai Mitchell, "Black Faith Leaders Weigh In on Next Steps for Nation After George Floyd's Death," CBS News, June 12, 2020, https://www.cbsnews.com/news/george-floyd-death-black-faith-leaders-discuss-next-steps-for-nation/.

9. Tim Perry and Jack Turman, "Covid Chronicles: Farms and Fisheries Hit Hard by Coronavirus," CBSN, June 14, 2020, https://www.cbsnews.com/video/farming-fishing-among-us-industries-hardest-hit-by-coronavirus-lockdowns/.

10. Cara Korte, "Covid Chronicles: Seasonal Changes Bring Challenges for

Colorado Tourism Amid Pandemic," CBS News, July 12, 2020, https://www.cbsnews.com/news/colorado-tourism-seasonal-changes-coronavirus-pandemic/.

11. Zak Hudak, "Covid Chronicles: Pennsylvania Graduates Continue to Face Uncertainty Amid Pandemic," CBS News, August 19, 2020, https://www.cbsnews.com/news/pennsylvania-graduates-continue-to-face-uncertainty-amid-pandemic/; Musadiq Bidar, "Covid Chronicles: California Artists Try to Adapt to New World Wrought by Pandemic," CBS News, September 16, 2020, https://www.cbsnews.com/news/california-artists-try-to-adapt-to-new-world-wrought-by-pandemic/.

12. "Covid Chronicles," CBS News, July 9, 2020, https://www.cbsnews.com/feature/covid-chronicles/, retrieved August 10, 2021.

13. LaCrai Mitchell, "Covid Chronicles: 'We're not at break-even yet': Black-Owned Businesses in Florida on Road to Recovery Amid Pandemic," CBS News, June 23, 2020, https://www.cbsnews.com/news/florida-black-owned-businesses-covid/.

14. LaCrai Mitchell, "Covid Chronicles: Black North Carolina Business Owners Adapt to Financial Uncertainty Amid Pandemic," CBS News, June 25, 2020, https://www.cbsnews.com/news/north-carolina-business-owners-coronavirus-pandemic-financial-uncertainty/.

15. Eleanor Watson, LaCrai Mitchell, Adam Brewster, Musadiq Bidar, and Ed O'Keefe, "Party Leaders Agree with Joe Biden—the Democratic National Convention Cannot Proceed as Originally Planned, CBS News, April 1, 2020, https://www.cbsnews.com/news/biden-democratic-national-convention-scheduled/.

16. Adam Brewster and LaCrai Mitchell, "Local Leaders Weigh In on COVID Uncertainty Surrounding National Conventions," CBS News, May 16, 2020, https://www.cbsnews.com/news/coronavirus-uncertainty-national-conventions-local-leaders/.

17. Caitlin Conant, "Trail Markers," CBS News, November 20, 2020, https://www.cbsnews.com/feature/trail-markers/.

Investigative Reporting

Assessing Covid's Lasting Impact

Mark Douglas Iusi

> "All of a sudden everyone needed medical journalism training"
> —University of Illinois journalism professor Brant Houston, co-founder of GIJN and former executive director of Investigative Reporters and Editors, Inc.

A Storm Is Coming

March 6, 2020, was the kind of day postcards are made from in St. Petersburg, Florida—a real Sunshine State spectacular. That Friday, two dozen foreign visitors awoke to sunny skies, cool temperatures and a light breeze that carried the promise of an early spring. But those investigative reporters and news editors visiting from 24 nations—including the Bahamas, Bangladesh, Malawi and Malaysia—didn't fly to Florida for the weather. They gathered indoors that day to improve their tradecraft and trade a few tricks. No one suspected the biggest trick of the year would be figuring out how to survive Covid-19.

They huddled around a long conference table without social distancing or other precautions that would soon dominate daily life. They had crossed oceans to learn about best practices in a program sponsored by the U.S. State Dept. Edward R. Murrow Program for Journalists. This day's midday session (organized locally by World Partnerships, Inc.) focused on investigative reporting. I was the guest speaker and, like others, just starting to get twitchy about Covid-19. The conversation of investigative journalism practices and challenges that day was serious business. But no one knew how serious the business of uncovering secrets and protecting the public was about to become and how profoundly it was about to change. CNN reported a total of 14 Covid-19 cases across the U.S. that day in early March 2020, half of which centered on a single nursing home in Washington State. The news about infections would soon get worse—much worse.

Two dozen international journalists gather around a table for an investigative training conference in St. Petersburg on March 6, 2020, just days before WHO declared a pandemic and most such in-person gatherings abruptly ended for more than a year. The day after this photograph most of these journalists returned to their home nations to face immediate quarantines and lockdowns due to COVID-19 and a dramatic change in how they performed their jobs. (courtesy Gary Springer, World Partnerships).

That evening some of the visiting journalists hit the town. It was Friday night and the next day they would leave for homes spread across other continents. They had reason to celebrate. After an all-expense paid extended visit to America, they were heading home with fresh ideas and maybe some swagger. Fifteen months later, Slovenian newspaper editor Antisa Korljan vividly recalled the carefree mood on that final night out in St. Petersburg:

> Streets were full, clubs were packed, and I particularly enjoyed the one in the basement of some restaurant. It was small and I could touch its ceiling with an

elbow.... People were dancing, touching, sweating their week out. I had no idea it was my last such experience for a year and more.[1]

Balmy weather aside, a global storm was creeping in. In fact, it had already arrived. Five days earlier Florida governor Ron DeSantis had declared a state of emergency when Florida's first two reported cases emerged within a few miles of the visiting group of international journalists.[2] CNN was reporting that there had been about 300 infections confirmed nationwide, and half of the nation's Covid-19 death toll was confined to that one nursing home in Washington State.[3]

Just days later CNN's news investigative team broadcast its first Covid-19 exposé, revealing that American first responders who processed U.S. citizens returning from abroad had inadequate protective gear.[4] "That sort of kicked off our coronavirus coverage," said Patricia DiCarlo, executive producer of CNN's investigative unit. It also foreshadowed our U.S. government's wobbly response to the coming plague. DiCarlo continued, "So all of these people being brought in directly from China, repatriated to the United States were all being handled by people who did not have the right PPE, and then [sent] out in the community. There's some schools of thought that perhaps these were some of the clusters in the United States started with some of these workers who were handling these people."

Warning signs abounded. Danger was spreading. And the kinds of stories investigative journalists wrote and how they produced them were about to change dramatically.[5] March 11, the same day as CNN's first investigative report on Covid-19, the World Health Organization declared a global pandemic due to Covid-19, with 118,000 known infections in 110 countries.[6] A metaphorical dam holding back the potentially lethal and highly contagious virus was suddenly bursting amid one of the most contentious presidential elections in modern history. All of that came against a backdrop of growing racial violence and civil unrest nationwide. "I didn't think it was possible that we could add anything more to our plate," DiCarlo recalled. CNN's investigative team nearly doubled story production over the course of 2020—even after a ferocious four years trying to keep up with the Trump administration. "Our busiest year since I began running the unit," DiCarlo said. CNN executives ordered everyone to work from home. DiCarlo and their team quickly grabbed essential office gear and migrated to their homes with just a few hours of advance notice. "It turns out CNN actually ended up renovating, so I never saw that office again," DiCarlo said.

Economies throttled down worldwide, travel nearly halted and millions of people died from viral infections that suffocated them in hospital isolation wards. Investigative journalism became more challenging overnight. And the stakes couldn't have been higher. Antisa Korljan arrived back in Ljubljana, Slovenia, exhausted after 19 hours spent on airplanes while traveling home from St. Petersburg, six time zones away. Within hours, his editor called to tell Korljan he would have to work from home for the next two weeks. "Within a week government imposed strict lockdown, hospitals started to fill, people were starting to die, the virus was here," he said. More than a year later, Korljan recalled:

> We were thinking—wishfully—the whole nightmare would be over by the end of the year. Well, we were as wrong as one could ever be. Pretty soon almost everyone in the newsroom started working from home, the managing editor's ears were burning from the phone constantly ringing. Since there were no events, we had to resort to our imagination producing every day's edition. We introduced sections dedicated to staying sane in the pandemic. I remember ordering and editing an eight-pages section after one month of lockdown exploring how did our lives change due to pandemic. Never did I realize I might have as well waited for six months to do that. Or a year, for that matter. I was optimistic.[7]

According to Korljan, many readers were afraid of contracting Covid-19 from touching newspapers. That's because in Slovenia, newspapers are commonly passed from hand to hand in taverns and other gathering spots. When Slovenian bars closed due to Covid-19 restrictions, they cancelled subscriptions, and thus landed yet another financial blow against newspapers in that eastern European nation.

Back in the U.S., the Covid-19 viral plague would kill half a million Americans within a year's time and claim five times that many lives in 223 nations around the world.[8] The number of cases in Florida would grow from two to more than two million by April 2021.[9] Global pandemic restrictions on personal contact, travel and press freedoms tested investigative journalists worldwide and forced them to operate in new ways and places literally overnight.

The visiting foreign journalists like Korljan who attended that Florida seminar in early March 2020 returned home to an eerie landscape of quarantines, lockdowns and economic hardship. Many faced a triple hurdle: surviving the pandemic, informing the public, and battling information roadblocks imposed by their own governments.

Korljan's fellow visitor and investigative filmmaker Gali Ginatt landed in quarantine for 14 days immediately upon her return home to Israel after the Florida seminar. Months later, she was back in biologically dangerous territory working on a documentary in what Ginatt referred to as "the most infected city in Israel."[10]

Investigative journalists worldwide faced fresh danger and unique challenges, some of them logistical or biological and others politically

54   Part I. Reporting a Pandemic

Two dozen international journalists pose for a group photograph shoulder to shoulder after an investigative seminar in St. Petersburg, Florida, just days before the World Health Organization declared a pandemic, effectively ending such gatherings for more than a year due to the threat of Covid-19. Most of these journalists returned to their home countries the day after this photograph and immediately faced extended lockdowns, quarantines and a dramatic change in how they performed their jobs amid worldwide Covid-19 restrictions (courtesy Gary Springer, World Partnerships).

contrived or opportunistic. In the Philippines, celebrated investigative journalist Maria Ressa ended up in jail when that nation's authoritarian government exploited Covid-19 restrictions to control the flow of pandemic news and information. Ressa faced prosecution for cyber-libel in a court case few people saw. It happened when health-related Covid restrictions limited public access to the courtroom during the trial that resulted in her conviction.[11]

As Covid-19 infections spread sickness and death across manmade borders, many investigative reporters found themselves thrust into the role of journalistic "first responders" on the pandemic front lines. And it wasn't easy. From Detroit to Dubai, investigative journalists faced the same logistical obstacles: How to investigate wrongdoing and corruption without travel, close personal contact or the ability to report from news locations as eyewitnesses to history. They learned to operate in new ways, collaborate remotely with peers and explore creative methods to hold governments accountable. In the U.S., the pandemic intersected with racial violence, hate-laced extremism, economic collapse, and a tumultuous presidential election. As a result, 2020 was colored with politically driven disinformation about almost everything, including Covid-19 and its remedies.

The stakes were enormous. Secretary-General Christophe Deloire of Reporters Without Borders warned that the work of reporters during the global pandemic crisis would become a bellwether for journalism though the next decade. "We are entering a decisive decade for journalism linked to crises that affect its future," Deloire said.[12] "The coronavirus pandemic illustrates the negative factors threatening the right to reliable information and is itself an exacerbating factor. What will freedom of information, pluralism and reliability look like in 2030? The answer to that question is being determined today."

Meeting the Moment

In September 2019, on the eve of the pandemic, the Global Investigative Journalism Network hosted a training conference in Hamburg, Germany. An impressive roster of 1,700 journalists traveled from 130 nations to attend.[13] Worldwide interest in investigative journalism wasn't just thriving, it was soaring. "That was I believe the largest international investigative conference," said GIJN staff reporter Rowan Philp.[14]

One year later, there was no such in-person GIJN conference, and prospects for a return to personal gatherings remained dim in the early months of 2021. "There is something someone loses without personal interaction just as a reporter does with sources," Philp said. "But, I'll tell you what, it's been a very successful year nevertheless."

Like other investigative journalism networks and nonprofit training organizations, GIJN switched to webinars, virtual conferences and digital networking as substitutes for physical gatherings while the worldwide demand for investigative content intensified. Tips on how to cover the pandemic permeated GIJN efforts.[15] "The pandemic probably occupied half of my work last year (2020), specifically interviewing journalists about how they're handling it," Philp said. After monitoring the Internet and his organization's network of listening posts, Philp listed dozens of global Covid-related stories on the GIJN website over the course of 2020 and shared creative methods that investigative reporters used to count Covid-19 cases—a task made more difficult when some governments tried to minimize the crisis and interfere in the newsgathering efforts of reporters.[16]

Antisa Korljan wrote that during the final months of 2020 in his country, the Slovenian government was trying to suppress news coverage by limiting access to newspapers: "For instance, for a few days in December they closed down kiosks in which papers are being sold. Why? 'Fighting the pandemics,' they claimed. Totally unsubstantiated. The government ceased funding the state-owned press agency and conflict escalated to Brussels so the EU commission and parliament had to deal with it."[17]

Regardless of national borders, a fundamental change in working conditions for investigative reporters arrived almost without warning. *Washington Post* investigations editor Jeff Leen said his teams began reporting remotely from home offices on March 11, 2020—the same day WHO declared a global pandemic. At the time of our interview with Leen in late February 2021, he noted it had been 353 days since reporters abandoned the *Post* newsroom for the relative safety of their own home offices. Almost a year into the new operational game plan, Leen was literally counting the days, still from home. By then, the *Post* website was overflowing with stories on Covid, federal relief spending, racial unrest, domestic extremists and the superheated presidential race.[18]

"We're just doing everything by email, phone and Zoom now and so much information is available digitally," Leen said.[19] Despite the operational challenges of social distancing and travel restrictions, Leen said the productivity of the *Post*'s investigative teams increased after reporters began working remotely. Now, that was a bonus few predicted. "We can work at a pace that is faster than we have previously thanks to the technology," Leen said. "One of the surprising things is how well we could work remotely."

Leen said the *Post* responded nimbly to the Covid challenge partly because it already had two investigative teams—one for deeper, long-range dives and the other designed as a rapid response to the kind of ground-shaking news events that permeated 2020. "We did COVID, we did the racial reckoning and we also did the election," Leen said. "We can move deep or we can move fast and with two separate teams. It's like having two engines and so we are busier than we've ever been. We're producing more than we've ever been." Leen said the "old school" method of going out for lunch with investigative sources may have already been waning due to the Internet, long before Covid-19 induced social distancing.

"The reporters do miss some of the camaraderie ... the water cooler conversations, the synchronicity and serendipity you have from those conversations that people just bump into each other in the hall," Leen said. "So, that sort of thing is missing and is a negative, but these other things fill in to allow us to keep doing our job."

In Tampa, Florida, Kylie McGivern had been reporting for several years as a news investigator at WFTS-TV, the local ABC Network affiliate. She faced many of the same hurdles as *Washington Post* reporters and also had to change her methods. "Some of the challenges back in the beginning I felt like I was tapping back into my skills as a multimedia journalist," McGivern said.[20] As a local TV reporter, McGivern needed to keep her stories looking professional while working alone from home during her forced exile from the WFTS-TV Tampa studios. "I just can't prop my phone up on the back of a candle or something. Let me get a ring light, let me figure out how to make this look good where I am getting my interviews." McGivern would record interviews and her voice track (the story's narration) in her makeshift home studio and email those TV story ingredients to her videographer or video editor, who would assemble the video story in isolation and then feed it electronically to the TV station as a completed package. Her story focus changed as well. McGivern's investigative reporting, which generally had centered on long-term projects, suddenly shifted to the fast-breaking pandemic story. Like investigative reporters at the *Post* and around the globe, McGivern found herself working as a journalistic "first responder" along with her primary role as a slower-paced truth detective. "The news has been changing not just day by day but hour by hour so you know meeting the moment so to speak and getting what you can out as quickly as possible, knowing it can change very quickly," McGivern said.[21]

Just like at the *Washington Post*, where Leen said every staff reporter seemed to eventually have some piece of the pandemic story, McGivern recalled an "all hands on deck" response at WFTS in the early days to daily developments about the spread, danger and death toll of the virus. McGivern said she was eventually able to take a breath, dig deeper and help discover new ways to report on the unfolding pandemic. "I had done a story on the fact that local funeral homes were running out of storage for bodies because there was a backlog in waiting for the medical examiners to review COVID deaths," McGivern said.

Data, Science and Technology

No working journalist in 2020 had ever had the opportunity to report on a health issue of this magnitude. It was the most pervasive public health emergency since the 1918 pandemic that infected an estimated 1/3 of the world population and killed more than 675,000 victims in the U.S. and 50 million victims worldwide.[22] A century later, a later generation of investigative reporters had to suddenly school themselves on the science surrounding epidemiology, virology, and the relative efficacy of vaccinations. "All of a sudden everyone needed medical journalism training," said University of Illinois journalism professor Brant Houston, co-founder of GIJN and former executive director of Investigative Reporters and Editors, Inc. (IRE).[23]

Investigative reporters around the world also needed to learn a new lexicon of medical terms and be able to parse the nuances of "death toll," "positivity rate" and "recovered." "We got better at understanding definitions," said Houston. But that part turned out to be tricky. "There are at least five different kinds of ways of classifying 'recovered' and they did a survey of 50 different state definitions," Houston said. "In Illinois if you're not dead in 42 days after your diagnosis, you're considered 'recovered.'" That probably surprised Covid-19 "long haulers" in Illinois who survived the initial infection but had not returned to their former health—or anything close to it—a year or more later.[24] Houston said contradictions and confusion surrounding government Covid-19 statistics helped lead to "deep-dive" data reporting by investigative journalists in Illinois about the differences in "recovered" definitions and why some southwest Illinois counties failed to report any recovery rate statistics when Illinois residents were getting infected by the thousands.[25]

Advanced data reporting techniques by investigative reporters also became important in New York State. As early as July 2020, *New York Times* reporters used data analysis to decipher the controversy over nursing home deaths in that state that was growing increasingly political.[26] Six months after the *Times* investigative report, the New York State attorney general validated the news investigation with an official report that faulted Governor Andrew Cuomo and his administration for undercounting nursing home deaths by as much as half. That same AG report alleged that a failure to follow Covid-19 protocols put some New York nursing home residents at increased risk.[27]

GIJN's Philp said a number of the investigative journalists he monitored on five continents on behalf of GIJN not only worked from home during the 2020 pandemic but increasingly made use of open-source intelligence made famous by Bellingcat—the group of "citizen" investigators who surfed the Internet to uncover government plots, solve murders and reveal criminal conspiracies.[28] By April of 2021, Bellingcat itself was partnering with traditional news organizations like NBC News to investigate such things as the U.S. Capitol insurrection, which had occurred three months earlier.[29] Such partnerships exemplified the kind of collaboration between organizations and skill sets Houston had predicted would increase in his essay about the future of investigative journalism published in *Daedalus* eleven years earlier.[30] Pandemic pressures in 2020 appeared to put those predicted partnerships into high gear.

During the pandemic, investigative journalists helped elevate the science of solving mysteries with publicly available (open source) clues to a new level of prominence. Covid-19 investigative reporting highlighted the value of geocoding software programs such as CrowdTangle and Twitter, as well as the embedded metadata in photos posted online. Not only were such tools helpful for reporting on the rise and location of Covid-19 infections, but also for unrelated political events that later became important to investigative journalists as well as the FBI and other law enforcement investigators. Take, for example, the political mob that stormed the U.S. Capitol on January 6, 2021. "The use of geocode in TweetDeck which we saw as recently as the Capitol Building attack, those are the kinds of tools that are taking off," Philp said. Investigative reporters at the *New York Times* used geocoding, leaked smartphone data and social media posts to identify and locate some of the suspects eventually arrested for that attack.[31] NBC's Richard Engel also employed geocoding technology in his partnership with Bellingcat while investigating the Capitol attack.[32]

Investigative journalists had been honing their data skills long before the pandemic—in my case, sporadically for decades. I attended my first National Institute for Computer-Assisted Reporting (NICAR) seminar in 1995 and learned how to find (and close) cases on dead fugitives and expose sex offenders working in Florida as licensed massage therapists. How about violent convicted criminals and schizophrenics with Florida concealed weapons permits? Bet you didn't know dozens of South American pit vipers were living in your neighbor's bedroom. But the state did, and they approved it. The possibilities were endless. Most of the nation's large news organizations and even smaller newsrooms that promote investigative journalism had been training staff on the use of spreadsheets, pivot tables and data mapping for a generation prior to the pandemic. That meant hundreds of investigative reporters, producers and editors were already experienced in managing "big data" long beforehand. In 2020, there was no more important data set across the planet than the number, location and severity of Covid-19 infections.

In 2020, TV newscasts announced the daily infection tally with the same frequency as sports scores or stock market reports. But it was up to investigative journalists to fact-check and make sense of those statistics. "By the time the pandemic hit here in the U.S. we had 25 years of intense training and using machines—that is computers and software—to understand bad data and really correctly visualize data," Houston said.

As part of an ongoing project to visualize the human toll of Covid-19, the *New York Times* broke new ground when it published a front page "Wall of Grief" graphic on February 21, 2021. That one illustration represented every reported Covid-19 death in the U.S. by using black dots on a timeline.[33] The timeline's density of "death dots" turned black in January 2021—just at a time when some U.S. political leaders were declaring victory over the pandemic in order to re-open the economy. The actual darkness of that moment—the truth of it—was on stark display in black and white. It was a stunning illustration of the disconnect between the facts of the moment and wishful thinking. "The *New York Times* 'COVID Project' is a poster child for that," Houston said.

When Houston wrote about the future of investigative journalism in *Daedalus* a decade ago, the journalism profession was still reeling from the 2008 Great Recession, and investigative budgets in newspapers had withered. Houston noted that over time, budgets improved and collaboration between news outlets and nonprofit investigative organizations filled the gap. "Then Donald Trump came along," Houston said. The so-called "Trump Bump" changed everything.

No Slow News Days

Before the so-called media "Trump Bump" arrived in 2015, the *Washington Post* was already heavily invested in news investigations. Four years later, with Trump running for re-election, the *Post* found itself well-situated to report on the Covid-19 crisis while backed by a billionaire as the paper's owner and a renowned champion of investigations as executive editor. "[Amazon founder] Jeff Bezos bought the place and our newsroom doubled in size," Leen said. "[Executive editor] Marty Baron put an emphasis in investigative reporting," Leen added. "So every single staff from sports to financial to local engages in investigative reporting now as part of their mission." Baron retired from the *Post* on February 28, 2021, but the investigative emphasis he had nurtured and promoted during his tenure showed little sign of waning after his departure.[34]

When the pandemic arrived, two separate teams of WP investigators were already working under Leen, which he said was the *Post*'s largest commitment to news investigations since the unit's formation with 1970's Woodward and Bernstein Watergate investigation. On March 7, 2020, the *Post* published one of its first big investigative stories surrounding Covid-19, days before the World Health Organization (WHO) declared a pandemic. "We broke the story that it was the contamination of the Centers for Disease Control [CDC] lab that held up the testing in the United

States," Leen said. It was like lighting a fuse for what was to follow. "I mean, that story went viral and got more than a million hits," Leen said.

For investigative journalists across the United States, little else mattered as fatalities mounted, economies shut down and pandemic fears worsened, all of it unfolding amid racial discord, violent protests and rising political extremism on both ends of the political spectrum. January 6, 2021, nearly a year into the pandemic, a mob of President Donald Trump supporters sought to reverse the November 2020 presidential election outcome by attacking the U.S. Capitol while Congress was meeting to certify the election results. Investigative reporters now had to deal with an insurrection layered over a pandemic on top of racial violence and national unrest. There would be no more slow news days for anyone.

Follow the Money

Despite the danger and aggravation, the pandemic gave investigative journalists an opportunity to do what they had always done best: *follow the money*. And what a bonanza that turned out to be. There were trillions of Covid relief dollars to account for in the U.S. alone. In other nations, where investigative journalists had been writing about kleptocracies for years, Covid-19 opened the door for more cash grabs by corrupt leaders, this time under the guise of public health.[35]

Poynter Institute media trainer and news analyst Al Tompkins said the pandemic prompted a flood of news investigations on government spending and financial relief linked to the Covid crisis. "We have a lot of really important stories going on not just pandemic related but also related to all sorts of things including the trillions of dollars-worth of relief funds that are floating around all over the place," Tompkins said.[36] In the early months of the pandemic, investigative reporters revealed that much of the first CARES Act relief funding ending up in the wrong hands. *Time* magazine reported that the rich were getting richer with the first $2.2 trillion Covid-19 relief package passed in March 2020 at the expense of struggling taxpayers.[37]

Growing Collaboration

A trend toward collaboration between media organizations was already well underway before the pandemic when former IRE executive director Houston wrote about the future of investigative journalism a decade ago.[38] Large media organizations had been partnering on projects with investigative nonprofits on a regular basis even before the pandemic arrived.

Several years prior to the pandemic, data sharing on a global scale had taken place with great success with the "Panama Papers." In that investigative journalism project, a consortium of more than 100 media partners analyzed more than 11 million leaked bank and financial records to uncover corruption on a global scale in 2016.[39] When Covid-19 alarms started going off in early 2020, global journalism networks such as the International Consortium of Investigative Journalists (ICIJ), which analyzed the Panama Papers, and the Global Investigative Journalism Network (GIJN), which has members in 80 nations and staff on five continents, were already well established and flourishing.

When Covid-19 hit, the GIJN discontinued in-person training and focused on supplying resources and networking opportunities to journalists who found themselves more isolated than ever and now faced with some of the most challenging investigative stories of a lifetime. Philp said GIJN had already established a global network of editors from Peru to Pakistan by the time the pandemic emerged. "I'll reach out to our regional editor in that region and say, 'who do you know who's done some amazing work using open source investigative techniques or on authoritarian surveillance technologies and they'll say 'oh' and they'll link me up with that person," Rowan said. The pandemic didn't spark the GIJN network of editors, but it helped forge a common purpose when reporters around the planet began covering local versions of the same global story. "The [GIJN] regional editors are really the backbone I would say of the whole organization ... people spread around the world monitoring the investigative landscape where they are." GIJN's ability to translate tips and tools into 14 languages was a boon for investigative journalists around the world covering the same pandemic.

The kind of journalistic networking and collaboration that Houston predicted back in 2010 was paying dividends during the pandemic. "It is so easy to see what others are doing and share it," Houston said. NBC's partnership with Bellingcat in the January 6, 2021, Capitol Insurrection investigation, referred to earlier, established that such partnerships had finally gone mainstream and could be a powerful tool to identify wrongdoers and hold them accountable.[40]

Pandemic Attacks on Press Freedom

One of the most damaging impacts of Covid-19 on investigative journalism and those who practice it is the extent to which some governments seized the moment to suppress press freedoms and target journalists for surveillance, harassment and even arrest.[41] Under the political cover of pandemic public health protocols, some governments deliberately restricted journalists' freedom to gather and accurately report on some of the most pressing issues of the day: the spread of infections, government inaction and incompetence, economic hardship, and the deaths of millions. The repressive trend was repeatedly noted by journalism organizations as well as human rights activists worldwide.[42]

In the Philippines, strongman Rodrigo Duterte's disdain for journalists had been festering for years before the Covid-19 outbreak.[43] During the pandemic his power to bully the press was unleashed even further. The 2020 RSF report painted a frightening picture:

> When sworn in as president in June 2016, Rodrigo Duterte issued this cryptic but grim warning: "Just because you're a journalist, you are not exempted from assassination, if you're a son of a bitch. Freedom of expression cannot help you if you have done something wrong." Three Philippine journalists were killed in 2019, probably by thugs working for local politicians, who can have reporters silenced with complete impunity.[44]

In 2020—amid the fear and chaos of the Covid-19 pandemic—Duterte's regime brazenly seized the moment in attempt to silence the Rappler news operation[45] with "cyberlibel" charges and even jailed its besieged manager Maria Ressa for alleged journalistic wrongdoing. Duterte's crackdown may have been intended to muzzle Ressa, but in some ways it had the opposite impact. It raised Ressa's previous status as a cause célèbre of journalism advocates such as the #HOLDTHELINE coalition. Duterte's public harassment helped pushed Ressa to the center of a world stage as a crusader for press freedom.[46] Ressa was the focal point of a PBS *Frontline* documentary titled "A Thousand Cuts," broadcast on January 8, 2021; it detailed Duterte's relentless campaign to silence Ressa, culminating in her arrest amid the turmoil, distraction and distress of the Covid pandemic.[47] The documentary concluded that Covid-19 gave Duterte perfect cover for retaliation against Ressa and Rappler and helped send a menacing message to other watchdog journalists in the Philippines. Meanwhile, investigative organizations were sending their own message back by publicizing journalistic bullying and injustices.

In the United States, there was friction from the Trump administration and some U.S. governors when investigative journalists held government leaders accountable for their handling of the pandemic and the vaccine roll-out. Trump adapted his running battle over what he called "fake news" by focusing on pandemic reporting. In the final weeks of his 2020 re-election campaign, Trump assailed the press for reporting on a new surge of Covid-19 infections at a time when he and his allies were trying to end pandemic restrictions in order to help revive the economy and put the final days of his first term in a positive light.[48] Meanwhile, state and regional leaders in the U.S. also sparred with investigative reporters as public criticism over the pandemic response piled up.

CBS's *60 Minutes* broadcast a story on April 4, 2021, that alleged Florida governor Ron DeSantis favored campaign contributors in a "pay-to play" scheme during the early days of the vaccine distribution, when demand far outstripped supply. A day after the broadcast, DeSantis threatened unspecified "consequences" as a retaliation against what he called "false narrative."[49] DeSantis had refused a *60 Minutes* interview request prior to the CBS report, but he hosted a one-hour news conference days after the CBS broadcast to dispute the facts. DeSantis went on the offensive, telling reporters he refused to be bullied by big corporate media organizations such as CBS.[50] DeSantis's rant against CBS paled next to threats of violence against reporters by foreign leaders like Duterte, or constant criticism from Trump. But it was more evidence of the friction between investigative reporters and government leaders that grew hotter under the pressure of the pandemic.

The *2020 World Press Freedom Index*,[51] compiled by Reporters Without Borders, concludes that authoritarian governments took advantage of the public health crisis to implement a "shock doctrine" intended to throttle journalists and control the flow of pandemic information to the public. In that 2020 analysis, RSF secretary-general Christophe Deloire wrote that the health crisis opened the door for some governments "to take advantage of the fact that politics are on hold, the public is stunned and protests are out of the question, in order to impose measures that would be impossible in normal times." The 2020 RSF analysis of 180 nations specifically calls out China, Iran, Iraq and Hungary as some of the most flagrant oppressors of press freedoms related to the pandemic:

There is a clear correlation between suppression of media freedom in response to the coronavirus pandemic and a country's ranking in the *Index*. Both China (177th) and Iran (173rd) censored their major coronavirus outbreaks extensively. In Iraq (down 6 at 162nd), the authorities stripped Reuters of its license for three months after it published a story questioning official coronavirus figures. Even in Europe, Prime Minister Viktor Orbán of Hungary (down 2 at 89th) had a "coronavirus" law passed with penalties of up to five years in prison for false information, a completely disproportionate and coercive measure.[52]

Those nations may have grabbed some of the biggest headlines of that 2020 report, but the *Index* concluded that press freedoms suffered even greater losses in Haiti and two seldom-discussed countries—Comoros (an Indian Ocean island nation located off the east coast of Africa) and the West African nation of Benin.[53]

One of the most ironic examples of the government repression of investigative journalists shares the same epicenter as the pandemic itself. On March 25, 2021, the *Press Gazette*'s Dominic Ponsford reported—more than 15 months after the first reported Covid-19 infections in Wuhan, China, became public knowledge—on the harassment of the *Telegraph* correspondent Sophia Yan.[54] Among other things, Yan "exposed the extent of a state-led coverup in the city where COVID-19 is believed to have emerged." Yan's reporting on Covid and other sensitive matters resulted in her "being tracked, intimidated and assaulted by the Chinese state," according to the Press Gazette.[55] That was a lot of government firepower aimed at the professional musician turned Beijing correspondent. Yan became a journalist after switching from a career as a concert pianist. Yan apparently hit sour notes with the Chinese state by trying to tell the story of Covid-19.

Spy Tools and Burner Phones

During the pandemic, some governments allegedly re-purposed a powerful spyware tool called Pegasus to snoop on reporters by tapping into their cell phones. Privacy warnings about Pegasus emerged as far back as April 11, 2017, in a blog by John Snow of the Kapersky global cybersecurity firm.[56] Pegasus can steal data from an infected mobile phone and then erase all of that phone's data when it's done, mimicking a real-life *Mission Impossible* moment. According to one news report, written five months before the pandemic by David Binod Shrestha of the *Deccan Herald*, Pegasus is so insidious that it can infect a phone without a single response by the intended target, something known as a "zero-click vector." Shrestha wrote, "Basically, the phones were infected via an incoming call, which even when ignored, would install Pegasus on the device."[57] In one such instance of cell phone "cyber-peeping," *Al Jazeera* reported how Israeli government snoopers hacked into the phones of that Mideast-based news organization's investigative team using Pegasus spyware.[58] That privacy incursion occurred while the creators of Pegasus were reportedly marketing a new variant of that spyware to governments for a more benevolent purpose—as a software tool for tracking Covid infections.[59]

GIJN reporter Rowan Philp expressed concern about the misuse of surveillance tools to monitor investigative reporters during the pandemic. "This business about surveillance—increased surveillance—has been a real problem for reporters that I've spoken to in the last year [2020]," Philp said. Philp believes the pandemic only made such spying on reporters more pervasive. "It's useful cover," Philp said. "Many states have wanted to track down and surveil reporters anyway. This has given them justification—even the legal justification in some cases—to legally track down and start monitoring reporters in a more detailed fashion." Philp said Pegasus software can mine a reporter's cell phone contents such as geo-location data, phone logs, contacts and even photos. And as Kaspersky pointed out years earlier, the target—in this example a reporter—does not even have to answer the phone. "You can get a missed phone call, that's it and Pegasus can redirect your phone to a site that just begins harvesting your details," Philp said.

He noted one of the most chilling examples involved Moroccan investigative journalist Omar Radi in the run-up to and early days of the pandemic. Radi had been the target of harassment in the past, which reportedly intensified during and after the alleged phone hacks. On June 21, 2020, the *Guardian* reported on the depth of Radi's harassment by government officials[60]: "He has in the past faced interrogations and detention in solitary confinement. He was given a suspended four-month prison term in March [2020] for a tweet he posted in April 2019 in which he criticized a trial of a group of activists." Because of government surveillance of them, some investigative reporters like Radi have turned to burner phones and encrypted communications alternatives to common Internet meeting platforms such as Zoom that are harder to hack and monitor by authorities.

Exiled Saudi filmmaker and investigative journalist Safa Al-Ahmad became renowned for her gutsy reports on suffering in war-torn Yemen prior to the pandemic. Covid-19 restricted her ability to travel and presented other roadblocks for Al-Ahmad due to the increasing threat of government surveillance. Philp said, in 2020, that Al-Ahmad operated in a constant state of vigilance—and, like other journalists wary of Pegasus, had stopped using traceable cell phones and other digital tools subject to government surveillance. "She has to use a burner phone constantly," Philp added. "She has to be paranoid during any digital interaction."

At the *Washington Post*, investigative journalists also used defensive technology to safeguard their privacy and protect sources. Even prior to Covid-19, they did not typically meet with confidential sources in parking garages—like they famously did back in the Woodward and Bernstein days—because they now had access to relatively secure digital communication tools to avoid the prying eyes and ears of government. "We still get sources that reach us through encrypted [means]—like Signal or WhatsApp," said *Post* news investigations editor Jeff Leen. But that doesn't mean the Woodward and Bernstein garage days are all in the past. Leen said there are still times when a clandestine rendezvous is necessary and appropriate. "We still have meetings with sources with really sensitive material," Leen said.[61]

For thousands of investigative journalists around the world, government surveillance and new restrictions on press freedoms during the pandemic added a troubling layer of difficulty to the Covid-19 news coverage conundrum.[62] Reporters Without Borders warned that not only did the pandemic have a negative impact on press freedoms in 2020, but reporters also entered a decisive decade for journalism at the same moment: "With the COVID-19 pandemic highlighting and amplifying the many crises that threaten the right to freely report, independent, diverse and reliable information."[63]

New Skills and Methods

While the pandemic may have helped give rise to new Big Brother technology to monitor, harass and censor investigative journalists, it also fostered fresh tools for reporters to track what governments were doing and how well they were doing it. Look at what happened when Florida governor Ron DeSantis sparred with journalists who annoyed him with anecdotes about breakdowns in the state's unemployment insurance system. At the time, thousands of consumer complaints were pouring into Florida news outlets. By May of 2020, Florida's unemployment rate had swelled to 14.5 percent due to the pandemic lockdowns, an alarming fact that was minimized in DeSantis's press releases at the time. DeSantis preferred talking about Florida's expanding workforce as he attempted to "safely" re-open the state's economy.[64]

In contrast to DeSantis's rosy economic projections, many out-of-work residents complained they were not getting the State of Florida unemployment relief checks they deserved.[65] DeSantis insisted the system was working well at the time and challenged journalists to forward their consumer complaints instead of hectoring him at news conferences with anecdotal questions he could not answer.[66]

WFTS-TV investigative reporter Kylie McGivern said her TV station and other news outlets turned to technology and took up the governor's challenge. "You want a list," McGivern responded. "We have a list."[67] But creating that list required a new way of collecting and organizing consumer complaints that were overwhelming WFTS and other Florida news organizations at the time.[68] "When you are a local news station and all of a sudden you have hundreds and hundreds of people reaching out to you with these issues how do you capture that[?]" McGivern asked. Rather than individually fielding calls, emails and letters, as had been done in the past, McGivern's investigative team set up a fill-in-the-blanks Google Docs page where unemployed Floridians with grievances could enter their complaint information. "It goes into a spreadsheet that we can sort through and send it directly to the state," McGivern said. "So, in terms of capturing a huge amount of people we shifted our reporting way to be able to handle that in a way we've never thought of before."

The "rise of machines" that Houston predicted in 2010 would play a prominent role in the future of investigative journalism helped provide an effective 2020 pandemic solution to the WFTS investigative team and other news outlets. It wasn't brain surgery; they just compiled crowd-sourced spreadsheets. "As of now [March 5, 2021] we [WFTS-TV] have sent more than 26,000 names to the [Florida] Department of Economic Opportunity," McGivern said. Other investigative reporters in Florida used the same methods to hold the state accountable.[69]

During the pandemic, Houston was teaching data analysis skills to journalism students as the Knight Chair in Investigative Reporting at the University of Illinois. Houston said the pandemic proves that literacy in data analysis, spreadsheets and pivot tables should be among the basic skills of investigative reporters. On a more advanced level in some newsrooms, artificial intelligence (AI) is already in play for some investigative journalists (see Dr. Casey Frechette's essay in this collection), but Houston urges caution. "We need to proceed slowly and carefully," Houston said. He has long taught that data reporting can go wrong with a single click of a mouse, and the proper implementation of AI algorithms can be even trickier.

A year before the pandemic hit, the Nieman Journalism Lab at Harvard published a list of grants and projects advancing the use of AI for metadata analysis and investigative journalism projects to help analyze government contracts for patterns of fraud, promote the understanding of AI itself, and advance its journalistic use.[70] On November 18, 2019— just months before the pandemic became a worldwide threat—Professor Charlie Beckett of the London School of Economics and Political Science published an AI status report after surveying 71 news organizations in 32 nations.[71] Beckett found that less than half of the worldwide news outlets surveyed at that time indicated they were using AI for newsgathering purposes. Roughly two-thirds of them said they employed AI for production purposes. Many of those who did use AI as a reporting tool spoke enthusiastically about how AI eliminates robotic tasks that waste time for reporters as well as helps sift through metadata with algorithms to reveal newsworthy trends along with patterns of fraud, corruption and government failures.

The use of AI revealed shopping habits during the pandemic and helped explain the surprising shortage of toilet paper and other paper goods during the pandemic. It also revealed some weaknesses in the technology.⁷² Yet there are many possibilities for using AI to explore important questions. A few months before the pandemic, GIJN reported how investigative journalists at the *Atlanta Constitution* had used AI years earlier to narrow the search for physicians who had sexually abused their patients but continued to practice medicine.⁷³

Just weeks after WHO's official declaration of a pandemic, Alex Engler of the Brookings Institution published a report (on April 2, 2020) called "A Guide to Health Skepticism of Artificial Intelligence and the Coronavirus." In that report Engler cautioned against too much reliance by journalists on AI as a panacea for pandemic data analysis.⁷⁴

Professor Beckett's AI journalism report listed numerous possibilities as well as pitfalls in the application of AI to journalism. Professor Beckett wrote that while AI brings a new set of ethical questions and pitfalls to the profession, it is also critical to helping journalists operate more efficiently and to helping the public cope with an overload of information:

> Perhaps the biggest message we should take from this report is that we are at another critical historical moment. If we value journalism as a social good, provided by humans for humans, then we have a window of perhaps 2–5 years, when news organisations must get across this technology. The good news that we take from the responses to our survey, is that a significant part of the global journalism industry is facing up to that challenge and working hard to make it happen. They are enthusiastic about the new powers, but also accept the new responsibilities.⁷⁵

Whether through AI algorithms or simpler forms of data analysis, journalistic fact-checking efforts became even more crucial during the pandemic to help combat misinformation and disinformation about the virus, vaccines and related political issues. The Google News Initiative said it helped train thousands of journalists in India alone during the pandemic but had to switch its methods to online training instead of person-to-person seminars as a safety measure.⁷⁶ Those training efforts became more important than anyone might have imagined. By May 2021, India had become the World's hotspot for Covid-19, with nearly 23 million reported infections, a quarter million reported deaths, and a worldwide plea for oxygen, ventilators and other depleted medical supplies.⁷⁷

A Defining Moment

Even savvy journalists didn't start raising concerns about a possible "SARS" epidemic until January 2020. Even then, in a January 3, 2020, report about a "China pneumonia outbreak," the BBC relied on statements by Chinese authorities who wrongly insisted "there had been no human-to-human transmission" among the 44 confirmed cases in Wuhan at that time.[78]

Two weeks after that BBC report, the Global Investigative Journalism Network (GIJN) published predictions of the investigative journalism landscape by a dozen investigative journalists from China to Colombia in a report titled "What Investigative Journalism Will Look Like in 2020."[79] The GIJN report accurately predicted intensified press censorship by authoritarian regimes, the growth and necessity of collaboration, and increased use of technology including not just spreadsheets but also satellites and artificial intelligence. But not even one of the GIJN writers foresaw the coming pandemic that would consume the world's attention, kill millions worldwide and alter the course of history. It was not even on their radar. Just a few months earlier, GIJN held its 11th Global Investigative Conference in Hamburg, Germany, with the highest number of attendees ever. The conference generated countless discussions about technology, kleptocracy and collaboration but nary a word about the coming storm called Covid-19, which just six months later dominated the global news cycle 24/7.

Investigative journalists may have been caught flat-footed at the start of the pandemic, but many also "met the moment," as McGivern said. "In the beginning we were so 'hair on fire' working incredibly long days. Nine in the morning until 11:15 at night every single day, it was just to get it done," said CNN's DiCarlo. She said investigative journalists felt compelled to step up as a matter of personal and professional survival. "I wish I had kept a journal of every day and what it was like because when you're going through this and this incredible moment you're just trying to get through your work and do the best you can," said DiCarlo.[80]

Like everyone impacted by the pandemic, investigative journalists learned how to gather information while roaming about with computer keyboards instead of their feet. Cyberspace became the forced alternative when travel restrictions and social distancing limited physical interactions. Investigators by necessity learned how to work from home and collaborate using new and more secure means of communication. "We figured out a way to put television on—great television on—every single day—with every single person being at home," said DiCarlo. "I think we were a lot more nimble that we believed ourselves to be."

All this happened while simultaneously untangling a gordian knot of medical misinformation that infected the Internet faster than the virus itself. The Covid-19 pandemic created unprecedented obstacles for investigative reporters, but it also allowed them to apply reporting methods and data tools that had been decades in development. It also fostered creativity in the face of adversity. When Somali journalists suspected that government officials were under-reporting the Covid-19 death toll, they interviewed medics, funeral workers and gravediggers for a more accurate, visceral and compelling account of the unfolding tragedy.[81]

The pandemic also gave investigative journalists a bottomless well of topics to write about. "It was hard to get a hearing [for reporters] in any other kind of story," Houston recalled. "It was a major story of the century in so many ways." At CNN, investigations ranged from failed government Covid-19 testing to state prisons where inmates produced hand sanitizer for the nation but were banned from using it themselves. The germicide contained alcohol and was considered "contraband."

In a world roiled by pandemic panic and fear, journalists somehow had to make sense of it or at least describe accurately the gravity of what was going on. This is how newspaper editor Antisa Korljan starkly described pandemic life in his native Slovenia:

> The administrations went into lockdown, sports events were cancelled, festivals, culture, everyday life, even criminals took a break. It was possible to take a selfie in the middle of the busiest road of the capital without risk of being hit by a car. As there was absolutely no traffic in the city centre one could hear birds from the park around the corner. Never before nor later did I have such an experience.[82]

One year after the first two Covid-19 cases in Florida spiraled into two million infections, it was hard to focus on anything else. Around the globe possible pandemic stories proliferated faster than journalists could tackle them. But working through travel restrictions, government roadblocks and physical separation from colleagues and sources—now, *that* was the trick. During most of 2020, heading to the office typically meant walking to another room in your own home. "Now a year later, no one actually has to go into the [CNN] building to get anything done," DiCarlo said. As of May 2021, DiCarlo was still running CNN's investigative unit out of her parent's home in Tampa. "We had to pivot in the way we do news," DiCarlo said.

During 2020 and 2021, investigative journalists dramatically altered their work methods and personal lifestyle as a matter of basic survival in the global pandemic. In some cases, these "truth hunters" became "hunted" by authoritarian governments using spyware, surveillance and arrest powers. New tricks, tools and technology helped investigative reporters worldwide speak truth to power despite government resistance, travel restrictions and even the threat of prosecution or actual imprisonment. In the end, collaboration, creativity and a call to duty carried the day in what historians may someday regard as the most important years to date for investigative journalism.

Notes

1. Antisa Korljan, email to author, May 13, 2021, 10:25 a.m.
2. State of Florida, Office of the Governor, Executive Order Number 20-51, https://www.orlandoweekly.com/media/pdf/executive_order_20_51.pdf.
3. "DHS Denies 241 People Entry at US Ports and Airports," CNN, March 5, 2020, https://www.cnn.com/world/live-news/coronavirus-outbreak-03-06-20-intl-hnk/h_9714 62988f8d70b53f06d9214a629cc9.
4. Patricia DiCarlo, CNN Investigative Unit Executive Producer, phone interview, April 13, 2021, 2 p.m.
5. Scott Bronstein, Drew Griffin, and Scott Glover, "They Didn't Protect Us," CNN, March 11, 2020, https://www.cnn.com/2020/03/11/health/coronavirus-first-responders-invs/index.html.
6. Dave Alsup, "8 Cases of Coronavirus Confirmed in Colorado," CNN, March 6, 2020, https://www.cnn.com/world/live-news/coronavirus-outbreak-03-06-20-intl-hnk/index.html.
7. Antisa Korljan, email to author, May 13, 2021, 10:25 a.m.
8. "Coronavirus Disease (COVID-19) Pandemic," index to topics, World Health Organization, https://www.who.int/emergencies/diseases/novel-coronavirus-2019.
9. State of Florida Covid Dashboard, April 6, 2021, https://experience.arcgis.com/experience/96dd742462124fa0b38ddedb9b25e429.
10. Gali Ginatt, email to author, May 6, 2020, 9:16 p.m.
11. Rebecca Ratcliffe, "Journalist Maria Ressa Found Guilty of 'Cyberlibel' in Philippines," *Guardian*, June 15, 2020, https://www.theguardian.com/world/2020/jun/15/maria-ressa-rappler-editor-found-guilty-of-cyber-libel-charges-in-philippines.
12. "2020 World Press Freedom Index: 'Entering a Decisive Decade for Journalism, Exacerbated by Coronavirus,'" Reporters Without Borders, n.d., https://rsf.org/en/2020-world-press-freedom-index-entering-decisive-decade-journalism-exacerbated-coronavirus.
13. 11th Global Investigative Journalism Conference, https://gijc2019.org.
14. Rowan Philp, Zoom interview, February 17, 2021, 1 p.m.
15. "GIJN Launches Webinar Series: Investigating the Pandemic," Global Investigative Journalism Network, April 2, 2020, https://gijn.org/2020/04/02/join-gijn-and-guests-for-our-webinar-series-investigating-the-pandemic.
16. Rowan Philp, "How to Tackle the Global Undercount in COVID-19 Deaths: Reporters Offer Tips and Techniques," Global Investigative Journalism Network, May 26, 2020, https://gijn.org/2020/05/26/how-to-tackle-the-global-undercount-in-covid-19-deaths-reporters-offer-tips-and-techniques/.
17. Antisa Korljan, email to author, May 13, 2021, 10:25 a.m.
18. "National Investigations," *Washington Post*, https://www.washingtonpost.com/national/investigations/.
19. Jeffrey Leen, *Washington Post* investigations editor, phone interview, February 25, 2021, 2:00 p.m.
20. Kylie McGivern, WFTS-TV investigative reporter, phone interview, March 5, 2021, 11 a.m.
21. Kylie McGivern.
22. "1918 Pandemic (H1N1 Virus)," Centers for Disease Control, https://www.cdc.gov/flu/pandemic-resources/1918-pandemic-h1n1.html.
23. Brant Houston, University of Illinois journalism professor, phone interview, March 9, 2021, 3:30 p.m.
24. Anthony Komaroff, "The Tragedy of Long COVID," Harvard Health Publishing, October 15, 2020, 2:30 p.m., updated March 1, 2021, 1:02 p.m., https://www.health.harvard.edu/blog/the-tragedy-of-the-post-covid-long-haulers-2020101521173.
25. Mike Koziatek, "Some Counties in Southwest Illinois Track Coronavirus Recoveries," *Belleville News-Democrat*, April 10, 2020, https://www.bnd.com/news/coronavirus/article241909731.html.

26. Luis Ferré-Sadurni and Amy Julia Harris, "Does Cuomo Share Blame for 6,200 Virus Deaths in N.Y. Nursing Homes?" *New York Times*, July 8, 2020, https://www.nytimes.com/2020/07/08/nyregion/nursing-homes-deaths-coronavirus.html.

27. New York State Office of the Attorney General, "Nursing Home Response to COVID-19 Pandemic," revised January 30, 2021, https://ag.ny.gov/sites/default/files/2021-nursinghomesreport.pdf.

28. Bellingcat, https://www.bellingcat.com/.

29. "New Insights into How Capitol Riot Carried Out," NBC News, April 9, 2021, https://www.nbcnews.com/nightly-news/video/new-insights-into-how-capitol-riot-carried-out-109951557517.

30. Brant Houston, "The Future of Investigative Journalism," *Daedalus*, spring 2010, pp. 45–55, https://www.amacad.org/sites/default/files/daedalus/downloads/Sp2010_On-the-Future-of-News.pdf.

31. Charlie Warzel and Stuart A. Thompson, "They Stormed the Capitol. Their Apps Tracked Them," *New York Times*, February 5, 2021, https://www.nytimes.com/2021/02/05/opinion/capitol-attack-cellphone-data.html.

32. "Richard Engel Investigates the January 6 Capitol Insurrection," Yahoo News, April 9, 2021, https://news.yahoo.com/richard-engel-investigates-january-6-165349920.html.

33. Nancy Coleman, "On the Front Page, a Wall of Grief," *New York Times*, February 21, 2021, https://www.nytimes.com/2021/02/21/insider/covid-500k-front-page.html.

34. Marc Tracy, "How Marty Baron and Jeff Bezos Remade the Washington Post," *New York Times*, February 27, 2021, https://www.nytimes.com/2021/02/27/business/marty-baron-jeff-bezos-washington-post.html.

35. Natalie Rhodes, "Corruption and the Coronavirus," Transparency International, March 18, 2021, https://www.transparency.org/en/news/corruption-and-the-coronavirus.

36. Al Tompkins, Poynter Institute instructor, phone interview, March 5, 2021, 1 p.m.

37. Alana Abramson, "'No Lessons Have Been Learned.' Why the Trillion-Dollar Coronavirus Bailout Benefited the Rich," *Time*, June 18, 2020, 4:13 p.m. https://time.com/5845116/coronavirus-bailout-rich-richer.

38. Warzel and Thompson, "They Stormed the Capitol."

39. "About the investigation," International Consortium of Investigative Journalists, n.d., https://www.icij.org/investigations/panama-papers/pages/panama-papers-about-the-investigation.

40. "Our House—The Police," MSNBC, April 11, 2021, https://www.msnbc.com/on-assignment/watch/in-a-joint-investigation-by-nbc-news-bellingcat-and-its-volunteers-on-assignment-with-richard-engel-takes-a-closer-look-at-the-insurrection-at-the-capitol-on-january-6th-watch-part-five-of-our-investigation-the-police-110189637727.

41. "2020 World Press Freedom Index: 'Entering a Decisive Decade.'"

42. Sarah Repucci and Amy Slipowitz, "Democracy Under Lockdown," Freedom House, n.d., https://freedomhouse.org/report/special-report/2020/democracy-under-lockdown; Louisa Loveluck, Robyn Dixon, and Adam Taylor, "Journalists threatened and detained as countries on multiple continents restrict coronavirus coverage," *Washington Post*, April 5, 2020, https://www.washingtonpost.com/world/journalists-threatened-and-detained-as-countries-on-multiple-continents-restrict-coronavirus-coverage/2020/04/05/90d9953e-6eb7-11ea-a156-0048b62cdb51_story.html; ForeignPolicy.com, https://foreignpolicy.com/2020/12/30/press-media-freedom-2020-journalists-covid-19-pandemic/; "Press Freedom Must Not Be Undermined by Measures to Counter Disinformation About COVID-19," Council of Europe, March 4, 2020, https://www.coe.int/en/web/commissioner/-/press-freedom-must-not-be-undermined-by-measures-to-counter-disinformation-about-covid-19.

43. Bill Whitaker, "Maria Ressa: Reporting in the Philippines," CBS News, November 10, 2019, https://www.cbsnews.com/news/rappler-news-ceo-maria-ressa-60-minutes-interview-2019-11-10.

44. "Holding the Line Against Duterte's Attacks," Reporters Without Borders, n.d., https://rsf.org/en/philippines.

45. Rappler, https://www.rappler.com.

46. "#HoldTheLine Coalition Sounds Alarm over Escalating Legal Harassment of Maria Ressa," Reporters Without Borders, February 2, 2021, https://rsf.org/en/news/holdtheline-coalition-sounds-alarm-over-escalating-legal-harassment-maria-ressa.
47. "A Thousand Cuts," PBS *Frontline*, January 8, 2021, https://www.pbs.org/wgbh/frontline/film/a-thousand-cuts.
48. Berkeley Lovelace, Jr., "Trump Claims the Worsening U.S. Coronavirus Outbreak Is a 'Fake News Media Conspiracy' Even as Hospitalizations Rise," CNBC, October 26, 2020, https://www.cnbc.com/2020/10/26/coronavirus-trump-claims-the-worsening-us-outbreak-is-a-fake-news-media-conspiracy-even-as-hospitalizations-rise.html.
49. Steve Lemongello, "DeSantis Threatens CBS with 'Consequences' over 'Pay-for-Play' Vaccine Story on '60 Minutes,'" *Orlando Sentinel*, April 6, 2021, https://www.orlandosentinel.com/politics/os-ne-desantis-threat-60-minutes-20210406-t6eamy2uljewdidrmthsuaqkhy-story.html.
50. Charlotte Klein, "Ron Desantis Is Taking His *60 Minutes* Feud All the Way to the Bank," *Vanity Fair*, April 7, 2021, https://www.vanityfair.com/news/2021/04/ron-desantis-is-taking-his-60-minutes-feud-all-the-way-to-the-bank.
51. "2020 World Press Freedom Index."
52. *Ibid.*
53. *Ibid.*
54. Dominic Ponsford, "Telegraph's Sophia Yan on Being Tracked, Intimidated and Assaulted by Chinese State," *Press Gazette*, March 25, 2021, https://www.pressgazette.co.uk/reporting-china-sophie-yan-journalism.
55. Ponsford, "Telegraph's Sophia Yan."
56. John Snow, "Pegasus: The Ultimate Spyware for iOS and Android," Kaspersky Daily, April 11, 2017, https://usa.kaspersky.com/blog/pegasus-spyware/11002.
57. David Binod Shrestha, "Pegasus Spyware: All You Need to Know," *Deccan Herald*, November 2019, https://www.deccanherald.com/specials/pegasus-spyware-all-you-need-to-know-772667.html.
58. "The Spy in Your Phone," *Al Jazeera*, January 6, 2021, https://www.aljazeera.com/program/al-jazeera-world/2021/1/6/the-spy-in-your-phone.
59. Lorenzo Franceschi-Bicchierai, "We Saw NSO's Covid-19 Software in Action, and Privacy Experts Are Worried," Vice, April 2, 2020, https://www.vice.com/en/article/epg9jm/nso-covid-19-surveillance-tech-software-tracking-infected-privacy-experts-worried.
60. Stephanie Kirchgaessner, "Israeli Spyware Used to Target Moroccan Journalist, Amnesty Claims," *Guardian*, June 21, 2020, https://www.theguardian.com/technology/2020/jun/21/journalist-says-he-was-targeted-by-spyware-from-firm-despite-its-human-rights-policy.
61. Jeffrey Leen, Washington Post investigations editor, phone interview, February 25, 2021, 2:00 p.m.
62. Rowan Philp, "How Journalists Are Coping with a Heightened Surveillance Threat," Global Investigative Journalism Network, August 26, 2020, https://gijn.org/2020/08/26/how-journalists-are-coping-with-a-heightened-surveillance-threat.
63. "2020 World Press Freedom Index."
64. "The Florida Department of Economic Opportunity Announces Florida's Workforce Is Increasing as Governor DeSantis Safely Reopens the State," Florida Department of Economic Opportunity, https://floridajobs.org/news-center/DEO-Press/deo-press-2020/june-press-releases-2020/2020/06/19/the-florida-department-of-economic-opportunity-announces-florida-s-workforce-is-increasing-as-governor-desantis-safely-reopens-the-state.
65. Lawrence Mower and Kirby Wilson, "Florida's Unemployed Still Haven't Been Paid. And They Don't Think It's Their Fault," *Tampa Bay Times*, May 31, 2020, https://www.tampabay.com/news/health/2020/05/31/floridas-unemployed-still-havent-been-paid-and-they-dont-think-its-their-fault.
66. Greg Angel, "'Who's Been Waiting?': DeSantis Denies State Isn't Paying Valid Unemployment Benefits Claims," Bay News 9, https://www.baynews9.com/fl/tampa/

news/2020/05/18/desantis-disputes-that-florida-is-failing-to-pay-valid-unemployment-benefits-claims.

67. Kylie McGivern, WFTS-TV investigative reporter, phone interview, March 5, 2021, 11:00 a.m.

68. Victoria Price, "Florida Unemployment: Fill Out 8 on Your Side Survey About Application Struggles," New Channel 8, https://www.wfla.com/community/health/coronavirus/florida-unemployment/florida-unemployment-8-on-your-side-fighting-to-get-answers-for-struggling-applicants.

69. Heather Monahan, "Still Waiting on Florida Unemployment? Fill Out 8 on Your Side's Form to Send Your Name to DeSantis," News Channel 8, https://www.wfla.com/community/health/coronavirus/florida-unemployment/whos-been-waiting-desantis-says-floridians-waiting-on-unemployment-likely-filled-out-application-wrong.

70. Laura Hazard Owen, "Whatsapp Fact-Checking, Deepfake Detection, and Five Other AI/News Projects Get Funding," NiemanLab, https://www.niemanlab.org/2019/03/whatsapp-fact-checking-deepfake-detection-and-five-other-ai-news-projects-get-funding.

71. Charlie Beckett, London School of Economics, (2019, November 18). https://blogs.lse.ac.uk/polis/2019/11/18/new-powers-new-responsibilities.

72. Will Douglas Heaven, "Our Weird Behavior During the Pandemic Is Messing with AI Models," *Technology Review*, May 11, 2020, https://www.technologyreview.com/2020/05/11/1001563/covid-pandemic-broken-ai-machine-learning-amazon-retail-fraud-humans-in-the-loop.

73. Jonathan Stray, "Beyond the Hype: Using AI Effectively in Investigative Journalism," Global Investigative Journalism Network, September 9, 2019, https://gijn.org/2019/09/09/beyond-the-hype-using-ai-effectively-in-investigative-journalism.

74. Alex Engler, "A Guide to Healthy Skepticism of Artificial Intelligence and Coronavirus," Brookings Institution, April 2, 2020, https://www.brookings.edu/research/a-guide-to-healthy-skepticism-of-artificial-intelligence-and-coronavirus.

75. Charlie Beckett, "New Powers, New Responsibilities: A Global Survey of Journalism and Artificial Intelligence," London School of Economics, November 2010, p. 92.

76. "Google News Initiative India Training Network," DataLeads.co.in, https://dataleads.co.in/pdf/GNI-Two-Year%20Report-2018-20.pdf.

77. "Tracking Coronavirus in India: Latest Map and Case Count," New York Times, May 11, 2021, https://www.nytimes.com/interactive/2020/world/asia/india-coronavirus-cases.html.

78. "China Pneumonia Outbreak: Mystery Virus Probed in Wuhan," BBC News, January 3, 2020, https://www.bbc.com/news/world-asia-china-50984025.

79. Eunice Au, "What Investigative Journalism Will Look Like in 2020," Global Investigative Journalism Network, January 15, 2020, https://gijn.org/2020/01/15/what-investigative-journalism-will-look-like-in-2020.

80. Patricia DiCarlo, CNN Investigative Unit executive producer, phone interview, April 13, 2021, 2:00 p.m.

81. Jason Burke and Abdalle Ahmed Mumin, "Somali Medics Report Rapid Rise in Deaths as Covid-19 Fears Grow," *The Guardian*, May 2, 2020, https://www.theguardian.com/world/2020/may/02/somali-medics-report-rapid-rise-in-deaths-as-covid-19-fears-grow.

82. Antisa Korljan, email correspondence, May 13, 2021, 10:25 a.m.

The Future of Collegiate Journalism in the Wake of Covid-19

Jennifer Fleming *and* Teresa Puente

> "It will help them better understand the challenges they face, to have destigmatizing conversations, and to be advocates for their peers (and even, perhaps, their professors, because mental health challenges can affect all of us)"
> —Prof. Bonnie Gasior, California State University, Long Beach

Discussions in higher education about the mass and instantaneous move to online teaching and learning since the pandemic hit typically focused on college courses. Hot topics included how to deliver course content, how to encourage engagement and how to assess achievement in online or hybrid formats. However, student media also changed dramatically and overnight in response to orders to stay at home, stay off campus and stay away from other people to stop the spread of Covid-19. Thousands of student journalists could no longer meet in newsrooms, interview sources in person or produce stories inside campus facilities. Collegiate journalism had gone virtual like its professional counterpart, yet student journalists and their advisers were for the most part on their own navigating the brave new world of covering their campuses and putting together newspapers, newscasts, podcasts and other types of content alone and from home.

In this essay, we examine the changes and challenges student journalists experienced during the pandemic at four California State University (CSU) campuses—California State University, Long Beach (CSULB), California State University, Fullerton (CSUF), California State University, Northridge (CSUN) and San Francisco State University (SFSU). We explore the effects on news gathering, communication, organization and camaraderie as campuses and newsrooms shut down, and we highlight unexpected opportunities, achievements and future directions brought on by at-a-distance reporting and storytelling. While the pandemic wreaked havoc on nearly every facet of college life, the pivot to online teaching, learning, reporting and producing inadvertently transformed collegiate journalism outlets into more intentional, collaborative and innovative digital-first operations with a renewed focus on local coverage, mental health and the civic and public service function of student-run campus news sources.

Campus Settings and News Sources

The California State University (CSU) system is the largest and most diverse four-year higher education system in the United States. It is made up of 23 campuses, close to half a million students and tens of thousands of faculty members and staff. While student demographics vary slightly from campus to campus, they generally reflect surrounding communities and the majority-minority balance of the state. Roughly 4 percent of CSU students are African American, 16 percent Asian or Pacific Islander, 45 percent Hispanic or Latinx, and 22 percent White; and another 10 percent or so identify as other, unknown, two or more races, or foreign. CSU tuition is about $6,000 a semester, and around 80 percent of students receive some form of financial aid, making CSU a national leader in accessible and affordable higher education.[1]

CSULB is a large comprehensive campus with about 40,000 students located in the city of Long Beach near the southwest corner of Los Angeles County, a few miles from the Pacific Ocean. Student news operations affiliated with the CSULB Department of Journalism and Public Relations include the *Daily Forty-Niner*, an independent student newspaper founded in 1949; *DIG Magazine*, a lifestyle and culture publication; and *DIG en Español*, a Spanish-language magazine serving Latinx audiences. CSUN is in the San Fernando Valley in northwest Los Angeles County; it has roughly 40,000 full-time students. Student media affiliated with the CSUN Department of Journalism include the *Daily Sundial*, founded in 1958, and *El Nuevo Sol*, in operation since 2003, a cross-platform bilingual publication covering social justice issues. CSUF is another large comprehensive campus in southern California. It also has around 40,000 full-time students; it is about a ten-minute drive from Disneyland in Orange County. *The Daily Titan*, an independent news source founded in 1959, *Tusk Magazine*, a lifestyle publication, *OC News*, a current-affairs television program, and *Al Día*, a Spanish-language television newscast, call the CSUF Department of Communications home. Meanwhile, SFSU is located in the heart of San Francisco city and county. It has roughly 27,000 students. Student media affiliated the SFSU Department of Journalism include the *Golden Gate Xpress* newspaper, which has been published since 1927, and the feature-focused *Xpress Magazine*. Even though the four campuses are located in different regions, and therefore different health boards dictate their Covid-19 restrictions, CSULB, CSUN, CSUF and SFSU were bound by the same CSU system-wide calls to move classes (and news production) online in March 2020 and keep university activities there for more than a year.

Of note, CSU was the first major university system to suspend face-to-face instruction in the early days of the pandemic. It subsequently was the first to make a definitive decision about the 2020–2021 academic year, keeping the vast majority of courses offered across the CSU online and hundreds of thousands of students off campus.[2] CSU Chancellor Timothy White[3] wrote in a letter that the sweeping and conservative approach was the "only responsible" choice available to ensure the safety of all CSU constituents and to facilitate degree progression for the largest number of students in a system that awards roughly half of all undergraduate degrees in the state each year. The fact that instruction and student media in the CSU by and large remained online throughout the duration of the pandemic provides a unique window into the future of collegiate journalism in the wake of Covid-19.

Changes to Practice, Challenges to Connect and Mental Health Struggles

The most obvious and immediate changes to student journalism at CSULB, CSUN, CSUF and SFSU mirrored the all-encompassing changes to modern life and professional journalism—changes *Daily Forty-Niner* adviser Barbara Kingsley Wilson at CSULB described as "sudden and disheartening." Students who once gathered together in newsrooms, classrooms and studios had to complete projects, report stories and produce newscasts remotely and independently. In scenarios similar to those described elsewhere in this book, our students connected via technological tools such as email, Zoom, Slack and the good old-fashioned phone to rejig editorial calendars and reporting practices and come up with new story topics and angles. While the video conferencing tool Zoom became a household name early in the pandemic, Slack is not as widely known. Slack is a business communications platform that is increasingly used in a variety of higher education contexts, especially in courses and programs that require group work.[4] Slack's simple interface allows users to communicate and share materials through two methods, channels for group chats and direct one-on-one messages.

For the most part, the transition from buzzing campus newsrooms to decentralized off-campus operations was manageable, and student journalists continued to pursue critical stories about how the crisis was affecting their colleges. However, meeting and reporting by Zoom and other mediated means were not always seamless or equal experiences. Some sought refuge in their cars for privacy and quiet when there was little in their homes, or they parked close to a business to tap into a strong Internet signal. Technical issues also plagued students with older laptops that could not support various software programs essential for media design and multimedia storytelling. *Golden Gate Xpress* adviser Laura Moorehead at SFSU commented that the pandemic exacerbated structural issues that have plagued student media for years in the Bay Area with its high cost of living, adding that the department was increasingly worried that some students, particularly those from historically underrepresented populations, were not participating in student media because of the time commitment and their need to work elsewhere for pay.

Mining the Opportunities

Reporting was also a challenge for a variety of reasons, one being that some student journalists moved back home, sometimes hundreds of miles from campus, making covering local stories, issues and events difficult. CSUF professor Jesús Ayala Rico, who teaches a broadcast journalism course that produces the weekly 30-minute Spanish-language Emmy-winning newscast *Al Día*, turned the distance into an opportunity to expand coverage. Shortly after the move online, he realized that his students could report from their own communities, so they formed a statewide team of correspondents: "They were scattered through the entire state and we did a show on how COVID is affecting everything in the state. They filed from their different locations."[5] *DIG Mag* adviser Robin Jones at CSULB remarked that her editorial team had to constantly keep their eyes on what was open, what was canceled, what was closed because the editorial emphasis of the lifestyle magazine is food, culture and the arts.[6] CSUN journalism department chair Linda Bowen said that during the lockdown students were advised to continue reporting, but not to put themselves at risk: "This could mean conducting interviews via phone/Zoom, or asking for 'courtesy of' photos rather than taking photos on-site."[7]

In addition, students who often spent dozens of hours each week in newsrooms were putting in just as many, if not more, hours telling the biggest stories of their lives from home. This forced them to find new ways to communicate and connect. CSUF communications department chair Jason Shepard commented, "Zoom can't replace the comradery of newsrooms and TV studios, but I think in some ways the tools we've all gotten used to during remote learning will have some positive effects going forward." *Daily Forty-Niner* newsroom leaders at CSULB turned to phone calls for check-ins with editors, and they launched Instagram Live meetings to help with recruitment, while Slack quickly became the preferred newsroom connection tool across CSU student newsrooms. At CSUN, journalism chair Bowen agreed that the virtual environment spawned beneficial changes to newsroom practices: "Access to experts and other guest speakers will become more routine, and many of the tools, like Slack and Zoom, will remain as powerful enhancements to the teaching and learning process." She added that students use Slack for all sorts of purposes including sharing scholarship information and story examples, and it is also a "water cooler" place for students to gather, talk and bond over non-work-related topics.[8]

Mental Health Concerns

While tools such as Zoom and Slack helped keep news production going, student journalists were not immune to the mental health crisis brought on by widespread illness and death, disruptions to daily life, economic uncertainty and the perils of isolation. Kingsley-Wilson commented that *Daily Forty-Niner* journalists were often on tight deadlines, and they had to do "real world" journalism work along with school and outside-work responsibilities. Student journalists' struggles with mental health mirrored the experiences of college students in general and their professional journalist counterparts. Numerous studies indicate that college students had trouble coping with distance living and learning. Meanwhile, Messer argues that covering Covid-19 was "trauma reporting" because it became nearly impossible for journalists across the profession—from news anchors in New York to campus news reporters—to distinguish between the stories they were covering and their personal lives. The increased attention on mental health led to changes to practices in the long term. For example, the *Daily Forty-Niner* hopes to integrate mental health first-aid training into orientation programs so student media editors, producers, reporters and advisers are better prepared to help themselves and each other when mental health issues and topics arise in newsrooms and news stories.

The premise of mental health first-aid training is similar to that of traditional first aid in the sense that it is positioned as an immediate and temporary intervention to stabilize a situation until appropriate professional help is received or the crisis is resolved. Spanish literature professor Bonnie Gasior has led efforts to train faculty at CSULB in mental health first aid (MHFA), given that they are often the first to learn about, see or meet with students in distress yet are rarely adequately prepared to offer initial support. The CSU Chancellor's Office is committed to expanding the training created by Gasior and Darci Strother, a colleague from CSU San Marcos, across the system. While the primary training target audience would remain faculty, Gasior is excited about sharing MHFA principles and tactics with student journalists at CSULB because "it will help them better understand the challenges they face, to have destigmatizing conversations, and to be advocates for their peers (and even, perhaps, their professors, because mental health challenges can affect all of us)."

The Changes Mount

Another change prompted by the pandemic that affects future directions in student media was the disappearance of print journalism on CSU campuses, at least temporarily. There was no one to receive delivery of newspaper and magazine hard copies and, most importantly, the audience for print issues was gone too. CSU campuses by order of the chancellor were supposed to be ghost towns. This meant a substantial drop in advertising revenue used to supplement news production costs and editor salaries on some campuses, a drop similar to the revenue hit other news sources experienced around the same time. Paradoxically, the suspension of print journalism also created an opportunity to digitize editorial strategies and practices more fully, leading to an increase in the quantity and quality of digital content across student media newsrooms at CSULB, CSUF, CSUN and SFSU. Now SFSU's *Golden Gate Xpress* and CSULB's *Daily Forty-Niner* are considering suspending print operations altogether, traditions that trace back decades, when life and classes return to their campuses.

Expand, Experiment and Engage

Increased awareness of mental health issues and improvements in digital storytelling were not the only positive effects of the pandemic on collegiate journalism. Campus outlets also experienced an increase in audience size, and they expanded coverage to serve diverse audiences. Student news sources were often the only sources covering the pandemic for their communities, thereby elevating the interest, importance and reach of their work at critical times during the transition to remote learning, again during the social justice movements that erupted in early summer 2020, and later during the tumultuous presidential election in fall. At CSUF, for example, the monthly audience for the *Daily Titan*'s website shot up immediately after the pandemic began, nearly tripling readership to more than 1.5 million pages and 100,000 unique visitors. Online readership remained high into summer 2020, with 1.1 million pages delivered in June, about quadruple the *Titan*'s normal readership.

Also at CSUF, *Al Día* adviser Jesús Ayala Rico said that his students noticed a lack of in-depth pandemic coverage by the Spanish-language networks Univision and Telemundo, so they sought to fill the void by producing a 45-minute TV news magazine-style show called *Coronavirus Pandemia Mundial*. It won awards from the College Media Association for best newscast and from the Associated Collegiate Press for best Covid-19 coverage. *DIG en Español* at CSULB included articles in its digital issues about the financial, health and educational impact the pandemic had on local Latinx communities that were unproportionally affected by the pandemic economically and medically, especially during the post–Thanksgiving surge that ravaged Los Angeles County.[9]

Digital expansion also meant experimentation. Before the pandemic, *DIG en Español* students completed multimedia stories with in-person interviews. That was changed to Zoom interviews because face-to-face reporting was not safe. For the next academic year, storytelling was adapted again to a Zoom broadcast project the students recorded with the logo as a virtual background. It was promoted on the *DIG en Español* Instagram account, and students created content for a new TikTok page; three of *DIG en Español*'s TikTok videos subsequently exceeded 10,000 views, far eclipsing the audience of its website. The use of digital tools such as TikTok and Zoom enhanced cross-platform storytelling at CSUN, too. At CSUN, Zoom evolved from a basic tool to conduct meetings to a vibrant virtual newsroom open 9 a.m. to 9 p.m. Monday thru Friday, where *Daily Sundial* editors worked shifts to meet with contributors in groups or private breakout rooms. The setup allowed student media leaders and advisors to conduct demos and workshops and host guest speakers. CSUN journalism chair Linda Bowen said these activities would have been logistically more difficult if students had to drive to campus and physically attend the sessions.

Another example of experimentation that inspired more collaboration and more journalism during the pandemic was the Cal State Journalism Newswire. The wire was the brainchild of Aidan McGloin, a reporter for the campus newspaper at California Polytechnic State University in

San Luis Obispo, the *Mustang News*. McGloin rounded up student journalists at other CSUs and launched the Newswire March 1, 2020, in an effort to address the lack of resource sharing among CSU student news organizations. The service now includes more than 10 student-run CSU newspapers, the *Daily Forty-Niner* at CSULB, the *Daily Sundial* at CSUN and the *Golden Gate Xpress* at SFSU among them. Participating reporters and editors communicate through Slack, and the wire is available on the self-publishing platform Substack for free. Stories submitted to Substack can be republished by member organizations or they can be used as reference for leads, ideas, sources, background information and images.[10]

The spirit of collaboration and connection seen between CSU journalism students extended to CSU journalism faculty. Rachele Kanigel, journalism department chair at SFSU, led the formation of a CSU journalism administrators' working group soon after classes and student media operations went online in March 2020. More than a dozen program directors from nearly every CSU were invited to join and many met monthly throughout the pandemic to share ideas, tactics and solutions to address changes and challenges inherent in running a program and supporting student journalism from afar. The meetings transformed from deer-in-the headlights discussions to collegial and collective sounding boards for a wide range of issues related to collegiate journalism education during and after the pandemic, including how student media labs are structured, pandemic graduation plans and the various and differing governing structures on CSU campuses.

Pandemic, Protests and the Public Service Mission of the Collegiate Press

Normally, a once-in-a-century global pandemic would be the biggest story of a collegiate journalist's career, and for many it was. Student journalists broke stories, and their outlets were go-to resources for breaking news about their campuses and surrounding communities. CSUF *Al Día* adviser Jesus Ayala described the pandemic as the biggest story since 9/11. He said that news directors told him that they're going to "judge students on how they covered COVID." However, another once-in-a-lifetime story emerged in the middle of the pandemic, the murder of George Floyd. Floyd's horrific and prolonged death was captured on camera; the images and sounds of the nearly 10-minute homicide spread like wildfire across social media, igniting outrage and a racial justice and reconciliation movement not seen since the 1960s.[11] Lillian R. Dunlap's essay, later in this collection, addresses the monumental impact of the Floyd murder as a change agent for diversity in our nation's newsrooms.

On a collegiate level, CSULB, CSUF, CSUN and SFSU exemplify diversity, each being located in highly diverse urban areas that were the sites of protests in the weeks and months that followed Floyd's death. Protests are popular and important story assignments for student journalists, but the pandemic posed unique challenges because in-person reporting and gathering in crowds were banned. Student journalists thus faced a conundrum: The Black Lives Matter movement was one of the most impactful stories of their lifetimes, yet university policies dictated that they sit on the sidelines and cover the events via Zoom. Some students subsequently blurred the line between journalist and private citizen, and their experiences at the protests provided opportunities to further develop, define and refine reporting protocols during and after the pandemic, one example being the case of a CSULB student who captured and shared on social media a controversial image taken at the most disruptive and dangerous BLM protest in Long Beach in May 2020.[12]

The photo's angle made it seem as though a Long Beach police officer was aiming a weapon at a toddler in a Batman costume perched on an adult's shoulders. Some commentators used it as proof of police brutality and racism; others labeled the student anti-cop for taking the picture and sharing it, while still another group of online commentators questioned the accuracy and ethics of the image. All the while, the student was bombarded with licensing requests from news organizations around the world. At first, more reputable news organizations reached out, but tabloid-style outlets seemed the most interested in paying to publish what was at first glance a shocking image.[13] The Long Beach Police Department subsequently issued a statement and announced an investigation into the incident, later recommending that the adult who brought the toddler to the protest should be arrested for child endangerment.[14]

The viral and inflammatory nature of the image served as useful case study in photojournalism ethics, the power and reach of social media, the responsibility of the press, and the distinction between reputable news organizations and tabloids. Another takeaway for student media advisers and student journalists was a reemphasis on university policies that if students opt to attend protests when in-person reporting and gathering in crowds are strictly prohibited, they were to do so as private citizens, not representatives of student news organizations. The experience also triggered an evaluation of protest coverage policies in general after the pandemic because student news organizations and their associated universities do not have the resources or security to ensure the safety of student journalists during protests.

Issues of freedom of expression and of the press and the role of journalism in democracies were front and center as part of efforts to bring student journalists back to campus during the pandemic. Even though the default was to stay at home, CSULB, CSUN and CSUF managed to eventually secure limited on-campus presence for a small number of editorial staff. The exemption was not easy to attain given the CSU systemwide preference was to have no one on campus, even if they wore masks and stayed at least six feet away from each other. Advisers and administrators turned to California governor Gavin Newsom's executive order and accompanying list of "essential critical infrastructure workers" to make their case. Communications professionals, including journalists, were among more than a dozen sectors deemed essential for in-person activities to ensure the functioning of society during the pandemic.[15]

The essential function of the student press was underscored by the fact that student journalists were often the only independent sources of information reporting on how the pandemic was affecting students, faculty and other campus constituents. For example, student journalists were regularly the first to report on Covid-19 outbreaks among students, they called out professors for inappropriate conduct or content during Zoom classes, and they were consistently holding those in power accountable for decisions that affected tens of thousands of people. For those reasons and others, a commentator in a *Washington Post* article deemed college news reporters "heroes for the pandemic era,"[16] especially since local news sources had dwindled or disappeared altogether.

Conclusion

The experiences at four journalism programs and their associated student media operations in the California State University system provide a unique view into changes, challenges and opportunities in collegiate journalism brought on by Covid-19. Changes to the campus news organizations were instant and sweeping. Reporting and producing practices kept students off campus and away from each other and their sources; they amplified economic inequities in terms of access to technology and availability to take part in time-intensive student journalism operations, and they brought into sharp focus mental health issues. However, Covid-19 also triggered innovation, collaboration and changes to collegiate journalism practice that will sustain themselves long after the pandemic ends. Student journalists experimented with digital media to enhance storytelling; they expanded their reach and they increased their audience size; they connected with sources and each other through digital platforms such as Zoom and Slack, and they filled information voids left open by the commercial press.

From March 2020 to May 2021, the pandemic news cycle was in overdrive. Members of the collegiate press covered—and to some degree were part of—stories that made their time in student media memorable, impactful and busy. They published important stories on campus shutdowns and local Covid-19 outbreaks; the BLM protests and other racial reconciliation movements in response to attacks on Asian Americans; and the presidential election and insurrection. It is said that college newsrooms are living laboratories, incubators for young journalists to develop skills and sharpen news judgment, and a rite of passage for those serious about pursuing careers in the field. The pandemic era revealed that collegiate journalism is all of these things. It also demonstrated the relevance and influence of college press sources that are often the only ones reporting on communities that rival the size of small cities. The pandemic thus inadvertently confirmed without a doubt that student journalists are pivotal to the health of the modern journalism ecosystem and essential to the free flow of information in their communities.

NOTES

1. California State University, 2021.
2. Nina Agrawal, "Cal State Universities Will Stay Online All Year Amid Covid-19 Pandemic," *Los Angeles Times*, September 10, 2020; Maggie Angst, "Cal State Will Not Return to In-Person Classes for Spring 2021," *The Mercury News*, September 10, 2020; "California State University Campuses to Accelerate Transition to Virtual Instruction," California State University news release, March 17, 2020, https://www2.calstate.edu/csu-system/news/Pages/California-State-University-Campuses-to-Accelerate-Transition-to-Virtual-Instruction.aspx.
3. Timothy White, "Chancellor Message," California State University, Office of the Chancellor, September 10, 2020.
4. Stacy Forster, "Instructors Encourage Slack-Ing in the Classroom," *MediaShift*, August 18, 2016; Kathleen Kole de Peralta and Sarah Robey, "4 Reasons Slack Will Change How You Teach," *Inside Higher Ed*, September 18, 2018; Spencer M. Ross, "Slack It to Me: Complementing LMS with Student-Centric Communications for the Millennial/Post-Millennial Student," *Journal of Marketing Education* 41, no. 2 (2019): 91–108.
5. Daniel Eisenberg, Sarah Ketchen Lipson, and Justin Heinze, "The Healthy Minds Study," Healthy Minds Network, 2021; Lauren Lumpkin, "Coronavirus Has Made Already-Stressed College Students Even More Anxious and Depressed, Study Finds," *The Washington Post*, July 24, 2020; Lauren Lumpkin, "A Mental Health Crisis Was Spreading on College Campuses. The Pandemic Has Made It Worse," *The Washington Post*, March 30, 2021.
6. Olivia Messer, "The Covid Reporters Are Not Okay. Extremely Not Okay," *Study Hall*, May 7, 2021.
7. Hazel Kelly, "First Responders for Mental Health Challenges," *CSU System News*, May 26, 2021; Sarah Ketchen Lipson, Amber Talaski, and Nina Cesare, "The Role of Faculty in Student Mental Health," Boston University School of Public Health, 2021.
8. Brad Adgate, "Newspaper Revenue Drops as Local News Interest Rises Amid Coronavirus," *Forbes*, April 13, 2020; Jessica Guynn, and Michael Braga, "Coronavirus' Next Casualty: The Nation's Biggest Story Could Devastate News Industry," *USA Today*, March 31, 2020.

9. Akilah Johnson, "Death in the Prime of Life: Covid-19 Proves Especially Lethal to Younger Latinos," *The Washington Post*, March 15, 2021; Brian Melley, Associated Press, January 1, 2021, https://Apnews.Com/Article/Travel-Pandemics-Los-Angeles-Thanksgiving-Coronavirus-Pandemic-D21fdd1e5395812e6155258c70896eba; Alexandra Villarreal, "'Everywhere You Look, People Are Infected': Covid's Toll on California Latinos," *The Guardian*, January 11, 2021.

10. Mike O'Sullivan, "California Student Journalists Pool Resources to Create Online Newswire," Voice of America, 2021; Hanaa Tameez, "California State University's Student Journalists Launched a Wire Service to Share Their Work with Each Other. Here's How They Did It," *NiemanLab*, March 16, 2021.

11. Audra Burch, Amy Harmon, Sabrina Tavernise, and Emily Badger, "The Death of George Floyd Reignited a Movement. What Happens Now?" *New York Times*, April 20, 2021.

12. Kelly Puente, "Long Beach Police Spent Nearly $1 Million in Overtime for Night of May 31 Civil Unrest," *Long Beach Post*, August 25, 2020; Emily Rasmussen, "National Guard Summoned to Long Beach after Looting, Fires," *Long Beach Press Telegram*, May 31, 2020; Ruben Vives and Hannah Fry, "Long Beach Hit Hard by Looters as Crowds Roam Through Downtown," *Los Angeles Times*, May 31, 2020.

13. Stephanie Rivera, "Viral Photo from Sunday's Protest Shows Tense Scene with Police; Here's the Backstory," *Long Beach Post*, June 3, 2020.

14. Jeremiah Dobruck, "Man in Viral Protest Photo Should Be Arrested for Child Endangerment, LBPD Chief Says," *Long Beach Post*, June 23, 2020.

15. Sonia Y. Angell, "Order of the State Public Health Officer," California Department of Public Health, 2020; California Public Health Officer, "Essential Workforce," news release, 2020, https://covid19.ca.gov/essential-workforce/; Gavin Newsom, "Executive Order N-33–20," Executive Department, State of California, 2020.

16. Elahe Izadi, "College Newspaper Reporters Are the Journalism Heroes for the Pandemic Era," *Washington Post*, September 19, 2020.

Community Journalism
The Pandemic as a Catalyst for Change

BERNARDO H. MOTTA

> "Engaged journalism refers to a range
> of practices that aim to build relationships between
> journalists and the public and involve the public
> in the process of co-creating journalism"
> —Andrea Wenzel, community journalism researcher

As shown elsewhere in this book, in a world in which journalists have already been under attack, the pandemic made everything exponentially worse as the costs and risks of reporting increased, travel and freelancing budgets were slashed, and access to places and people was curtailed by governments more than happy to take control over the narrative. This intensive attack provoked an intensive reaction. In addition to the above, there are specific ways in which the pandemic affected traditional community newspapers. To start, a number of organizations and "alternative" community newsrooms developed mechanisms that made it possible for journalists out of the mainstream to finally access resources mostly available to traditional media outlets. These efforts ultimately played into a series of movements to reform journalism and turn certain longstanding journalism principles on their heads.

When Covid-19 Came to Town, 1: The View from the Inside

One of the best overviews of the impacts of the pandemic on community newspapers comes from Teri Finneman and Ryan J. Thomas.[1] In four questions, they painted a bleak scenario at the beginning of the pandemic that, almost instantaneously, became catastrophic. The slow and continuous erosion of traditional business models for local newspapers was suddenly compounded by one powerful blow to the already diminished pillar that barely supported regular operations. The first question concerns the causes of local newspapers' financial stresses. Finneman and Thomas, as well as Elliot Weiser in his essay found in this collection, each describe the immediate and substantial loss of ad revenue. *The Tampa Bay Times* reported a $1 million loss in just two weeks at the end of March. *The Philadelphia Inquirer* published a story on May 19, 2020, describing a plunge of 30 percent to 50 percent in advertisement sales while also referring to an interview with news industry analyst Ken Doctor, who said that 10 percent of daily American newspapers were already unprofitable before the pandemic.[2]

Finneman and Thomas also identified the fact that overloaded and burned-out journalists were already at the brink when the pandemic hit and described how journalists saw the legacy role of multigenerational newspapers. "The critical incident of a global pandemic prompted these journalists to demonstrate to their audiences that the market-driven business model of journalism was no longer sustainable,"[3] they concluded.

It is fundamental here to distinguish what Finneman and Thomas defined as "community newspapers," though. In their words:

> Because of our focus on mainstream daily and weekly newspapers, we removed alternative publications from our sample, leaving 249 articles and columns for analysis. In addition, we visited the websites of 44 state newspaper associations to pull content from member newsletters and/or organizational online articles that specifically mentioned the pandemic to better understand how the industry was conversing with itself.[4]

All around the world the problem was similar: failing business models, overburdened journalists, attacks against press freedom, and lack of vision before the pandemic. Add to those factors more mental health stress for individual journalists, more restrictions to reporting, less income from traditional sources, and more attacks against journalists' credibility.[5]

When Covid-19 Came to Town, 2: The View from the Outside

If on the one hand, mainstream daily and weekly newspapers were being ravaged by the failures of traditional business models when the pandemic hit, on the other hand, networks of independent small news organizations have been skyrocketing. "Nonprofit outlets have launched at a pace of a dozen or more a year since 2008,"[6] and INN (Institute for Nonprofit

News) has reached 300 members this year, while LION Publishers (Local Independent Network News) reports that the number of independent local news organizations has grown by 50 percent in the last five years.[7] And that is just in the U.S. and Canada.

Small, local independent news outlets have not only been on a rapid rise but have also been building their own support networks to become both more resilient and more effective in serving their communities.[8] Such outlets in the U.S. include Resolve Philadelphia, Reveal News (Center for Investigative Reporting), Capital Public Radio, Free Press New Voices, Your Voice Ohio, The LAist, the Discourse, Listening Post Collective, Flynt Beat. Funding organizations such as LION Publishers, Democracy Fund, Lenfest Institute and the Knight Foundation have partnered with Google, Facebook and other mega-donors to create new forms of revenue that fund training, resources, and support networks. That helps ensure new community media will thrive, especially those outlets serving and owned by marginalized communities. A great example is the Tiny News Collective, which uses LION Publishers' funding to provide funding, technology, training, and financial planning for founders of color, women, and gender-diverse people.[9]

University of British Columbia scholars Candice Callison and Mary Lynn Young[10] reported on another move away from the traditional White-male-dominated commercial model of journalism. Their focus is on populations that have been marginalized by mainstream news, especially Indigenous nations:

> In following this thread, we find journalists, startup founders, sources, activists, and citizens holding a mirror, resisting prior journalisms by using social media and other forms of digital media to reflect, resist, talk back, counter, and refuse to participate in legacy media or journalism conversations. These case studies of journalists and audiences, dealing with gaps scholars have left underexplored, explain the reckoning in both the internal and external conversations of journalism. We find many journalists responding and struggling with journalism's dominant authority, history, and reckoning at individual, structural, and organizational levels.[11]

Among the numerous opportunities for entrepreneurial journalists popping up all around the world, Casares described the rise of the constructive or "solutions" approaches to journalism; that approach has recently been reinforced by an independent media research firm, SmithGeiger for the Solutions Journalism Network.[12] SmithGeiger's research shows that solutions journalism fared better with a sample of 638 respondents from six media markets (Austin, Texas; Chicago, Illinois; Cleveland, Ohio; Kansas City, Missouri; Phoenix, Arizona, and Portland, Maine) on all of the measured outcomes, including being seen as more trustworthy, interesting, educational, and uplifting, with margins of 20 percent or more when compared to traditional problem-focused (watchdog) stories. Smith-Geiger and Casares also found the approach to be more economically viable than traditional watchdog journalism.

During the pandemic, the Solutions Journalism Network (SJN) started a worldwide program in 2020 called Solutions Journalism LEDE Fellowship, targeted at entrepreneurial, independent journalists trying to develop solutions journalism projects locally. LEDE Fellows get financial support, training, and access to a support network including journalists, educators and trainers all over the world. Connectas (https://www.connectas.org), ICFJ (https://www.icfj.org) IJNET (https://ijnet.org/en), and GIJN (https://gijn.org), among others, have created multinational collaborations mixing small, independent journalism outlets, freelancers and traditional media, including collaborations involving training, networking and support. These are just a few examples in a constellation of different but connected movements in journalism associated with dozens of organizations and collaboratives that promote their connectivity and intersectionality very much in the way Callison and Young described.

Because of the Covid-19 pandemic, what had been brewing at the margins suddenly had an opportunity to flood into the mainstream spaces left empty by the megalithic news corporations. While parachute journalists from the main media markets were confined to their own home markets due to the pandemic restrictions, the local, grassroots, community-based reporters and tiny news organizations everywhere finally could hear their own voices through the fading noise of the massive corporate behemoths leaving town. For community journalists everywhere in the world, the immeasurable tragedy brought by the pandemic to their towns and neighborhoods also brought affirmation and confirmation of their valuable work and of their ethical approach in ways that are both evolutionary and revolutionary.

The changes are evolutionary because those media outlets and their community-centered approaches were already present in one shape or another, such as the Black Press, Indigenous news organizations, local weeklies, community radio stations, independent investigative reporting outlets, and a plethora of niche and specialized news organizations in all types of media and business formats. The most recent evolution of these many different journalism organizations, usually referred to as "ethnic" or "alternative" (as in contraposition to "mainstream"), has focused mostly on cooperation and association (a great example of this is the Center for Cooperative Media at Montclair State University). These arrangements are sometimes forced upon them by economic and political needs, sometimes led by grassroots organizing, and they are made easier and cheaper by social media as well as by other digital spaces online.

In response to the devastating mix of job scarcity, dwindling work conditions, low salaries, and even lower investment in professional development within mainstream newsrooms (think mentorships, apprenticeships and other training programs), networks of journalists and small media owners became the primary centers of learning, discussion, and improvement of professional standards and conditions. Both traditional professional associations,[13] which saw the need to adapt to a new majority of members becoming detached from traditional newsrooms (i.e., freelancing or working for small startups), and relatively new networks[14] designed to fill the gap in support roles left by the declining work conditions in legacy media emerged. In addition to those, new academic programs and networks started to take a more proactive role in covering local communities, either by associating with local newsrooms or taking the responsibility for themselves after the closing or consolidation of the local newspaper. Again, Finneman and Thomas noted that, amid all the dreadfulness of the pandemic's impact on the industry, "state associations didn't just use their roles to offer a sympathetic ear but also to take a proactive approach to assisting the industry, including promoting new innovations to go beyond the market-driven model to help newspapers survive into the future."[15]

Due to funding from the Lenfest Institute, the Democracy Fund, and even tech behemoths such as Facebook and Google, small independent outlets and freelancers now have a better reach. They have also been helped due to the new influx of experienced and well-trained journalists who left or were laid off from mainstream outlets. On the other side, the traditional mainstream newsrooms saw a new wave of reporters brought in as "diversity hires" after many scandals in prominent newsrooms based on sexual harassment and gender equity,[16] racism[17] and disability[18] have also helped accelerate the current revolution in journalism, especially at the hyperlocal level.

Moreover, collaboration became not only a mode of reporting but also a system of covering the news and protecting journalists. In Canada, large media outlets were mostly silent when the Royal Canadian Mounted Police (RCMP) increased its attacks against journalists, blocking access, imprisoning reporters under bogus charges (that were later dropped), and corralling reporters in ways to impede coverage of RCMP's illegal actions to protect corporate interests and attack local land defenders and water protectors from Indigenous Nations.[19] Genocide against Indigenous peoples in Canada has been recognized by its own government in a report that implicates police forces, especially RCMP, in the process, but most of the reporting on the topic has come from small, independent outlets such as *Ricochet* and *The Narwhal* and from Indigenous reporters and organizations. Instead of waiting for larger media outlets to take the case with their much better financed legal teams, these small outlets worked together with the Canadian Association of Journalists, CPJ and other press freedom organizations to get legal representation to sue the RCMP.[20]

This effort mirrors the work of the Reporters Committee for Freedom of the Press (RCFP) in the U.S. With investment from the John S. and James L. Knight Foundation, RCFP offers the Local Legal Initiative, which "provides local news organizations with direct legal services they need to pursue enterprise and investigative stories in their communities"[21] in five U.S. states (Colorado, Oklahoma, Oregon, Pennsylvania, and Tennessee). Free or affordable legal representation is crucial for small, community-based news outlets to be able to fight the increasing attacks on press freedoms and do more in-depth investigative work without fear of being shut down by a strategic lawsuit against public participation (SLAPP), which can be too onerous for independent outlets and reporters to defend against. Thanks to integrative networks, financial support from grant-giving organizations, business-management support, data and technology partnerships, and reporting collaborations, stories that were out of reach for small, community-based newsrooms are now possible.

Covid-19 Closed Doors and Opened Windows

In 2019, as many of these smaller revolutions were starting to pick up speed, news of a new coronavirus epidemic rose from Wuhan in China. Soon, the Covid-19 pandemic shut down travel, workspaces, and direct access to sources, and so raised new barriers to the work of journalists in mainstream media. On the other hand, many of the very costly traditional barriers to professional development and to networking opportunities that took place in conferences and gatherings were suddenly lifted for the overworked and underpaid community journalist. Within weeks, cheap and even free web-based training and networking events became widely accessible for journalists with basic Internet access or even a phone anywhere in the world.

Suddenly, a one-person news operation covering a small community could be in the same online webinar as a well-funded top journalist from Washington, D.C. More important, she/he could be in the same online room with funders, trainers, and networking professionals. The tragedy of the pandemic that devastated the world and traditional newsrooms also served as the catalyst, the push that brought in a massive new market for journalism trainers and exponentially increased the chances for new organizations to get funding. In addition, a new batch of energized entrepreneurial journalists who were already looking for new, better ways of doing journalism with their communities could now collaborate with each other in a low-to-no-cost manner and, in the process, begin to create a new ecosystem for journalism.

Praxis: Committing Community Journalism After the Pandemic

What does all of this mean in practice? It's helpful to talk and write about paradigmatic changes and revolutions in journalism academically, but what does it actually mean to the reporter, the journalism student, the editor, and the public in practical tangible ways? It means waking up in the morning thinking in a different way, acting in a different way, and producing journalism in a different way. It means improving curricula for journalism programs (not just in higher education, but everywhere). It means changing the ethics, the practice and even the worldview that has sustained journalism in the past century or so. But how?

Casares describes the specific traits of constructive journalism, a framework very similar to "solutions journalism" and other community-building reporting initiatives (e.g., empowerment journalism, restorative journalism, humanistic journalism):

- Although it can employ characters as a narrative axis, it focuses the narrative on the character's work, projects and the change they produce.
- It centers the results achieved and the verification based on data, not on good intentions or plans.
- It includes the project's limitations with the questioning from critiques.
- It includes lessons learned that can be useful to others.
- It doesn't take the side of a specific solution.
- It is critical and balanced.
- It attempts to build bridges and avoid polarization.
- It brings in new voices to the conversation about each issue.
- It looks forward to the future.
- It uses the reporter in the essential role of facilitator and catalyst for conversation.
- It connects people and institutions working to solve a problem.
- It brings people together and creates spaces for conversations.
- It aims to achieve social impact and measure it.[22]

Andrea Wenzel, who has both worked in and extensively researched community-centered and solutions journalism, explains both the solutions and the engagement approaches to journalism:

Solutions journalism holds that a journalist's role is not only to report on problems but also to rigorously report on "responses to social problems." Solutions journalism initiatives offer an alternative for residents ... who are alienated by the constant drumbeat of negative local news. Engaged journalism refers to a range of practices that aim to build relationships between journalists and the public and involve the public in the process of co-creating journalism....

...I argue that when applied in combination, local solutions journalism and engaged journalism practices can contribute to a communication environment with greater trust between media, community members, and organizations, where residents feel more connected and invested. But, I caution that these practices will neither strengthen storytelling network ties nor build trust with marginalized communities unless they are reflexive about journalistic norms, like objectivity, that reinforce hierarchies of race, class, and geography.[23]

On the ground, this means that journalists are in constant contact with community members, looking at what each individual, organization and institution has to offer, and telling stories that help communities tackle their most urgent and important challenges. It still holds those in power accountable, but it exposes not only the problems but also solutions that have been produced within the communities themselves or produced elsewhere and applied locally. By serving the community locally, this kind of journalism brings new perspectives to the national and global mainstream. Communities don't exist in isolation, and the search for solutions elsewhere can bring them together more easily, especially in the digital world.

In the last few years, too many new networks of community-centered, engaged and solutions journalism have sprouted to list here, but great examples of these approaches are seen in relatively new organizations such as City Bureau, Resolve Philadelphia, the Discourse, Flynt Beat (U.S.), Progress Clock (Nigeria), Network 506 (Costa Rica), The Narwhal (Canada), StopBlaBla (West and Central Africa), and many others around the world that either fully embrace the new paradigm or are experimenting with special projects or ongoing programs.

This new engaged, community-centered, solutions/constructive approach may have taken many names and forms, but its proponents share a goal of enhancing their own communities while fostering an internal conversation about journalism on the national level. The main elements of this paradigm are not entirely new; they were already present at the beginning of the Black Press in the U.S. nearly two centuries ago:

> Because these exchanges also move beyond the African-American community, the writings in the Black press help us understand not just that community but the nation as a whole. Writers who wanted to successfully address their position in society had to craft a story that made sense of a country torn by an economic and social system based on racial injustice.[24]

The production and distribution of news also takes on any format needed to best reach the people who most need the information. At the Neighborhood News Bureau at the University of South Florida's St. Petersburg campus, for example, students and faculty work side by side with community members to produce documentaries, news stories, digital projects, oral histories, live performances and events, community conversations, academic and professional talks. It's a model also reflective of the Black Press, as Vogel describes:

> The difficulty Black writers faced in getting published made them work creatively to broadcast their ideas in a variety of mediums. This raises important genre questions for scholars. Black authors wrote for newspapers and magazines, self-published in pamphlets, and turned to large houses to put out their novels.[25]

Community journalism practiced by non–White communities in the U.S. has always been pushed to the margins, in particular when we refer to communities forced to the margins by White supremacy and classicist practices. However, it always has found ways to continue to bring its practitioners together, especially in the space of so-called "alternative media." In 2020–21, this development finally received a push when the Covid-19 pandemic allowed those in leadership positions of the community-led journalism movement to finally make their case to a wider public and to funding institutions, while also benefiting from the momentum of the Black Lives protests in the U.S. during the summer of 2020.

As we have seen, community journalists—the marginalized, the alternative, and others seen as outsiders—could now be seen by many of the power players in the media funding world. They were able to demonstrate the advantages of their community-centered approaches and make funders aware that they can be much more effective and efficient in bringing change and improvements both to their communities and to journalism in general. Community-based journalists already had a network through which to collaborate, educate, and participate in ground-up conversations with their communities with much more trust and support in those communities than large media conglomerates have. That became a major advantage during the pandemic when so much information, though essential, was suspect when disseminated by mainstream media.

As Wenzel and Casares have shown, these community-centered and solutions-oriented processes are a direct counter to the credibility crisis, the economic crisis, the information crisis, the workplace equity crisis, and the quality crisis of journalism today.[26] Community-based news services are as diverse and alternative as the communities they represent. Moreover, they not only represent their own communities but also carry the knowledge and experience that parachute journalists do not. They can be perceived as more accurate and truthful since they share the lived experiences of their communities.

With the new access to tools, techniques, funding and resources brought by the pandemic, community-based news services are also capable of doing better investigative journalism that works both as watchdog and as a conversation about the best solutions for systemic problems. The elitism and exclusionism of higher education programs that are both unaffordable and inaccessible to many can be turned on their axis as local associations and organizations begin to provide high quality, more accessible and practical training in journalism. Online communities and fellowships, such as Gather, the Cooperative Media Network, and the Solutions Journalism Network, bring together journalists from all over the word to share experiences and learn from each other.

Finally, a new community-driven approach allows the community to set the agenda, picking its own priorities instead of submitting to national and international news services, which usually force polarizing or meaningless issues onto the local information digest.[27] The very choice of topic comes from the needs of the community, protecting it against outside influences, from interest groups to political parties. Community journalism becomes, then, useful news that builds community because it is produced by the community for the benefit of the community it serves. It brings resources and money to the community while spotlighting community needs at the local, regional, and sometimes national level, and global conversations and decision-making processes.

Conclusion

No one can predict how quickly the new paradigm for journalism would have developed without a catalyst such as the Covid-19 crisis—in much the same way that we can't say with any degree of certainty how the Black Lives Matter protests would have reached a global audience as effectively without the pandemic. Nonetheless, a confluence of events and trends hit its peak at the same time that most people were stuck at home and traditional ways of doing journalism were directly affected. This confluence created a flood of opportunities for journalists who had seldom had access to training, while at the same time funders and large media associations were looking for responses to the crises of sustainability and trust for traditional media. What we can say with some level of certainty is that, once this genie was out of the bottle, it would not quietly return to the "old normal."

Notes

1. Teri Finneman and Ryan J. Thomas. "'Our Company Is in Survival Mode': Metajournalistic Discourse on COVID-19's Impact on U.S. Community Newspapers," *Journalism Practice*, February 15, 2021, 1–19, https://doi.org/10.1080/17512786.2021.1888149.

2. *Ibid.*, n.d.; see also Sam Wood, "News Industry Resorts to Layoffs, Cutbacks as Ad Revenues Plunge During Coronavirus Pandemic," *Philadelphia Inquirer*, March 27, 2020, https://www.inquirer.com/business/newspapers-coronavirus-stimulus-ken-doctor-jim-friedlich-lenfest-institute-20200327.html.

3. Finneman and Thomas, "Our Company," n.d.

4. *Ibid.*

5. Alfredo Casares, *La hora del periodismo constructivo: El poder transformador de la información orientada al futuro y a las soluciones* (Pamplona, Spain: Ediciones Universidad de Navarra S.A. [EUNSA], 2021); Damian Radcliffe, "The Impact of COVID-19 on Journalism in Emerging Economies and the Global South," SSRN, Advanced Online Publication, 2021, https://papers.ssrn.com/sol3/papers.cfm?abstract_id=3796666; Chindu Sreedharan, Einar Thorsen, Lee Miles, Jamie Matthews, Mike Sunderland, and Christopher Baker-Beall, "Impact of Covid-19 on Journalism in Sierra Leone," National Survey Report 2021, http://eprints.bournemouth.ac.uk/35463/1/Sierra%20Leone%20National%20Survey%20Report%20English%20with%20APPENDIX.pdf.

6. Institute for Nonprofit News, "The State of Nonprofit News: Entering a Crisis Year with Growing Audiences," *INN Index 2020*, https://1l9nh32zekco14afdq2plfsw-wpengine.netdna-ssl.com/wp-content/uploads/2020/06/INN.2020.FINA_.06.15.20.pdf; see also Gabby Miller, "'Where there is disruption, there is opportunity': What Does the Future Hold for Nonprofit Newsrooms?" *Columbia Journalism Review*, April 13, 2021, https://www.cjr.org/tow_center/where-there-is-disruption-there-is-opportunity-what-does-the-future-hold-for-nonprofit-newsrooms.php.

7. Chloe Kizer, "Introducing Project Oasis: A Deep Dive into the Fast-Growing World of Independent News Startups," *Lion Publishers*, March 11, 2021, https://lionpublishers.com/introducing-project-oasis-a-deep-dive-into-the-fast-growing-world-of-independent-news-startups-196f24881a2.

8. Casares, *La hora del periodismo constructivo*.

9. https://tinynewsco.org.

10. Candice Callison and Mary Lynn Young, *Reckoning: Journalism's Limits and Possibilities* (New York: Oxford University Press, 2020).

11. *Ibid.*, pp. 5–6.

12. Casares, *La hora del periodismo constructivo*; SmithGeiger, "The Secret Weapon for Any Newsroom That Wants to Be No. 1," Solutions Journalism Network, April 2021, https://sjn-static.s3.amazonaws.com/SmithGeiger2020.pdf.

13. Investigative Reporters and Editors (IRE), Society of Professional Journalists (SPJ), American Association of Journalists and Authors (ASJA), National Association of Black Journalists (NABJ), National Association of Hispanic Journalists (NAHJ), Native American Journalists Association (NAJA), Asian American Journalists Association (AAJA), and many other topic- and identity-specific associations.

14. Online News Association (ONA), Global Investigative Journalists Network (GIJN), International Center for Journalists (ICFJ) and its International Journalism Network (IJNET), Connectas (Latin America), Solutions Journalism Network, and many others.

15. Finneman and Thomas, "Our Company," n.d.

16. Abigail Edge, "How Newsroom Culture Is Being Re-Evaluated Following #MeToo," *Quill*, March 19, 2018, https://www.quillmag.com/2018/03/19/me-too-movement-journalism-matt-lauer-glenn-thrush-sexual-misconduct-media-news/; Alexandria Neason, Meg Dalton and Karen K. Ho, "Sexual Harassment in the Newsroom: An Oral History," *Columbia Journalism Review*, January 31, 2018, https://www.cjr.org/special_report/sexual-harassment-newsroom-survey-me-too.php; Julia Wallace and Kristin Gilger. "There Aren't Many 'Stranger Things' Than What Women Put Up With in the Newsroom," *USA Today*, July 8, 2019, https://www.usatoday.com/

story/opinion/2019/07/08/stranger-things-netflix-women-newsrooms-sexism-metoo-column/1655769001/; Lewis Raven Wallace, "How Trans Journalists Are Challenging–and Changing–Journalism," *NiemanReports*, August 15, 2019, https://niemanreports.org/articles/how-trans-journalists-are-challenging-and-changing-journalism/.

17. Jon Allsop, "The Ongoing Fight Against Racism in Newsrooms," *Columbia Journalism Review*, February 26, 2021, https://www.cjr.org/the_media_today/media_racism_reply_all.php; Clark Merrefield, "Race and the Newsroom: What Seven Research Studies Say," *NiemanLab*, July 22, 2020, https://www.niemanlab.org/2020/07/race-and-the-newsroom-what-seven-research-studies-say/; Amanda Zamora, "Overcoming Systemic Racism Begins in Our Own Newsrooms," *Poynter*, June 26, 2020, https://www.poynter.org/ethics-trust/2020/overcoming-systemic-racism-begins-in-our-own-newsrooms/.

18. Eline Jeanné, "Disability and the Intersectionality in the Media: Is Ableism the Last Acceptable Form of Discrimination?" *Media Diversity Institute*, 2020, https://www.media-diversity.org/disability-and-intersectionality-in-the-media/; John Loeppky, "Newsroom Accessibility in a Post-Pandemic World," *J-Source*, July 6, 2020, https://j-source.ca/newsroom-accessibility-in-a-post-pandemic-world/.

19. Jonathan Goldsbie, "Waiting for Manseu: At Fairy Creek, RCMP Efforts to Restrict Media Can Devolve into Theatre of the Absurd," Canadaland, May 31, 2021, https://www.canadaland.com/police-block-media-fairy-creek/; Cherise Seucharan, "What Police Are Hiding at Fairy Creek," May 31, 2021, no. 371, audio podcast episode, in *Canadaland*, hosted by Jesse Brown, https://www.canadaland.com/podcast/371-what-police-are-hiding-at-fairy-creek/.

20. Committee to Protect Journalists, "Canadian Police Bar Journalists from Covering Anti-Logging Protests," CPJ, May 26, 2021, https://cpj.org/2021/05/canadian-police-bar-journalists-from-covering-anti-logging-protests/; see also Goldsbie, "Waiting for Manseu," and Seucharan, "Fairy Creek."

21. RCFP, n.d.

22. Casares, *La hora del periodismo constructivo*, pp. 101–102; translated from the Spanish original by Bernardo H. Motta.

23. Andrea Wenzel, *Community-Centered Journalism: Engaging People, Exploring Solutions, and Building Trust* (Urbana, IL: University of Illinois Press, 2020).

24. Todd Vogel, ed., *The Black Press: New Literary and Historical Essays* (Piscataway, NJ: Rutgers University Press, 2001), p. 4.

25. *Ibid.*

26. Casares, *La hora del periodismo constructivo*, and Wenzel, *Community-Centered Journalism*.

27. Joshua Benton, "Maybe Just Shut Up About National Politics If You Want to Reduce Polarization?" *NiemanLab*, April 1, 2021, https://www.niemanlab.org/2021/04/maybe-just-shut-up-about-national-politics-if-you-want-to-reduce-polarization/.

Part II
Gaining Understanding

Coronavirus and the Bermuda Triangle of Public Health Reporting

MARK JEROME WALTERS

> "[The] narrative on covid-19 has often been reductive, tribally entrenched, and polarized. This has sometimes led to false dichotomies between seemingly contrasting positions that are in fact compatible, consistent propositions that can be supported at the same time"
> —David Oliver, *British Medical Journal*

Introduction

It's not news that science and journalism have a complicated, opposites-attract relationship. They both seek truth but in different ways. Science is based on hard evidence, while the best narrative journalism often thrives on human emotion. For a journalist, nothing's better than a moving anecdote, but for a scientist, few things are worse than n=1.

The currency of the realm for journalists is often inductive reasoning, while for the scientist, it's deductive. Scientists and journalists sometimes bring different meanings to words. To scientists, a "conservative" estimate of pandemic deaths means the highest possible number, while to journalists and their readers, it may mean the lowest. To one, a "fact" refers to the best evidence at a given time; to the other, a "fact is a fact," as fixed and immutable as the North Star.

Scientists and journalists even draw their basic vocabularies from different quarters of English. While one relies largely on words from the intellectualized, high-status Latinate roots, the other draws from the humbler Germanic tongue. As a clinician once scolded me during fourth-year veterinary rounds, "It's not 'a blood problem'; it's a 'hematological disorder.'"

While major fault lines separate science and journalism, the two fields are also bound by mutual benefits. Journalists need scientists to help them inform the lay public about breakthroughs in medicine, health and technology. Without journalists, many scientists would have a harder time getting public recognition and government funding for research. And so the rocky relationship between science and journalism continued into Covid-19, perhaps the biggest event to test the relationship in generations.

The relationship not only survived but prevailed. In many respects, it's probably even stronger than before. For one thing, the pandemic showed the indispensable role journalists play during public health crises. And by revealing some of the weak spots in coverage, the pandemic also showed ways that reporting can be improved. While some of my criticisms are pointed, they are all offered in the spirit of just that.

The pandemic put enormous professional pressure on practitioners in both fields. Scientists were under pressure to come up with effective public health recommendations, treatments and vaccines, while journalists, many of them conscripted general reporters, were drafted into the most difficult battle of their careers—reporting on suffering, death and related scientific matters. The imperatives of reporters' professional duties such as detachment and objectivity collided with their personal lives as offices merged with bedrooms and the main topic of reporting—a deadly virus—became intensely personal. Scapegoating became a parlor game where scientists blamed journalists for poor reporting, journalists accused the public health community of poor messaging, and large segments of the public lambasted both. All the while, many elected officials measured truth by whatever "facts" gave them the greatest political advantage.

As much as any event in modern history, the pandemic laid bare the different methods, goals, expectations and limitations of the journalistic and scientific methods. It created a panoramic view of the challenges journalists face in explaining scientific and public health information to the public. Perhaps above all, as Seth C. Lewis wrote, the pandemic enlarged "the blind spots in our work."[1]

First, with people's heightened anxiety about their own health, news consumers demanded even more certainty than usual, unaware (or in denial) that science is at its core the art of the uncertain. Journalists—not to mention many scientists—sometimes conveyed "facts" as final conclusions rather than as snapshots of evidence at given points. Then, when the "facts" changed, as they inevitably do, the public concluded that the scientists on whom reporters depended for information were unreliable—and by association, the reporters who conveyed them.

Second, during the pandemic, journalists faced an unrelenting plague of false choices, often promulgated by politicians seeking to score points with their constituencies, that defined some of the most dramatic pandemic rhetoric. Extreme, black and white choices, which brought drama to stories, often stole the news while the manipulative purpose of the rhetorical tool—a well-known form of political propaganda—went unaddressed or unnoticed.

Third, during the pandemic we learned that an anecdote, long a staple of American journalism, can do more than we thought—and not in a good way. When a sports writer uses an anecdote to covey a player's disappointment after a grueling loss, readers might be saddened or chagrined. But when a public health reporter uses an anecdotal lede to illustrate the rare side effects of a vaccine, some readers will choose to go without and suffer the consequences. In this sense, the pandemic showed how public health reporting—and science reporting in general—isn't just another news beat like sports or business. Because scientific research is built on a set of assumptions largely alien to the lay public, medicine and public health almost always need a broad context—including a remainder that science is rarely about absolutes—to be clearly understood.

Taken together, these three pitfalls—uncertainty, false choices and misleading anecdotes—created a kind of Bermuda Triangle of reporting during the pandemic. Although the Triangle is a fiction, the treacherous journalistic zone marked by these warning buoys is not. How well journalists navigated these perils depended in large part on their resources and level of experience. Large national papers tended to finesse the challenges better than the chronically understaffed regional news outlets, where journalists were lucky to find time for lunch, let alone time to ponder the finer points of their craft.

Mask-Confusion and Scientific Uncertainty

Perhaps few public health crises in history have generated as many rapidly evolving governmental recommendations as did Covid-19. And few recommendations generated more confusion and controversy than guidance about masks—for journalists and news consumers, the public, and even health officials themselves.

"Stop buying Masks! They are NOT effective in preventing general public from catching #Coronavirus, but if health care providers can't get them to care for sick patients, it puts them and our communities a risk!" the then-surgeon-general Tweeted in February 2020. About two months later, according to the same *New York Times* article, CDC was urging everyone wear masks outside their homes. By September of 2020, CDC was touting masks as "the most important, powerful public health tool we have" for controlling the pandemic.[2]

Many general reporters and a large segment of their readers thought this "sudden" about-face meant that scientists were incompetent and maybe even deceitful (a noble lie in telling people masks were ineffective so that enough remained for frontline workers). Reporting focused on the supposed flip-flops so often that this prescribed storyline often overshadowed news about recommendations themselves.

But to many scientists, the quickly changing recommendations marked a stunning success for research. An astonishing proliferation of studies had changed the scientific understanding of masks almost overnight. CDC's "sudden" recommendations in and of themselves were mostly straightforward and arrived punctually on the organization's website as studies were published. The mask-confusion storyline seemed to persist largely as a narrative device in which reporters could funnel an otherwise indigestible amount of evolving scientific information.

As Tara Haelle, a public health reporter and contributor to *Forbes*, explained to me, "Now there are dozens of studies on masks because so many have been done during the pandemic. But at the time that the pandemic started, the very most 12 studies, at that time, based on the evidence. We didn't have great evidence that wearing a mask would do much good. And we had a little bit of evidence that it might have been problematic."

In her article "Should Everyone Wear a Mask in Public? Maybe—But It's Complicated," published on the *Forbes* website on April 1, 2020, Haelle reported CDC's findings that masks were thought to be ineffective. Later, when she reported on the changed guidance, she was pilloried online, along with other journalists whose only crime was to accurately convey CDC's state-of-the-art information.

"I've been accused of killing people because I was 'against masks' in the beginning," she said. "And it wasn't like I was against masks. It was that in the beginning, we did not have evidence that masks would make much difference. For science to go from yes to no, that's really fast, but to the public, that was two months of being lied to, which is not true, but that's what it felt like to them. The science is moving very quickly and the public is not used to seeing science change in real time. And that means it's hard to keep the trust of your audience and explain no, it's totally normal for them to think one thing today and think another thing the next day. That's actually how science works."

The core of the confusion goes back to the different meanings people bring to "fact." To lay people, facts are facts, and facts don't change. To scientists, a fact is a placeholder in the march toward a better answer. Many non-scientists see the purpose of science as establishing absolute truth.

But science is really a process of measuring the likelihood that something is untrue. It's not about black and white answers but about reducing the size of the gray zone.

Much of the pandemic reporting lacked this context. As Ed Yong, the *Atlantic* science writer wrote, "If officials—and journalists—are clear about uncertainties from the start, the public can better hang new information onto an existing framework, and understand when shifting evidence leads to new policy. Otherwise, updates feel confusing. When the CDC suddenly reverses its position on wearing masks, without having previously clarified why the issue was so divisive, it seems like an arbitrary flip-flop."[3]

In fairness, scientists often fail to stress to journalists these uncertainties or even acknowledge them themselves. In more than thirty years of interviewing scientists, I have had few step forward to stress the uncertainty of their own work, the most memorable being an HIV researcher who flat-out told me, "I'm 95 percent sure that this is true, but in that other five percent I could be 100 percent wrong." Scientists seem as eager to feed the journalist's hunger for certainty as journalists do the public's. Admitting uncertainty opens us up to our own doubts, and it's humbling.

Without frequently reminding news consumers that science is about uncertainty, journalists risk turning scientists into antagonists, especially when the "facts" quickly change. According to Yong, journalists need to remind their readers that science is "less the parade of decisive blockbuster discoveries that the press often portrays, and more a slow, erratic stumble toward ever less uncertainty."

Of course, scientists sometimes add to the confusion by being human—that is, by simple mistakes. But the science-as-certainty myth allowed non-stories like the CDC's posting of wrong information about the virus on its website in September of 2021 to balloon into big news. CDC quickly corrected the mistake, but not soon enough. As the *Washington Post* reported, "It was the third major revision to CDC information or guidelines published since May."[4] Here, the correction of a honest mistake was conflated with regular science-based updates about the virus. This lack of nuance in the reporting reinforced the storyline that science is unreliable when it was actually just getting closer to the truth.

It's also true that flawed messaging from CDC and government officials occasionally fed the cycle of confusion over masks. When then-surgeon-general Dr. Jerome M. Adams Tweeted in February 2020 that masks are "NOT effective in preventing general public from catching #Coronavirus, but if health care providers can't get them to care for sick patients, it puts them and our communities at risk," he administered to the media a fill-in-the-blank test, and reporters could hardly be blamed for not getting the right answers (added by me in bold italics): Masks "are NOT effective in preventing general public from catching #Coronavirus *because most people wear them incorrectly, become complacent, or are not necessarily in places of high risk of getting the virus.* If health care providers, *who know how to wear masks properly and are near COVID patients much of the time,* can't get them to care for sick patients, it puts them and our communities at risk *because healthcare workers will become sick and be unable to care for others."* (Of course, those clarifications would have blown past Twitter's character limit, which raises a different question of how succinct a message can be without becoming cryptic.)

In late April 2021, the durability of the mask confusion storyline showed itself again, when President Biden announced from an open-air podium CDC's recommendation that vaccinated Americans "could safely drop their masks when outdoors, except in certain crowded settings and venues."[5] (Biden himself was wearing a mask as he strolled across the lawn to speak.) After the president spoke, a reporter asked, "If the risk is so low outdoors, wasn't doesn't this new guidance apply to everybody? And you choose to wear a mask as you walked out here. What message were you sending by wearing a mask outside alone?"[6] The president explained that he wanted people to see him taking his mask off and then not put it back on until he went back inside.

A few days later, an opinion piece on the CNN website echoed the "confusion-is-everywhere" narrative by again interpreting as contradictory the president's apparent deviation from the very guidance he was about to publicly deliver. "Vague rules are fodder for political dissension," read a subheading.

Again, much of the confusion could have been avoided by—earlier in the pandemic—normalizing the uncertainty of science with phrases like "according to the present state of knowledge," "based on the best scientific evidence," "at this point, scientists believe," "this guidance may change as scientists learn more from ongoing studies," or "science, like the weather report, is frequently updated for a reason."

Clarity in public health reporting depends on putting science in the context of uncertainty. As Jon Allsop wrote in the *Columbia Journalism Review*, "The press has got to slow down. Reporters need to accept ambiguity and uncertainty. Rather than rush toward facile answers or simplistic assertions, our stories must reveal the profound complexity of the problems at hand…. But that work cannot be done responsibly if we don't take the time to ask essential questions and open every possible window into understanding. Our coverage of vital public health information will not be truthful unless it's patient."[7]

On May 13, 2021, CDC, prompted by new studies, posted new and completely updated guidance for masks—that fully vaccinated people needn't wear them inside or out. That was followed by a spate of mask-confusion headlines, including in the *Washington Post*, "CDC's mask guidance spurs confusion and criticism, as well as celebration."[8]

The next day, CNN's Sanjay Gupta tried to explain the seemingly contradictory guidance. "That's a pretty big change from what you have been hearing for some time now," he said, explaining that several just-released scientific studies showed, "If you're vaccinated, you're very well protected against getting sick, you're very well protected against getting infected, and what we now know is you're very well protected against also transmitting the virus to other people. So that is in part why the mask mandate for people who are vaccinated is changing so much."[9]

Still, CDC's new guidance begged some serious public policy questions, but they were unrelated to the science per se. "The guidance shifts all the burden onto individuals to be 'on their honor' and choose the appropriate actions when deciding whether to wear a mask.... The likely result is that almost no one will wear a mask," Lisa Maragakis, an epidemiologist at Johns Hopkins University School of Medicine, told the *Washington Post*.[10]

In an interview with Axios, Anthony Fauci made a valiant effort to have it both ways, telling people the misunderstanding wasn't their fault and then blaming them: "I think people are misinterpreting, thinking that this is a removal of a mask mandate for everyone. It's not. It's an assurance to those who are vaccinated that they can feel safe, be they outdoors or indoors. It's not their fault. People either read them quickly, or listen and hear half of it. They are feeling that we're saying: 'You don't need the mask anymore.' That's not what the CDC said."[11]

But the mask recommendations continued to evolve. With the emergence of the new and more contagious Delta variant, in late July 2021 CDC recommended that even vaccinated individuals don their masks again. The advice was based on a new study showing that the virus, perhaps through a mutation, could now be spread by fully vaccinated people. But rather than simply posting the new guidance on its website, CDC acknowledged the change in guidance and released a report explaining the science behind it. CDC's approach evolved. The point had been gotten: scientists need to explain themselves to the public and journalists no less than journalists needed to explain the science behind the episodes of changing guidance to their readers.[12]

How could journalists, most of them non-scientists and new to the field of public health, possibly begin to explain what *New York Times* contributing columnist Leana S. Wen called at this point "a giant mess"?[13]

The age-old advice for journalists caught in a complicated who-done-it story is to follow the money. The advice for journalists caught in a complicated public health story might be to follow the science. Even in the most politically complex of public health stories, one finds that virtually all roads begin with the science. Following that and the conclusions of earlier pivotal studies, one can begin to cut through the clutter using a timeline of who knew what and when.

How does this mapping approach play out in practical terms?

- Use the science as starting points in interview questions. This will often elicit clearer lines of reasoning than scattershot questions about related controversies.
- In the stories, reference pivotal scientific findings. This will combat the anti-science strain of thought inherent to the "incompetent scientist" storyline.
- Emphasize uncertainty. This will help to undermine the science-as-certainty myth.

False Choices

Dramatic either/or choices often masqueraded as news during the pandemic. Some stories spoke of cancer patients in need of surgery being forced off the surgery schedules because of the overwhelming acute needs of Covid-19 patients, with the insinuation that cancer patients were dying because all the resources were being poured into caring for Covid-19 patients. In reality, the choice was rarely that stark. That is, whether there were the resources or not, there was a real risk of surgery patients catching Covid-19 while in the hospital for surgery. The tension between choices was real, but it was the black and white choices—the false dilemmas—that often made the news.[14] As David Oliver wrote in the *British Medical Journal*, "It can never be 'either/or' but rather 'both, at once…' [The] narrative on covid-19 has often been reductive, tribally entrenched, and polarized. This has sometimes led to false dichotomies between seemingly contrasting positions that are in fact compatible, consistent propositions that can be supported at the same time."[15]

Economy Versus Freedom and Health

In 2020, as the pandemic swept across the U.S., Lt. Gov. Dan Patrick of Texas stated on a television talk show, "I'm not living in fear of covid-19. What I'm living in fear of is what's happening to this country…. As a senior citizen, are you willing to take a chance on your survival in exchange for keeping the America that all America loves for your children and grandchildren? And if that's the exchange, I'm all in."[16]

It was a classic squeezing of a complicated question into two extremes: you must choose to protect granny or protect your freedom because you cannot have both. He was presenting the elderly with a false choice: give up your freedom and isolate or go out and live and shop—and risk dying—for the cause of freedom and a healthy economy. Many news stories that covered his interview condemned the questionable ethics of sacrificing old people for the supposed greater economic good.

The Washington Post ran a column excoriating Patrick and reporting that he faced a sharp backlash for suggesting that older Americans should sacrifice their lives for the sake of the economy during the coronavirus pandemic.[17] Extreme choices are obviously a big part of the story, but so is the deception inherent in its false choices. It's certainly understandable that journalists, pressed for deadlines and often working without adequate resources, leave the deeper analysis to the academics. But calling out propaganda for what it is can also add value and depth to a story.

In 2020, when the White House claimed that a lockdown would be "worse than the disease" and that "deaths of despair" from lost livelihoods, suicide and addiction could kill thousands of people, they were following a similar rhetorical script. So was the story in the *Washington Post*, "Oklahoma State's Mike Gundy Says His Team Needs to Play for Benefit of State Economy."[18] In it, the coach was quoted as saying the football players "have the ability to fight this virus off" and the school needs to "run money through the state of Oklahoma."[19] In both cases, the extreme choices became the story, while the false choice remained largely unchallenged.

The Wall Street Journal, on the other hand, directly challenged the premise in the story "The False Choice Between Lockdowns and the Economy." As the paper reported, "Even major countries without significant lockdowns are experiencing their worst economic conditions since the 2008–09 financial crisis."[20] Similarly, the *New York Times* ran the story "Some May Have to Die to Save the Economy? How About Offering Testing and Basic Protections?" In it the reporter asked, "How about we wait to have the discussion of how many deaths are acceptable among which sorts of people—elders? asthmatics?—until after we have taken common-sense measures to prevent the preventable. Such as, a ramped-up national testing and tracing system that would allow Americans to make legitimate personal-risk assessments and reduce the chance of new outbreaks as they return to work and to their amusements. People need to work—but they also need to know they won't carry the virus home."[21]

Vaccine Versus No Vaccine

Some of the storylines were predictable: The African American community was underrepresented in mass vaccination clinics. Early shortfalls of the vaccine made it almost impossible for state and local health officials and healthcare providers to meet vaccination goals. The availability of multiple vaccine formulations with varying contraindications caused confusion. People in some regions complained that some areas of the country were getting an unfair share of the vaccine. Many healthcare providers were regularly overwhelmed by frequently changing information about the vaccine and the supply. Faith-based organizations, usually a good partner in spreading messages in the community, were not generally effective this time because many didn't believe in this vaccine and didn't promote it because they weren't sure it was safe.

These narratives were not from the Covid-19 pandemic but from the swine flu pandemic of 2009.[22] Not that the same issues don't repeat themselves during pandemics. But journalists, with little time to deliver their stories, we often forced to follow established storylines rather than break new ground in their reporting. Formulaic reporting is both an essential fallback—it helps them quickly package stories—and an occupational hazard: the same plot is too often repeated.

For example, a perennial topic of pandemic reporting is vaccine side effects. Scientifically or statistically speaking, the question is not whether to risk the side effects of getting a vaccine but whether to risk the "side effects" of getting Covid. Then again, focusing on downside risk is not limited to vaccine. How many lead news stories do you read about how safe it is to fly on a commercial airliner? But there is a difference. Choosing not to fly on an airplane isn't going to kill you. Turning down a vaccination just might.

Of course, most readers and viewers must have known in their back of their minds that a more rational question than "Do I want to get the vaccine or not?" must have been, "Do I want to get the vaccine or get COVID?" Yet, many reports presented it as an either or question.

Some reports admirably broke through this misplaced emphasis. CNN, citing its own analysis, stated, "The risk of dying from Covid-19 is 40 times the risk of developing a rare blood clotting condition after getting the Johnson & Johnson vaccine." The report explained that CDC had gotten reports that out of 8.7 million people who had gotten J&J's Janssen coronavirus vaccine, 28 had developed a rare blood clotting syndrome. Three of them have died from the condition. The report continued, "However, in that same time period—March 2 to May 7—more than 2.2 million people were diagnosed with Covid-19 and more than 43,000 died."[23]

That fact that many "side effects" were wrongly blamed on the vaccine made the risks of the vaccine seem worse than they really were—an issue perhaps underreported. The *COVID-19 Vaccine Communication Handbook* offers some good advice for reporters on "misattributed side effects"[24]:

> If we vaccinate 10 million people and the vaccine had no side effects whatsoever, then over the following two months we can nonetheless expect that: 4,025 of those vaccinated will have a heart attack; 3,975 will have a stroke; 9,500 will have a new diagnosis of cancer; 14,000 will, unfortunately, die. The solution is to report with context.[25]

But as Ecker, Lewandowsky and colleagues pointed out in their paper "Correcting False Information in Memory," unless journalists are careful in refuting inaccuracies, they can make things worse through the "backfire" effect. That is, repeating misinformation in trying to refute it may actually reinforce it.[26]

Anecdotes

Mass media is the primary source of scientific and health information for non-experts once they graduate from school.[27] This places a high ethical burden on journalists to be fair and accurate. But this means more than just getting the information right. Without the right presentation of accurate facts, articles correct in every detail can mislead. Depending on the presentation, the wrong impression left by a story can overpower the data.

Headlines, for example, can create powerful first impressions and color a consumer's interpretation of all the subsequent information. If a journalist tells the story of 5-year-old who died of coronavirus and then cites statistics showing that such deaths are extremely rare, readers will tend to remember the death but forget the data.

Psychologist Jerome Bruner found that facts are far more likely to be remembered if included in a story, while organizational psychologist Peg Neuhauser found that people remember a well-told story more accurately and for far longer than statements of facts and figures.[28]

Anecdotes can be powerful scene- and tone-setting devices used to bolster the appeal of ledes or as building blocks of articles. They can frame the reader's or viewer's perception and largely shape their memory of what the story is about.[29] Because of this, one of the journalist's most trusted devices can become one of the most deceptive, especially during a public health crisis where impressions really matter.

For this and other reasons, the use of anecdotes sometimes causes friction between scientists and journalists. As scientists sometimes complain, "the plural of anecdote is not data." As mentioned, scientific and journalistic articles are often built on two different types of reasoning. The scientific method usually starts with generalizations and moves toward a specific observation. The journalistic method usually starts with a specific observation—an anecdote, for example—then generalizes. It's a tall order to ask journalists reporting on a furiously breaking crisis to know which of the processes is at play and to make the two complementary rather than contradictory. But an awareness could improve science journalism in general and public health reporting in particular.

At times, this clash of deductive and inductive reasoning was on full display as journalists rendered scientific information using journalistic devices. Sometimes their anecdotes allowed—in the supposed words of Socrates' accusers—the weaker argument to defeat the stronger. It is no wonder that the use of anecdotes can sometimes frustrate scientists and public health officials as much as it can delight readers. To do away with anecdotes is obviously not the answer. To use them judiciously when reporting about health is.

A case in point was the website for Fox10 News in Alabama, which posted a story in April 2021 with the ostensibly balanced headline "23 Alabama Deaths Reported After Shots—But Health Experts Warn Against Making Link." The article featured an anecdote about one of those deaths, that of an 89-year-old man. Beyond the disclaimer in the headline, the reporter dutifully included data and told readers that deaths from the vaccine were rare. Yet, by including the anecdote at all, there was little doubt that the emotional impacts of the article would long outlive the truth of the matter.

As if to make sure of this, the reporter wrote, "Still, the proximity of health crises to vaccinations has some people questioning whether it is just a coincidence," then went on to describe the death of one of the supposed victims: "This happened overnight," the daughter was quoted as saying; "This was like a light switch." The reporter reported that the "doctors concluded it to a vaccine side effect," but later quoted the head of the (Mobile, Alabama) County Health Department's Covid-19 response, who confirmed that none of the deaths had been shown to be caused by vaccines. Later in the story the reporter disclosed that "six weeks later, after his third trip to the hospital, that doctors spotted the culprit—lymphoma, a form of cancer."[30]

Conclusion

While the issues of uncertainty, false choices and misleading anecdotes are routine challenges reporters face when reporting on science, the pandemic brought them into dramatic relief. These issues not only revealed the perils of public health reporting but also deeper challenges faced by reporters who sometimes found themselves surrounded. As researchers Perreault and Perreault pointed out, "The needs that journalism satisfies in a crisis are at odds with practices of journalism itself."[31]

On one hand, many journalists effectively became public information officers for CDC and other agencies, dutifully reporting scientific findings and recommendations that they themselves couldn't be expected to fully understand. This disseminator role, with all the new complexities borne of the pandemic, differed dramatically from their traditional role.[32]

At the same time, health reporters faced a public that had been conditioned to mistrust even traditionally rock-solid sources such as CDC and government health experts.[33] This made journalists wary of dealing with their own once-trusted sources. General reporters without a stable of high-level health experts as sources often turned to local doctors. Even though many were eager to either help reporters or have their names in the media, about the only thing some of them knew about the pandemic was what they read in the news. The pandemic also forced journalists into non-traditional online relationships with sources, although they were used to and most comfortable working in person. Video chats from their living rooms with pets or family occasionally wandering in the background didn't make for the most professional of settings.

As Perreault and Perreault concluded, "Journalists working during COVID-19 ... placed themselves in a vulnerable position within the communication ecology [and] found their reporting difficult during the pandemic, in that the pandemic exacerbated weaknesses that have long existed." Journalists themselves saw "the pandemic as laying bare the endangered nature of journalism, which was a result of pressure from access to sources as well as market forces. This jeopardized journalists' ability to fulfill their responsibility to society."[34]

Worse yet, all this was occurring against a backdrop of an industry under siege by market forces. While advertising revenues had long been in decline, the pandemic made it worse, or as Allsop wrote in the *Columbia Journalism Review*, "the coronavirus didn't start the industry garbage fire as much as it threw accelerant on it."[35]

Despite many of the old challenges and some striking new ones, reporting on disease outbreaks had noticeably improved in some ways since the swine flu pandemic in 2011 and the Ebola crisis between 2014 and 2016. Then, the fascination with the exotic natures of the viruses too often become the story—to the exclusion of the illnesses' personal and societal impacts. By the time of coronavirus, reporters had grown wiser to the fallacy of the both-sides-ism that had traditionally prevented them from either ignoring or calling out proven frauds and lies.

By confronting the weaknesses revealed by the pandemic "stress test," the journalism professional can grow stronger. At the same time, the heroic efforts by so many reporters in the face of unprecedented challenges cannot be overlooked. Already stressed by financial pressures and dramatic cuts in staff and resources, journalists still managed to achieve the near-impossible. They covered the pandemic from head to toe, week to week, and hour by hour, and in the process managed to create what is undoubtedly the most complete journalistic record of a public health crisis in history. If there are weak spots in this coverage, they should not be seen as a blemishes so much as opportunities to learn.

Notes

1. Seth C. Lewis, "The Objects and Objectives of Journalism Research During the Coronavirus Pandemic and Beyond," *Digital Journalism* 8, no. 5 (2020).
2. Marie Fazio, "How Mask Guidelines Have Evolved," *New York Times*, April 27, 2021.
3. Ed Yong, "Why the Coronavius Is So Confusing," *Atlantic*, April 29, 2020.
4. Tim Elfrink et al., "CDC Reverses Itself and Says Guidelines It Posted on Coronavirus Airborne Transmission Were Wrong," *Washington Post*, September 21, 2020.
5. Peggy Drexler, "What's Behind the Trauma of Taking Off Masks," *CNN*, May 5, 2021.
6. NBC News, "Biden Delivers Remarks on New CDC Mask Guidelines," April 27, 2021.
7. Jon Allsop, "Unmasking Certainty," *Columbia Journalism Review*, Summer 2020.
8. Isaac Stanley-Becker, et al., "CDC's Mask Guidance Spurs Confusion and Criticism, as Well as Celebration," *Washington Post*, May 14, 2021.
9. Maggie Fox, "What's the Science Behind CDC's Decision to Say Fully Vaccinated People Don't Need Masks?," CNN, May 14, 2021.
10. Stanley-Becker, et al., "CDC's Mask Guidance Spurs Confusion and Criticism, as Well as Celebration."
11. Mike Allen, "Fauci Says People Are 'Misinterpreting' the New CDC Mask Guidance," *Axios*, May 19, 2021.
12. Emily Anthes, "The Delta Variant: What Scientists Know," *New York Times*, June 22, 2021.
13. Leana S. Wen, "Opinion: The CDC's Mask Guidance Is a Mess. Biden Needs to Clean It Up," *Washington Post*, May 17, 2021.
14. Ava Kamb, "The False Choice Between Public Health and Civil Liberties," *Voices in Bioethics* 6 (2020).
15. David Oliver, "David Oliver: The False Dichotomies in Pandemic Commentary," *The BMJ* 372 (2021).
16. Fox News, "Lt Gov Dan Patrick," *YouTube*, March 23, 2020.
17. Felicia Sonmez, "Texas Lt. Gov. Dan Patrick Comes Under Fire for Saying Seniors Should 'Take a Chance' on Their Own Lives for Sake of Grandchildren During Coronavirus Crisis," *Washington Post*, March 24, 2020.
18. Des Bieler, "Oklahoma State's Mike Gundy Says His Team Needs to Play for Benefit of State Economy," *Washington Post*, April 7, 2020.
19. Sally Jenkins, "Some May Have to Die to Save the Economy? How About Offering Testing and Basic Protections?," *Washington Post*, April 18, 2020.
20. Mike Bird, "The False Choice Between Lockdowns and the Economy," *Wall Street Journal*, April 6, 2020.
21. Jenkins, "Some May Have to Die."
22. National Academies Press, "Institute of Medicine (US) Forum on Medical and

Public Health Preparedness for Catastrophic Events: The 2009 H1n1 Influenza Vaccination Campaign: Summary of a Workshop Series," 2010.
    23. Deidre McPhillips and Maggie Fox, "Risk of Dying from COVID-19 40 Times the Risk of Rare Blood Clot After Receiving J&J Vaccine," May 12, 2021.
    24. University of Michigan Office for Health Equity and Inclusion, Covid-19 Vaccine Communication Handbook (University of Michigan, 2021).
    25. Dan Kennedy, "The Johnson & Johnson Vaccine Announcement and the Limits of Journalism," Media Nation, April 13, 2021, https://dankennedy.net/2021/04/13/the-johnson-johnson-vaccine-announcement-and-the-limits-of-journalism/.
    26. Ullrich K.H. Ecker, et al., "Correcting False Information in Memory: Manipulating the Strength of Misinformation Encoding and Its Retraction," *Psychonomic Bulletin and Review* 18, no. 3 (2011).
    27. Michael F. Dahlstrom, "Using Narratives and Storytelling to Communicate Science with Nonexpert Audiences," *Proceedings of the National Academy of Sciences* 111, no. 4 supplement (2014).
    28. Dolf Zillmann and Hans-Bernd Brosius, *Exemplification in Communication: The Influence of Case Reports on the Perception of Issues* (Mahwah, NJ: Lawrence Erlbaum Associates, 2000).
    29. Maria Konnikova, "How Headlines Change the Way We Think," *New Yorker*, December 17, 2014.
    30. Brendan Kirby, "23 Alabama Deaths Reported After Shots—but Health Experts Warn Against Making Link," *Fox10 News*, April 9, 2021.
    31. Perreault M.F., Perreault G.P. "Journalists on COVID-19 Journalism: Communication Ecology of Pandemic Reporting." American Behavioral Scientist. 2021;65(7):976-991. doi:10.1177/0002764221992813.
    32. Mildred F. Perreault and Gregory P. Perreault, "Journalists on Covid-19 Journalism: Communication Ecology of Pandemic Reporting," *American Behavioral Scientist* 65, no. 7 (2021).
    33. *Ibid.*
    34. *Ibid.*
    35. Jon Allsop, "The Media Industry's Preexisting Conditions," *Columbia Journalism Review*, May 18, 2020.

Social Media and the Pandemic

Myths and Misinformation

TONY SILVIA *and* CASEY FRECHETTE

"There is nothing either good or bad,
but thinking makes it so"
—William Shakespeare, *Hamlet*

One of the more surprising aspects of social media usage during the pandemic was its steep decline pre-pandemic and its sharp rise in usage during the pandemic's height. Starting in 2018, Americans were turning away from social media, cites one study.[1] Pre-pandemic, major platforms like Facebook, Twitter, and Snapchat had lost major audience shares. However, once the Covid crisis began, so did an uptick in usage, attributable in large part to the quest for shared experience and an antidote to isolation.

In March 2021, one year after Covid became an everyday word in homes across America, a study was done about its utilitarian value to people in lockdown: "These sites have been a social lifeline as well as a way to get new information about the disease spreading across the globe and upending life as we knew it. Twitter, especially, shone as a real-time news source." In addition, a year after the pandemic's onset, the claim was made that Covid altered everything, including how we use social media:

> The pandemic made social media, whose utility had languished and whose user growth was in decline, suddenly relevant. Some even mused that social media, though still under intense scrutiny for spreading misinformation and general toxicity, was good again. After years of social fragmentation, during which people were less likely to have watched the same shows or even share the same reality, people suddenly had something they could all talk about.[2]

To a certain, perhaps large extent, social media's access to others during crisis and lockdown was undoubtedly a good thing. It provided platforms for easing loneliness, desperation, anxiety, and even depression. For many, if not most, old and new social media platforms provided the only way to connect with family and friends. Conversely, those same platforms also provided opportunities to create and disseminate myths and misinformation surrounding the pandemic, and indoctrinate large numbers of the global population with these. Theories and falsehoods were spread virally either by those with little to no expertise or by others with an established agenda.

Social media also continued to create the "echo chamber" effect, a phenomenon in which exposure to a narrow set of views reinforces pre-existing opinions and biases. As much as social media created connections and shared experiences, it reinforced sharp partisan divides around mask-wearing, vaccinations, and other pandemic mitigation steps. One consequence of an echo chamber is the legitimacy that ideas circulating in a given bubble can enjoy, regardless of their basis in evidence or the extent of scientific consensus. Eli Parser, a technology author and activist, coined the phrase "filter bubble" to describe this effect,[3] underscoring the dynamics that not only perpetuate preconceptions but also prevent contrary or competing ideas from emerging.

You have read, hopefully, the insightful piece by our colleague Mark Jerome Walters earlier in this collection. He points out that among other problems with news media coverage of Covid-19, there was (and at this writing remains) a disconnect between science and journalism. Social media takes that disconnect to a new, higher level. The number of myths, misinformation, and outright falsehoods (often rising to the level of lies) was staggering at the pandemic's height and persisted even as vaccination rates plummeted, herd immunity slipped out of reach, and new, more contagious variants took hold in the U.S.

While social media was good in many ways for sharing and for establishing a platform of mutual concern, care, and connection for hundreds of millions of Americans, as well as billions more globally, it also had a dark side—one that is inherent in the medium itself. It can be used for good, for ill, or for ill-gain, often (but not exclusively) politically. Part of the dilemma is linked to those who share posts, unwittingly, that spread rumors, inaccuracies, and—by extension—fear or superstition about the virus, and suspicion of and skepticism towards public health professionals, government agencies, and state and local officials. A Harvard University analysis suggests that mainstream journalists themselves, rather than the public at large, may have been culpable, whether or not by intention:

> Mainstream media coverage has added to the problem, analysts say. At many major news outlets, reporters and editors with no medical or public health training were reassigned to cover the unfolding pandemic and are scrambling

to get up to speed with complex scientific terminology, methodologies, and research, and then identify, as well as vet, a roster of credible sources. Because many are not yet knowledgeable enough to report critically and authoritatively on the science, they can sometimes lean too heavily on traditional journalism values like balance, novelty, and conflict. In doing so, they lift up outlier and inaccurate counterarguments and hypotheses, unnecessarily muddying the water.[4]

Add to this assessment the reality of those with simply a phone, a laptop, and an Internet connection. Opinions become personal experience; fiction is taken at face value as fact; and truth becomes relative. In the storm of voices raging, social media followers select those voices that most adhere to their own worldview, a phenomenon known as confirmation bias. The pandemic became a bountiful ocean for self-validation. This, of course, is nothing new, but Covid-19 and its attendant uncertainty, fears, and the human need for resolution to dissonance magnified social media's already dubious ability to disseminate fact and not opinion. For heavy social media users, it arguably became less a tool and more a weapon.

The Pandemic "Weapon"

A quote from Shakespeare reinforces an earlier point made: "There is nothing either good or bad, but thinking makes it so."[5] Social media is a force for good, yielding much-needed, valuable information, especially during a pandemic. The degree of thought that goes into that information relay, in addition to the biases contained within the message itself, can also be bad for society. As a society, we trust in certain sources for our information and disregard others. That once defined the central role of what we term "legacy" media. Legacy news media, while occupying a central space in terms of Covid-19 coverage—platforms like the *New York Times, Wall Street Journal, Washington Post*, CNN, MSNBC, and Fox News—paled in comparison to the rapidity of social media transmission to an audience both anxious and fearful. With legacy media comes a "filter"—a characteristic of those trusted sources that is lost when individuals or groups advocating a specific viewpoint or agenda take precedence for a sizable percentage of the total media audience. When reliable, journalists entrusted with the public's well being provide a vital role in filtering information from misinformation. Debates have raged long before Covid-19 over whether social media platforms have or should have such filters or become a virtual village square where all facets of information—including misinformation—can proliferate, leaving the reader/viewer to decide for her or himself.

Concern over the spread of misinformation about Covid-19 grew to the point where the Centers for Disease Control undertook a strategy to help reduce the flow of falsehoods and myths surrounding how the virus originated, proliferated, and spread. The danger, the CDC recognized early in the pandemic, was very real. "Mitigating the risks associated with Covid-19 requires sustained public action, so misinformation that promotes false preventives or cures can hinder necessary behaviors to reduce the spread of the disease," the CDC asserted.[6] While no one would argue, journalists especially, that the free exchange of ideas is essential—even perhaps especially during—a global pandemic, deliberate falsehoods have a corrosive effect on society.

Complicating matters greatly was the reality that information didn't need to be outright false to do harm or have deleterious impacts on individual behavior. In line with the pitfall reporters routinely encountered when prioritizing novelty when assessing newsworthiness, many public health officials became increasingly alarmed at the tendency for journalists to cover so-called "breakthrough cases," instances when vaccinated people contract the virus. Likewise, they expressed concern about coverage of severe but exceedingly rare adverse reactions to vaccination. Such coverage, some argued, dissuaded many from getting vaccinated at a time when supply outstripped demand in the U.S. and communities with large pockets of unvaccinated people faced risks on a par with the threats of the early days of the pandemic.

These are murky waters from a media literacy perspective. Pandemic stories about adverse reactions or breakthrough cases were, by and large, fact-based and accurate; but they also created an impression about the dangers of vaccination or the efficacy of the shots that went beyond what many medical professionals saw as warranted. In their pursuit not only of what's accurate but also of what's interesting—and, indeed, marketable—journalists may have missed opportunities to capture and perpetuate larger truths. On social media, stories about vaccinated individuals becoming gravely ill, or about severe vaccine side effects, gained significant traction, despite representing outlier cases that ultimately proved the rule that vaccines worked and were the single greatest tool to combat the virus and prevent severe disease.

The Washington Post did one of the earliest analyses of social media's deleterious effect on the public's understanding of the coronavirus. First came the recognition that there was a relatively simple reason why so many turned so fast to social media for information, advice, and confirmation: "In a crisis, people struggle collectively to make sense of a complex and frightening situation—and as a result, misinformation spreads. For several reasons, that's been especially true during the novel corona virus pandemic. Scientists are still trying to understand everything about the virus's disease, covid-19, including how it spreads and which treatments work. Armchair epidemiologists are filling the Internet with their own interpretations of the emerging science." However, those interpretations were the most benign aspect of social media misleading the public. "Partisan polarization interacting with social media and cable news have amplified this dramatically, quickly spreading problematic beliefs about covid-19," the authors maintained.[7]

To support their point, the *Post* cited as one especially virulent example a Covid-19 article that on March 20, 2020, spread virally, influencing untold millions of readers on platforms like Twitter. The article was titled "Evidence over Hysteria—COVID-19" and was written by Aaron Ginn on the publishing platform Medium.[8] "He presented scientific findings and statistics related to the virus, arguing that the health risks were overstated and that social distancing would hurt the economy," stated the *Post*'s writers. "This article was heavily criticized by experts (including our University of Washington colleague biologist Carl Bergstrom) for misrepresenting the science and promoting misunderstanding. About 32 hours after it was posted, Medium removed the article for violating its platform policies."[9]

Initially, the article received scant attention, but by the following day, March 21, its viral momentum surged, "rapidly gaining visibility through tweets and retweets, surging to approximately 1,000 tweets an hour for several hours. Ginn's number of Twitter followers quadrupled in two days, from 4,000 to more than 16,000. This burst of attention was short-lived—Medium removed the article about 13 hours after the article began to spread widely, while Twitter added a safety warning to the link, discouraging users from clicking on it."[10] Despite that, its dissemination continued to gain steam. Fox News's Bret Baier and Laura Ingraham soon posted their own tweets that linked to the original article.

Ginn's case points to a dangerous dynamic that can arise when dubious information that would never first appear in a legacy news outlet's coverage nonetheless becomes mainstream news when it gains traction on platforms like Medium and Twitter, where little to no editorial oversight occurs, only to later gain official sanction after appearing in a news story as an embedded tweet or on a prominent anchor's timeline. Such reproductions are sometimes made under the auspices of calling necessary attention to popular, controversial, or even dangerous content. Attention on social media becomes a variable in the newsworthiness equation, and information that wouldn't otherwise appear in legacy channels gets prominent treatment and the legitimacy that legacy mastheads can provide. The net effect is an amplification of sharing trends in social media, but not necessarily of truth.

The *Post*'s research suggests that once these highly visible news "personalities" adopted the article's major premise—that Covid-19 was either a hoax or an overblown conspiracy that would harm the nation's economy—"the slope of the line showing the overall number of tweets increased." *The Post*'s analysis suggested "this is a typical story—and that's a problem." The problem resides in the methodology behind the misinformation's spread: "The spread of this story demonstrates some common patterns. First, a small group of key social media influencers can amplify the spread of misinformation and boost the long-term profile of previously obscure authors. Second, social media platforms like Twitter interact quickly with other media like cable news. Fox News personalities played a key role in spreading the story."[11] This suggests that rather than being at odds with one another, social media and legacy media were in a form of symbiosis during the height of the pandemic, reinforcing rather than fact checking one another.

It also reveals an important aspect of social media discourse: What can appear as unscripted, impromptu or organic—a raw temperature check of public sentiment—is often tightly orchestrated to shape public discourse and, ultimately, mold behavior, often to political ends.

The Rise in Fact Checking

A Reuters Institute study went further in exploring the types and sources of social media misinformation. Its authors analyzed 225 pieces of misinformation across social media between January and March 2020.[12] Among their findings was that in terms of scale, independent fact-checkers moved quickly to respond to the growing amount of misinformation around Covid-19; the number of English-language fact-checks rose more than 900 percent from January to March. (As fact-checkers have limited resources and cannot check all problematic content, the total volume of different kinds of coronavirus misinformation has almost certainly grown even faster. Furthermore, some research has suggested that incomplete fact-checking can do more harm than good, when problematic content isn't flagged and therefore receives an implicit seal of approval alongside content clearly labeled as suspect. Another problem is the "tainted truth" effect, a phenomenon that researchers believe causes us to become unjustifiably skeptical of legitimate information when something that had been presented as fact is later debunked.[13] Still others have argued[14] that the mere act of exposing false information gives it amplification, and that exposure does more potential harm than good.)

Interestingly, while the Trump administration played a role in disseminating Covid-19 information that could often be, at best, contradictory, and at worst false (such as claims of unproven, unscientific, and potentially harmful "cures" for the virus), the actual sourcing of much social media misinformation was found by Reuters not to be politically driven; however, those posts that did have either a political or a celebrity source were high on audience engagement.

"In terms of sources, top-down misinformation from politicians, celebrities, and other prominent public figures made up just 20% of the claims in our sample but accounted for 69% of total social media engagement," the study found. "While the majority of misinformation on social media came from ordinary people, most of these posts seemed to generate far less engagement. However, a few instances of bottom-up misinformation garnered a large reach and our analysis is unable to capture spread in private groups and via messaging applications, likely platforms for significant amounts of bottom-up misinformation."[15]

The "Infodemic" of Misinformation

The term "infodemic" was coined by the World Health Organization (WHO) in 2020 to describe what they saw as a crisis of great concern: "Mis- and disinformation about science, technology, and health is neither new nor unique to COVID-19. Amid an unprecedented global health crisis, many journalists, policy makers, and academics have echoed the WHO and stressed that misinformation about the pandemic presents a serious risk to public health and public action."[16] Their concern was broadly shared by others in the field of information dissemination. Cristina Tardáguila, associate director of the International Fact-Checking Network (IFCN), called Covid–19 "the biggest challenge fact-checkers have ever faced." The Reuters study referenced above asserted that the response to this "infodemic" went far beyond U.S. borders: "News media are covering the pandemic and responses to it intensively and platform companies have tightened their community standards and responded in other ways. Some governments, including in the UK, have set up various government units to counter potentially harmful content."

While there is little doubt that blatantly false information about Covid-19 festered on social media, Reuters found examples that suggest it was not the most persuasive content and made a differentiation between textual and image misinformation: "The most common form of misinformation, 'misleading content' (29%), contained some true information, but the details were reformulated, selected, and re-contextualized in ways that made them false or misleading. One very widely shared post offered medical advice from someone's uncle, combining both accurate and inaccurate information about how to treat and prevent the spread of the virus."[17]

The study's authors found,

while some of the advice, such as washing one's hands, aligns with the medical consensus, other suggestions do not. For example, the piece claims: "This new virus is not heat-resistant and will be killed by a temperature of just 26/27 degrees. It hates the sun." While heat will kill the virus, 27 degrees Celsius is not high enough to do so. A second common form of misinformation involves images or videos labelled or described as being something other than they are (24%). For example, one post shows a picture of a selection of vegan foods untouched on an otherwise empty grocery shelf and suggests that "Even with the Corona Virus [sic] panic buying, no one wants to eat Vegan food." AFP Australia observed this image is of a grocery store shelf in Texas in 2017, ahead of Hurricane Harvey. This is also an example of what some call "malinformation."

Mal- vs. Misinformation

The very term "mal," when applied to information, suggests information intended to mislead or harm, as opposed to "mis," which might not be anything other than posts containing inaccuracies without the author's intent to deceive. The problem is exacerbated by the reader's inability to discern what is simply false and what is intentionally false. It is especially harmful during a time of grave national and international concern. A 2015 study suggests that habitual users of Facebook, the largest social network, are far more susceptible to being deceived than light users.[18]

In part, that aspect of social media's influence is linked to the large number of Americans who take posts on their Facebook, Twitter, and other platforms as gospel, making them, in fact, gullible where truth alone is a factor, let alone malintent. The Pew study, done from November 2019 to December 2020, roughly corresponding to a period just before awareness of the pandemic and through the height of it, found, "Some 18 percent of respondents in the survey got most of their political and election news via social media."[19] How well informed was this group? According to Pew, just 17% of Americans who get most political news from social media displayed high levels of political knowledge, a figure almost three times lower than those who rely most on news websites and apps for political news.[20]

The study did discern a bright side to the social media usage of its 9,000 respondents: "Social media news consumers were more aware of specific false or unproven stories about the coronavirus and said they had seen more misinformation about the pandemic such as claims that Vitamin C could prevent infection." On the other hand, as stated in this book's first essay, the skepticism over social media's veracity splits along partisan lines. In the early days of the pandemic, in April 2020, about a third of Republicans said they relied mostly on Trump and his task force for pandemic news, according to Pew. As the pandemic unfolded, these Republicans paid closer attention to Covid-19 news, were more likely to think the government's pandemic response was strong, were more likely to think the media had overblown the threat, and were more likely to think election fraud was covered up, Pew found.[21]

Most interesting is that a majority of those surveyed said they distrusted social media as a news source, with Facebook considered to be the least trustworthy of all platforms. This finding points to one of several paradoxes in how we respond to misinformation: Awareness of the presence of false information does not appear to protect us from being swayed by specific instances of fake or manipulated content. Likewise, some research suggests those with higher levels of education are just as likely to share fake stories. More vexing, other scholars have found that belief in misinformation, once formed, is very difficult to shake off, even over long stretches of time, and even in the face of contradictory evidence. Put another way, false content not only spreads quickly, enabled by the design of social networks; it can also linger longer, both outpacing and outlasting the truth.

Another study, done by Northwestern University, delves more deeply into the relationship between false claims posted on social media and users' belief systems, leading to vaccine acceptance or rejection. Twenty-one thousand Americans were surveyed between August 7 and 20 in 2020. In this study, 28 percent of Snapchat users, 23 percent of Instagram users, and 25 percent of Wikipedia users believed false claims posted on those sites. In addition, Northwestern researchers found, "Of the 8% surveyed who received news from Facebook Messenger in the previous 24 hours, 26% were likely to believe a false claim. For the 4% who used WhatsApp, it was 31%. In contrast, the lowest levels of misperceptions emerged for those who received news about the pandemic from local television news, news websites or apps, and community newspapers (11% in each case)."[22]

The study's primary author, who completed his research as part of a consortium involving Harvard, Northeastern, and Rutgers universities, reached this conclusion: "The results confirm the initial fears that social media would contribute to misinformation about COVID-19. This misinformation may in turn have dire consequences when it comes to individual behaviors and group attributions." Among the study's additional findings:

- Those under age 45 were most likely to believe false claims, with older ages less likely. Those under age 25 had an 18 percent chance of believing a false claim, with people ages 25–44, 45–64 and 65+ having a probability of 17 percent, 12 percent and 9 percent, respectively.

- There also were racial gaps in misinformation. Black Americans held the highest average level of belief in the 11 false claims (17 percent), followed by Hispanics (16 percent), with White and Asian Americans at 13 percent. The most-believed claims by racial minority and ethnic groups were that antibiotics can prevent Covid-19: 23 percent for Black Americans. Meanwhile, 23 percent of White and Hispanic respondents believed that China created the coronavirus as a weapon.
- Those who believe Covid-19-related conspiracies are also less likely to seek the Covid-19 vaccine. In the largest gap, only 47 percent of respondents who believe that Covid-19 originated as a weapon in a Chinese lab said they would receive a Covid-19 vaccination, compared to 63 percent of those who did not believe the claim or were unsure.

This study is among many demonstrating the seriousness of the informational choices individuals and groups make, relative to their attitudes, beliefs, and actions. While social media may very well have served a useful purpose during the height of the Covid-19 pandemic, in terms of fostering connections with family and friends, and reducing feelings of anxiety and isolation, it simultaneously reduced many users' knowledge and understanding, and negatively affected their behavior during a critical time in global history.

Combating Misinformation Surrounding Covid-19

Some potential solutions to the spread of Covid-19 misinformation, "malinformation," and the resulting "infodemic" created by both reside within the tech industry that made social media possible from its earliest origins on the Internet. In February 2021, National Public Radio (NPR) did an analysis of efforts by the World Health Organization (WHO) and other groups to combat misinformation surrounding Covid-19. One problem NPR uncovered in its research for a story on the topic was somewhat obvious: taking down false, misleading, or otherwise problematic posts on social media often comes too late. The message once seen can't be unseen, and once it's gone viral (as we saw in an earlier example in this essay), little can be done to stem the tide of misinformation.

One especially illustrative example came on social media in October of 2020. Then-president Donald Trump claimed in a Twitter post that he had now had immunity from Covid-19 after being infected with the virus. According to the CDC: "There is no firm evidence that the antibodies that develop in response to SARS-CoV-2 infection are protective." Trump's post was removed from Twitter, after fact-checkers flagged it, but not before it was seen and shared by re-tweets among millions of his followers.

From 2020 to 2021, there was additional progress toward putting fact-checking tools in the hands of social media users. NPR lists the following tools among them:

- Pinned to the top of Instagram's search function, the handles of the U.S. Centers for Disease Control and Prevention and the World Health Organization are prominently featured. Click and you'll find posts and stories on how to keep safe during the pandemic.
- In the home section of the YouTube app, there's a playlist of videos that promote vaccination and counteract vaccination misinformation from WHO, the *Journal of the American Medical Association* and GAVI, the Vaccine Alliance.
- On the Twitter app, you might spot a warning under posts with fake or misleading Covid-19 information. A tweet from a user falsely proclaiming that 5G causes coronavirus, for example, has a big blue exclamation mark with a message from Twitter: "Get the facts about COVID-19." It links to a story debunking the claim from a U.K. media outlet called iNews.[23]

A professor of health communications at Harvard University is quoted in NPR's story as praising WHO efforts against the spread of false information. "The WHO deserves credit for recognizing that the sheer flood of misinformation—the infodemic—is a problem and for trying to do something about it," he says. "But the tech sector has not been particularly helpful in stemming the tide of misinformation."[24] The WHO's efforts began early in February 2020 when they teamed up with 40-plus tech companies to help counter misinformation with credible sources for accurate information, among the methods being the "learn more" and "for more information" labels on the major social media platforms.

According to NPR, these "learn more" and "for more information" Covid-19 labels can be found on almost every tech platform—yes, Twitter, Facebook and Instagram, but also Tinder, the dating app (every few swipes there are reminders to wash hands and observe physical distancing, with links to WHO messages) and Uber, the ridesharing app (a section on its website with rider safety information directs people to WHO for pandemic guidance). Future studies may bring light to how effective these efforts have been or continue to be. On the other hand, as Professor Viswanath of Harvard observes, "There are no guarantees that people are going to take the time to click on a link to credible sources to 'learn more,' as the labels suggest…. If I'm sitting in some community somewhere, busy with my life, worried about my job, worried about whether the kids are going to school or not, the last thing I want to do is go to a World Health Organization or CDC website."[25]

The Human Factor

Beyond what the tech industry, together with health professionals, can do to contain, combat, or curtail misinformation, several studies suggest that what I will call "the human factor," the determination of human beings to find the information they consider credible (whether it is or not), cannot be underestimated. The disinformation analytics company Graphika found that if one social media platform removed a suspect video, for example, it would often land on another platform with the same group of followers or, worse, create a new set of followers. That study showed the crackdown on anti-vaccine videos on YouTube has "led their proponents to repost the videos on other video-hosting sites like BitChute, favored by the far-right…. YouTube removes videos if they violate its COVID-19 policy. Videos that claim the COVID-19 vaccine kills people or will be used as a means of population reduction, for example, are not allowed. But other platforms may have less stringent policies."

The problem becomes increasingly complex when we see that there is no empirical evidence that fact-checking, whether done by journalists, tech companies, or the platforms themselves, changes an individual or group's behavior toward seeking out and embracing false information that accords with their own belief systems—whether that information was pro- or anti-vaccine, or pro- or anti-conspiracy theories related to the pandemic, its origin, or the progress toward bringing the pandemic to an end (or the failure to do so).

A group called "First Draft," which studies misinformation,[26] is quoted in NPR's story confirming the lack of evidence that fact-checking efforts and giving citizens the tools to separate information from disinformation results in the desired effect of steering users away from false claims and self-serving theories. "We can't just assume that things that seem to make sense (such as taking a post down or directing people to a trustworthy source) would actually have the consequences we expect," said Claire Wardle, the group's director.

One challenge fact-checkers face is that the effectiveness of their work hinges on their perceived credibility. If their efforts are seen as partisan, partial, or profit-driven, their judgments will be discarded out of hand, similar to the way a sizable contingent of Americans view with distrust the reporting of the "mainstream media," including legacy news organizations.

Another equally daunting challenge concerns the learning curve encountered, even by virologists and other medical experts, in building a reservoir of expertise about a virus that, in many ways, deviated from expectations. For months, evidence had accumulated, for example, that the virus can be transmitted not only by droplets, which can travel a few feet, but by tiny aerosols, which can circulate over a much wider area and without direct, face-to-face contact.

Yet it wasn't until May 2021 that the World Health Organization and the Centers for Disease Control, two of the most prestigious and influential health bodies, revised their official guidance to acknowledge the important role aerosols play in the transmission of the virus.

Zeynep Tufekci, an associate professor at the University of North Carolina, argued in the *New York Times*[27] that this omission had a drastic, deleterious effect on mitigation efforts. "If the importance of aerosol transmission had been accepted early," Tufekci wrote, "we would have been told from the beginning that it was much safer outdoors, where these small particles disperse more easily, as long as you avoid close, prolonged contact with others. We would have tried to make sure indoor spaces were well ventilated, with air filtered as necessary. Instead of blanket rules on gatherings, we would have targeted conditions that can produce superspreading events: people in poorly ventilated indoor spaces, especially if engaged over time in activities that increase aerosol production, like shouting and singing. We would have started using masks more quickly, and we would have paid more attention to their fit, too. And we would have been less obsessed with cleaning surfaces."

Tufekci attributed the slow updates to endemic problems with how we go about doing science and confronting data that conflicts with orthodoxy. "Clear evidence doesn't easily overturn tradition or overcome entrenched feelings and egos," she wrote. But she also pointed to human foibles: "Another key problem is that, understandably, we find it harder to walk things back. It is easier to keep adding exceptions and justifications to a belief than to admit that a challenger has a better explanation."

Whatever the cause of these shortcomings, a critical challenge remains for fact-checkers who rely on authoritative, official accounts from national and international organizations, when those very institutions don't provide or can't provide definitive answers.

As of this writing, there are ongoing efforts, however, to help determine how strong an influence fact-checking has had and can have in the future on human behavior—especially the tendency to imbue with truth claims that validate our deeply held beliefs. One example is a partnership between the WHO and Google. Since March 2020, Google has displayed pandemic-related public service announcements from the WHO above search results. In a 2022 study focused on these ads, Andy Pattison, the team lead of Digital Channels at the World Health Organization, along with research colleagues from the WHO and Google, found that message framing plays an important role in whether web users read public service announcements related to the pandemic. Descriptive frames, those that simply emphasized the information readers would find if they clicked through, tended to perform well; loss frames, those that emphasized costs tied to not following public health recommendations, tended to perform poorly.[28]

There is evidence to suggest that information alone will not automatically change people's behavior, at least in the short term. Another member of the WHO team, Melinda Frost, also interviewed by NPR in 2020, spearheaded a group of ethicists, sociologists, neurologists, and behavioral psychologists to help learn more about how information is spread and how it can be better managed to change people's minds—and behavior—for the greater good. So far, Frost maintains, "A lot of what we know about behavior change really requires something closer to the individual—making sure the information we have is relevant to individuals and makes sense in their lives."[29] Efforts like these will help guide future efforts to create spaces that promote credible, accurate, helpful information.

NOTES

1. The Infinite Dial 2021. Edison Research and Triton Digital. http://www.edisonresearch.com/wp-content/uploads/2021/03/The-Infinite-Dial-2021.pdf.

2. Rani Molla, "Posing Less, Posting More, and Tired of It All: How the Pandemic Has Changed Social Media," Recode, March 1, 2021, https://mail.google.com/mail/u/0/#inbox/KtbxLvGzbQlGHKhDMxfrNFnlXqjbQpjtnB, retrieved June 30, 2021.

3. Pariser elaborates on this concept in his 2011 book *The Filter Bubble: What the Internet Is Hiding from You*, written in the nascent years of social media and the "personalization" of the web that would come to dominate the online experience for billions of Internet users.

4. Christina Pazanese. "Battling the Pandemic of Misinformation," *Harvard Gazette*, May 8, 2020, https://news.harvard.edu/gazette/story/2020/05/social-media-used-to-spread-create-covid-19-falsehoods/, retrieved June 16, 2021.

5. Interesting comparisons have been made to Shakespeare's writing his greatest plays during three pandemics in London of his day and the COVID pandemic in our own. See Peter Marks, "Shakespeare Wrote King Lear During a Pandemic," *Washington Post*, November 6, 2020, https://www.washingtonpost.com/entertainment/theater_dance/great-artistic-works-during-plagues/2020/11/05/6575cac2-1d29-11eb-90dd-abd0f7086a91_story.html, retrieved July 1, 2021.

6. Emily Vagra and Leticia Bode, "Addressing Covid-19 Misinformation on Social Media Preemptively and Responsibly," *Emerging Infectious Diseases Journal* 27, no. 2 (February 2021), https://wwwnc.cdc.gov/eid/article/27/2/20-3139_article, retrieved June 5, 2021.

7. Kate Starbird, Emma Spiro, and Jevin West, "This Covid Information Went Viral," *Washington Post*, May 8, 2020, https://www.washingtonpost.com/politics/2020/05/08/this-covid-19-misinformation-went-viral-heres-what-we-learned/, retrieved June 29, 2021.

8. Zoe Schiffer, "How Medium Became the Best and Worst Place for Coronavirus News," Verge, April 14, 2020, https://www.theverge.com/2020/4/14/21219907/medium-coronavirus-covid-19-news-misinformation-conspiracy-theories-best-worst, retrieved July 1, 2021.

9. Ibid.

10. Ibid.

11. Ibid.

12. For more on the study's key findings, cited here, see Scott Brennen, Felix Simon, Philip Howard, and Rasmus Kleis Nielsen, "Types, Sources, and Claims of Covid-19 Misinformation," April 2020, http://www.primaonline.it/wp-content/uploads/2020/04/COVID-19_reuters.pdf, retrieved June 1, 2020.

13. See, for example, Gary Stix, "Attempts at Debunking 'Fake News' about Epidemics Might Do More Harm Than Good," February 14, 2020, *Scientific American*, https://www.scientificamerican.com/article/attempts-at-debunking-fake-news-about-epidemics-might-do-more-harm-than-good/, retrieved July 9, 2021.

14. For one roundup, see Harrison Mantas and Susan Benkelman, "Do No Harm: Debunking Without Amplification," June 11, 2020, Poynter.org, https://www.poynter.org/fact-checking/2020/do-no-harm-debunking-without-amplification/, retrieved July 8, 2021.

15. Brennen, Simon, Howard, and Nielsen, "Types, Sources, and Claims."

16. Oberin Apuke and Bahyiah Omar, "Fake News and Covid-19: Modelling the Predictors of Fake News Sharing Among Social Media Users," July 30, 2020, National Institutes of Health, https://www.ncbi.nlm.nih.gov/pmc/articles/PMC7390799/, retrieved May 30, 2021.

17. Brennen, et al., "Types, Sources and Claims."

18. Vishwanath, A. "Habitual Facebook Use and Its Impact on Getting Deceived on Social Media." *Journal of Computer-Mediated Communication*, 20(1), 2015, pp. 83–98. https://academic.oup.com/jcmc/article/20/1/83/4067561.

19. For a synopsis of the Pew research findings, see "Social Media Users More Likely to Believe Misinformation," Phys.org, Feb. 22, 2021, https://phys.org/news/2021-02-social-media-users-misinformation.html, June 21, 2021; for the full study, see Tom Infield, "Americans Who Get News Mainly on Social Media Are Less Knowledgeable and Less Engaged," Pew Trust Magazine, https://www.pewtrusts.org/en/trust/archive/fall-2020/americans-who-get-news-mainly-on-social-media-are-less-knowledgeable-and-less-engaged, retrieved June 21, 2021.

20. Pew Trust Magazine.

21. "How Americans Navigated the News in 2020: A Tumultuous Year in Review." Pew Research Center. https://www.pewresearch.org/journalism/2021/02/22/how-americans-navigated-the-news-in-2020-a-tumultuous-year-in-review/.

22. Stephanie Kulke, "Social Media Contributes to Misinformation About Covid-19," Northwestern Now, September 23, 2020, https://news.northwestern.edu/stories/2020/09/social-media-contributes-to-misinformation-about-covid-19/, retrieved June 12, 2021.

23. Malaka Gharib, "WHO Is Fighting False Covid Info. on Social Media," National Public Radio, February 9, 2021, https://www.npr.org/sections/goatsandsoda/2021/02/09/963973675/who-is-fighting-false-covid-info-on-social-media-hows-that-going, retrieved June 28, 2021. Subsequent references from the story are from this site.

24. Ibid.

25. Ibid.

26. For more on the group's ongoing efforts to intercept misinformation, see https://firstdraftnews.org/research/.

27. Zeynep Tufekci, "Why Did It Take So Long to Accept the Facts About Covid?," *New York Times*, May 7, 2021 https://www.nytimes.com/2021/05/07/opinion/coronavirus-airborne-transmission.html.

28. Pattison, A.B., Reinfelde, M., Chang, H., Chowdhury, M., Cohen, E., Malahy, S., O'Connor, K., Sellami, M., Smith, K.L., Stanton, C.Y., Voets, B., & Wei, H.G. "Finding the Facts in an Infodemic: Framing Effective COVID-19 Messages to Connect People to Authoritative Content." *BMJ Global Health*, 7(2), e007582. https://doi.org/10.1136/bmjgh-2021-007582.

29. Malaka Gharib, "WHO Is Fighting False Covid Info."

Part III
Charting a Course

Shifting Newsroom Economics
A Lasting Impact
Elliott Wiser

"Working remotely isn't always optimal in a news environment, but it does work. I don't see operations going back to the cacophony of crowded newsrooms and twice-daily in-person editorial meetings in a conference room. It's simply not as efficient as what we were able to do in the remote environment"
—Ron Lombard, TV and cable news veteran[1]

Changing News Consumption

The winds of change were already blowing through newsrooms long before the first case of Covid-19 was diagnosed. People were reading fewer newspapers and watching less news on television. Social media and news websites were the most popular choices, with social media becoming the medium of choice for people under 40.

A 2018 Pew Center study showed 36 percent of 18- to 29-year-olds said their primary source of news was social media, with news websites the second choice at 27 percent. Only 16 percent obtained news from television and a paltry 2 percent from print. Among the 30- to 49-year-olds, news websites were first choice, followed by television, social media, radio, and newspaper. The 50-plus age group turned to TV first, followed by news websites, radio, print, and social media.

Of special note in these numbers:

- Even among people over 50 years old, only 18 percent said print was their primary source for news. That number dropped to just 8 percent among 30- to 49-year-olds.

- The television number included network, cable, and local news viewing.
- Local television news ratings continued to decline, although many newscasts enjoyed a bump in ratings early in the pandemic as people stayed home and sought information. But the long-term trend is not good. In 2018 viewership for local news stations continued to drop in all key news time periods: morning, evening and late night. People are turning away from local television news.
- Radio viewership has remained steady, although there are methodology issues. Many studies do not differentiate between network radio (NPR), local radio, satellite, and podcasts.[2]

The decline in readership and viewership resulted in a decline in revenue, so jobs were disappearing even before the pandemic. According to the Bureau of Labor Statistics, in 2008 there were approximately 114,000 newsroom employees (that includes reporters, editors, photographers, and videographers) in the news producing business. By 2019, that number had declined to approximately 88,000.[3]

And then came the pandemic. It was like pouring gasoline on a fire. The global outplacement firm Challenger, Gray & Christmas reported that across broadcast, digital and print news, the news industry suffered more than 16,000 job cuts. That was 13 percent higher than the previous record of 14,265 newsroom job cuts that occurred during the "Great Recession" of 2008.[4]

Remote Newsrooms

Having fewer jobs in journalism was one impact of the pandemic. The second was the necessity to shut down newsrooms and ask all employees to work from home. Initially this resulted in TV anchors reading the news from makeshift sets situated in their homes. As the pandemic progressed, more newsrooms allowed "essential personnel" back into newsrooms. Anchors, producers, and managers returned to work; however, many reporters, writers, photographers, and editors remained at home.

As an aside, working from home as a journalist is not new. The author began his TV career in the 1980s working out of a basement apartment in Charlottesville, Virginia. Yet the practice was often relegated to bureaus located outside a media outlet's main sphere of influence. In 2020, working from home became the norm. As the pandemic becomes part of history, many reporters will return to the newsroom, but many will not. The advent of video conferencing applications like Zoom and Teams makes it easier for reporters to start their day from home and not travel to a newsroom for an editorial meeting. That can be done remotely. Stories can be filed from anywhere for both print and broadcast. Editing broadcast stories can be done on a laptop in the field. The pandemic proved a hypothetical often discussed among news managers before Covid-19: "Why have a reporter drive to work only to drive somewhere else?"

Deborah Collura, the general manager at CBS46 in Atlanta, writes, "The other big change is Return to Work or what we are calling, 'The new workflow.' We are putting together schedules where some employees may work remotely some or most days (depending on the job position). The way we scheduled prior to the pandemic will not be how we schedule employees in the future."[5]

More reporters will work from home because it is efficient and it saves money. The latter is a key factor post-pandemic for media companies. There will no longer be a need for large newsrooms and the expensive assets they require. Practicality meets cost savings.

Video App Interviews

Television reporters will now follow their print brethren in the way they conduct interviews. Newspaper reporters often do their work over the phone, while broadcasters needed a photographer, camera, and vehicle to travel to the interviewee to record an interview. That changed during the pandemic, as video app interviews became standard procedure for getting sound bites. That is here to stay.

No matter what platform a reporter uses (Zoom, Teams, WebEx) the reporter can stay home and record a video interview. As video quality improved for these platforms the audience became more accepting of hits, pauses, and blips. This will also reduce the amount of time it takes to produce a television story because crews will no longer need to travel to record an interview.

Post-pandemic, television crews will still travel to the story, especially for breaking news; however, it will not be a requirement. Employing video app interviews in a television story will become standard procedure. Also, video apps will negate the need to roll a microwave or satellite truck for an interview. Pre-pandemic that was required, except in breaking news when a phone interview was tolerated. The pandemic taught us that video apps are an effective tool to conduct interviews. Guests no longer will be required to come to the station or the live truck location.

The practicality of video app interviews is only surpassed by their ability to cut costs. Microwave and satellite trucks costs hundreds of thousands of dollars. Television stations will reduce their fleets and replace them with laptops loaded with video apps. Many stations are required to staff these trucks with driver/operators. Fewer trucks will mean fewer driver/operators. Media executives have surely already taken note of this cost-saving dynamic.

There is a positive aspect to the use and acceptance of video app interviews. A local reporter can now reach an expert anywhere in the world to conduct an on-camera interview. Pre-pandemic, a reporter could record audio or ask the long-distance interviewee to travel to a nearby affiliate to partake in a satellite interview. In special circumstances, the reporter and their photographer would travel long distances for the interview. The video app interview replaces expensive trips or satellite time. Again, media executives have already taken note of this cost-saving measure, and this will accelerate its acceptance post-pandemic.

Centralized Operations

Pre-pandemic, many newspapers chains were consolidating printing presses, sharing costs within a company, and in some cases, with another media entity. Further consolidation will occur post-pandemic.

In 2021, the *Tampa Bay Times* began outsourcing the printing of its newspaper to Gannett. The *Times* closed its 27-acre production facility in downtown St. Petersburg, laying off 150 workers. The newspaper put the property up for sale to pay down debt.[6] (For more on post-pandemic economic impact, read the interview with Poynter Institute president Neil Brown at the end of this essay.)

Finding ways to save money will be essential for all media properties, but for newspapers it will be critical. Industry consultant FTI predicts 20 percent of pre–Covid ad dollars might not come back to newspaper companies after the pandemic.[7] And many newspapers have new owners who are experienced budget cutters. Hedge funds have bought or merged with large properties like Tribune Publishing and Gannett. Tom Rosenstiel with American Press Institute astutely observed, "these companies (newspapers) got hedge fund owners who have a liquidation strategy."[8]

For broadcast and cable news operations, consolidation began taking place long before Covid-19. Stations within an ownership group were sharing master control operations, human resource management, marketing, web operations, engineering, business operations, weather forecasting, and feature stories.

The general manager of CBS46 in Atlanta, Deborah Collura, says station owner Meredith has embraced centralized operations: "Creative Service is now hubbed for us in Phoenix for better efficiency and greater coordination of our creative strategy on all platforms."[9]

Centralizing operations will accelerate post-pandemic as media owners reduce costs to make money. This will mean fewer jobs and require that employees demonstrate multiple skills.

Post-Pandemic Media Economics

The law of supply and demand is a tenet of economic theory. The greater the supply, the lower the demand, and that lowers prices. Something in great demand often results in lower supply and higher prices. As mentioned at the beginning of this essay, there are fewer jobs today in journalism than there were a decade ago. Yet the supply of journalists increases as veterans lose their jobs and re-enter the work market. Every year they are joined by thousands of college graduates. This simply means enormous competition for open positions that pay less and expect more.

The post-pandemic world will not see a groundswell of full-time jobs returning to the workplace. Companies have found economies of scale and face billions of dollars of debt. They will work hard to keep costs under control. To do so they will control one of the largest lines in a media budget: salary.

CBS46 general manager Deborah Collura says, "We will put each position through the microscope moving forward to see if they are essential workers. We are also examining if their job descriptions/functions change as we change some of our workflow."[10]

Media managers will be challenged like never before to control costs and expand output. This could lower the bar of what is deemed acceptable product in traditional media. Less experienced and lower paid employees producing more product is hardly the recipe for high quality journalism; therefore, the new media, as described later in this essay, will fill the void.

And more will be expected of newsroom employees. An increasing number of reporters will shoot and edit their own video ("multi-media journalist" is the term often used for this position). Reporters are being asked to write web stories and post to social media. Producers and writers work on multiple platforms and projects. Executives are asked to oversee more product in multiple markets.

Media job seekers would be wise to expand their skills beyond just writing and reporting. It would be sensible to have a robust knowledge of social media, the ability to shoot and edit video, and the flexibility to write for various news platforms (web, print, broadcast).

News veteran Ron Lombard offers the best advice: "The more you can show a potential employer, the more of an edge you will have against the competition. And don't forget the most important skill for any journalist:

strong writing and communication skills, command of the language. That's critical."[11]

News managers would be wise to take more business classes and focus on finance, strategy, and management. An MBA, rather than an advanced journalism degree, may be necessary for future media managers.

Colleges and universities should be attuned to these changes, and journalism curriculums must be adjusted. It would be unwise to offer a print versus electronic media track. University journalism departments must ensure students can write for all platforms while ensuring they have strong video, social media, and computer skills. At the graduate level, more classes on media economics should be offered.

Newsrooms will produce more product while saving money by employing freelancers. Freelancers do not get paid as much as full-time employees, and companies avoid the cost of benefits like medical, unemployment insurance, and retirement contributions. Freelancers are frequently asked to work varied schedules and are only employed when there is work to do. Post-pandemic, there will be more freelance positions available in journalism as media entities try to control costs.

Theresa Collington, one of the top freelance journalists in the country, comments, "I can't think of a current newsroom position that a freelancer couldn't fill in the future. I can envision a time where freelancers will work in areas of expertise and regularly serve multiple properties, and the content will become even more granular and relevant. When the health insurance market changes better for gig workers, I can see almost all newsroom positions becoming gig work, including management."[12]

Writing in *Forbes Magazine*, author Jon Younger predicts, "The acceptance of remote work will continue to lubricate freelancing." He calls the pandemic a "freelance accelerator" and says Covid-19 proved that hiring more freelancers was "feasible, attractive and productive." Younger also predicts the freelance market expansion will spawn more platforms like Catalant, where freelancers and companies can easily meet one another.[13]

The New Media

Overall, there are fewer news outlets. The Tow Center reports that 66 news outlets have shut down during the pandemic;[14] however, there will be post-pandemic growth in one media product. The digital realm will continue to expand as independent news sites launch around the world. These sites can be topic-driven (sports, business, politics, entertainment); location-centric, covering neighborhoods, small towns, and cities; or just blogs. Prior to the pandemic thousands of writers stayed home and worked. They produced independent news digital products. The pandemic kept most people home and that accelerated independent digital production, both written and verbal. Podcasts exploded as well.

In the 1990s, 24-hour local news channels proliferated. This author published an early history of 24-hour local news through the RTDNA (Radio Television Digital News Association). Local news channels provided local coverage that was lacking. For instance, in the New York market, the first news channel was created. News 12 Long Island provided coverage of Long Island, an area ignored by New York City stations. Bay News 9 in Tampa Bay promised coverage beyond the cities of Tampa and St. Petersburg. News products were created to provide coverage where there was none. But cable news channels are expensive to create and run. And now they are losing audience to hyper-local digital products. The pandemic is responsible for accelerating the growth of independent news sites, which have become the new media.

Recently, micro digital news sites have sprung up in such places as West Seattle in Washington State; St. Petersburg, Florida; and Fayetteville, North Carolina. As mainstream media slashes their budgets and coverage, there will be gaps in local coverage. These microsites will fill the gaps in neighborhoods, small towns, and cities where coverage is lacking. Digital sites focusing on a singular topic are also being launched. From politics to entertainment, digital products are proliferating.

Entrepreneurial journalists are launching these sites, some out of necessity. The pandemic has further reduced the number of media jobs, so journalists are introducing their own products. These sites are often accompanied by social media and podcasts. Costs are kept low as the business model to generate revenue is evolving. Ken Doctor wrote in his visionary book *Newsonomics*, "The Internet has made specialized reading easier, and consequently, it is making specialized reporting and writing more valuable."[15] The post-pandemic world will be dominated by the new media.

Interview with Poynter Institute's Neil Brown

To better understand the changing media economic landscape, there is no better person to speak with than Neil Brown. Brown is the president of the Poynter Institute, the preeminent journalism think-tank in the world. Brown is the former executive editor of the *Tampa Bay Times* and is considered by many one of the most innovative print people in the country.[16]

Q: *In your opinion, what is the biggest lasting impact the pandemic will have on the newspaper business?*

The coronavirus posed the most serious health threat to people with "underlying conditions." The local newspaper business had its own underlying conditions and has been devastated by the pandemic. Before the virus struck, newspapers reliant on traditional advertising revenue were seriously struggling to chart a future, taking regular but largely incremental cost-cutting steps. The so-called secular decline of print revenue—due to reader shift to online sources and the fragmentation of advertising opportunities—meant that any meaningful turnaround was unlikely. So, the pandemic was a body-blow to an already stressed local news industry and it hastened dramatic actions that might have come a year or two from now. The economic shutdown caused by the pandemic, devastating to small businesses, including restaurants and retailers, gutted print ad revenues and led to drastic actions, including:

- A widespread closing and sell-off of printing plants. Simply put: many local newspapers are no longer printed in your local area.
- A dramatic reduction of local journalists. Poynter has tracked newsroom layoffs and closures. Thousands of journalism jobs have been lost across the industry, including TV, radio and digital outlets, and several newsrooms have been consolidated into hubs, rather than being locally based. There will continue to be a growth in "news deserts,"—communities that have no local news coverage.
- Many newspaper companies abandoned traditional newsrooms—they didn't want to pay the costs of empty office space—with everyone working remotely. Given the strain on the economics of newspapers, it remains to be seen if a work-from-home environment or other remote work arrangements will become the norm.

Q: *Post-pandemic, will we see more newspapers embrace digital publishing and move away from printing an actual newspaper?*

Newspapers had already been moving more fully to serving their communities online. Before the pandemic, gains had been made to diversify revenue with distribution of both journalism and advertising through the newspaper websites and related products like newsletters. The pandemic will force many to jump with both feet. *The Tampa Bay Times* reduced the frequency of its print edition from 7 to 2 days a week (Sundays and Wednesdays).

Two days a week was certainly not sufficient to sustain the expense of its large printing and distribution operations, so the *Times*, and many other newspapers, will now outsource printing. It's sad, and it changes the character of the local business. But it was relentlessly logical. Beyond the sizable cost savings, it does force companies to become more effective digital publishers. So yes, digital will now become a core part of the newspaper company's business, not just an add-on. Again, the pandemic hastened action that was likely anyway.

Q: *Please share your thoughts about newsroom staffing and having more reporters and editors work remotely post-pandemic. Will there be more freelancers and part-timers?*

The workforce is changing. Some newspapers have very capable beat reporters working from outside their local market. I think that is unfortunate, but the reality is that many journalists have found ways to be very effective by working remotely. Yes, we'll be using more freelancers and part-timers. The challenge is the business model. Until we can find more sustainable revenue sources—probably more revenue from readers (print and digital subscriptions, or even membership models) and perhaps foundation or grant support—to offset the decline in advertising, the loss of feet on the street will continue. That's not great for the quality of reporting or connection to the local audience. But increasingly, organizations will only be able to pay for some of the journalistic work when they have the need and the revenue, so more journalism will be by the piece.

Q: *Digital publishing (micro news sites, independent news websites) was growing pre-pandemic. What do you see happening post-pandemic to digital publishing?*

Digital publishing will continue to grow, and the user experience will continue to get better and better. There will be more niche sites, and local news digital startups are attracting foundation support. National digital news companies like ProPublica and Axios are starting to expand into local markets. The pandemic did accelerate the digital habit for traditional print readers. And many news companies saw well-deserved growth in digital customers because local consumers became more comfortable receiving local news and information on their phones from their trusted local newsroom as the pandemic spread. That's been a good consequence for local news companies: their customers found renewed value as journalists helped people navigate this pandemic experience. Our relevance was clear as audiences found good digital journalism about the virus to be an essential part of their information diets.

Q: *Please discuss the potential for further consolidation in the newspaper business post-pandemic.*

Most newspapers are now owned by a handful of companies—a consolidation that started before the pandemic. The harsh economic realities are that consolidation has become a key component of creating scale in reaching audiences and a network of advertisers. What's more, it makes infrastructure costs like IT, HR and even sales teams more affordable by consolidating across markets. It's unfortunate that most local newspapers are not locally owned. Community connection is a casualty to some degree. That's not good for journalism or democracy. But as I mentioned, several locally unknown digital news websites are sprouting. Many will be funded through grants, donations, or membership efforts. This will help. The business model for local news remains challenging and the future is not entirely clear.

Projections

Will local media survive the pandemic? A Medill Media Industry Survey asked that question of 1,400 members of the U.S. news media. Almost 82 percent said they were very concerned about the sustainability of local news.[17] Before March 2020, media owners were confronting a decline in advertising revenue that made it problematic to service an enormous debt from years of corporate buyouts and consolidations. The pandemic has accelerated corporate losses and executives' desires to cut costs and streamline.

Employment levels at traditional media outlets will continue to decline, while salaries will increase only marginally. News coverage will change as video apps make it easier to interview and cover news. Newsrooms will be smaller as more journalists work from home. Those newsrooms will feature more centralized operations. Journalists will be asked to do more, and in many cases, they will be paid less to do so. Freelancing will become more pervasive throughout the industry.

There are calls for Congress to create a public journalism trust fund, a government program supported by tax revenue that would support news organizations. The idea is not farfetched. In 2020, the Canadian government created a $600 million spending plan to help that country's newspaper industry. Given the political polarization in America, a taxpayer supported bailout of the media industry would be a difficult bill to pass, to say the least.

The pandemic has become the demarcation point in the transition of power between traditional media and new media. Before Covid-19, people were turning away from newspapers and local television newscasts. Digital news consumption was on the upswing. As people remained at home for months, they had time to discover new online products that captured their interests versus general interest news from the traditional media.

Entrepreneurial journalists will become the new media leaders. The job market will see fewer positions in traditional media and growth in digital media. Facing a shrinking market, many young journalists will be forced to do their own thing. Generational research shows young people are more entrepreneurial than the older generations. They will boldly venture into a post-pandemic workplace reshaped by economic necessity. The post-pandemic media workplace will be different, but the question that remains unanswered is, "Will it be better?"

Notes

1. Ron Lombard, email to author, January 21, 2021.
2. Pew Research Center, "Local TV News Fact Sheet: State of the News Media," July 12, 2018, https://www.pewresearch.org/topics/news-media-trends.
3. Pew Research Center. "Newsroom Employees by News Industry, 2008 to 2019." April 20, 2020. https://www.pewresearch.org/topics/news-media-trends.
4. Ibid.
5. Deborah Collura, email to author, February 8, 2021.
6. "Times to Outsource Printing to Plant in Lakeland," Tampa Bay Times, January 7, 2021, https://www.tampabay.com.
7. Doctor, Ken. "Newsonomics: How will the pandemic panic reshape the local news industry?" NiemanLab. Nieman Foundation at Harvard, May 6, 2020, https://www.niemanlab.org/2020/05/newsonomics-how.
8. Jacob, Mark. "Covid-19 Accelerates Local Trends, for Bad and Good," Northwestern/Medill Local News Initiative, April 22, 2020, https://localnewsinitiative.northwestern.edu/posts.
9. Deborah Collura.
10. Ibid.
11. Ron Lombard.
12. Theresa Collington, email to author, February 6, 2021.
13. Jon Younger, "Freelancing 2021: Trends I See for the Freelance Revolution," Forbes, December 16, 2020, https://www.forbes.com/sites/jonyounger/2020/12/16/freelancing-2021-the-trends-i-see-for-the-freelance-revolution.
14. Harris, Lauren. "Five big findings from the Journalism Crisis Project," Columbia Journalism Review. March 3, 2021, https://www.cjr.org/business_of_news/five-findings.
15. Ken Doctor, Newsonomics: Twelve New Trends That Will Shape the News You Get (New York: St. Martin's, 2010).
16. Neil Brown, email to author, January 31, 2021.
17. Mark Jacob, "Covid-19 Accelerates Local Trends, for Bad and Good," Northwestern/Medill Local News Initiative, April 22, 2020, https://localnewsinitiative.northwestern.edu/posts.

Zooming the Pandemic
Developing New Technologies

CASEY FRECHETTE

> "The pandemic is the ultimate data story ... a news detection tool"
> —Chris Collins, senior executive editor, *Bloomberg News*

Throughout the pandemic, journalists approached technology in both evolutionary and revolutionary ways. On one hand, technological innovation in 2020 reflected the data and visual skills journalists had spent the previous decade finessing. Newsrooms had invested in graphics teams and data reporters, and their products had for years increasingly reflected a more visual, data-centric approach to reporting.[1] The pandemic accelerated these trends.[2]

But the story of pandemic coverage wasn't just about journalists adapting old tricks. They also adopted new reporting strategies enabled by the latest advances in recording gear. And they delved into emerging machine learning techniques that gave editors and reporters insight into where the pandemic story was likely to go—even before it happened.

Indeed, the pandemic gave newsrooms a chance to flex technological muscles that had been developed over years, but it also provided opportunities to experiment with new techniques. This essay goes behind the scenes to explore how newsrooms placed graphics editors and multimedia journalists at the center of their pandemic coverage, quickening advances in visual storytelling that were already years in the making. It reviews the opportunities and pitfalls in working with a vast public dataset and reveals how the *New York Times*, Johns Hopkins University, and the *Atlantic's* Covid Tracking Project aggregated and standardized dozens of local, county, and state-level datasets. And it considers the new workflows, techniques, and products that have emerged and will likely shape news coverage well beyond the pandemic for many years to come.

Technological innovation in the pandemic wasn't unilaterally positive. To a great degree, existing inequities deepened.[3] Newsrooms with resources to hire specialized designers, programmers, and data scientists flourished; those with small teams with more general skill sets struggled. Journalists with access to cutting-edge recording gear captured great footage while staying safe; those with fewer resources took more risks, often only to capture lesser-quality footage.

A deluge of data also prompted new ethical concerns and unexpected challenges to accuracy, as pointed out in relation also to social media (see "Social Media and the Pandemic: Myths and Misinformation" and "Ethical Reporting in the Pandemic and Beyond," both later in this collection). Newsrooms relied heavily on government-provided datasets, with little to no oversight to ensure veracity. And attempts to simplify complex scientific concepts to create more easily digestible graphics meant coverage sometimes forfeited accuracy for accessibility. This essay will also explore these and other technological pitfalls.

A Technological Leap, 30 Years in the Making

The pandemic story came at a particular moment in the evolution of journalism technology. For three decades, news organizations had been grappling with the move online and the ensuing turmoil to their business models and production cycles. The Internet offered new ways to tell stories, unprecedented immediacy, and unlimited space and time to publish. But with the advent of Craigslist in 1995, Google in 1998, and Facebook in 2004, it also upended every possible revenue stream, from classifieds and display advertising to subscriptions. The fraught move to the web— especially for the newspaper industry—made technological innovation difficult.

Despite growing audience demand for digital products, newspapers continued through the 2000s to see the lion's share of their revenue come from their print products—even as print readership and advertising revenues continued to decline.[4] Steady but very slow online growth discouraged bold investments in a strong technological infrastructure and workforce at all but the most elite publishers. Instead, digital journalism has flourished most in visual storytelling, a realm already familiar to newsrooms.

Decades of experience with visual storytelling, and more recent but very successful forays into data storytelling, meant journalists were poised to cover the pandemic deftly through photography, video, illustrations, animations, charts, graphics, and a range of other data visualizations, and much of the technological innovation has centered on these tools. At the outset of the pandemic, newsrooms had just begun to grapple with the implications of other technological innovations, including natural language processing, machine learning, and other forms of artificial intelligence—a broad set of tools and techniques that enable computers to perform tasks previously only achievable by humans. Coverage of the coronavirus has provided opportunities to explore the potential of these approaches to transform reporting and storytelling, but efforts remain less mature.

Data, the Mother of Invention

The pandemic put relentless pressure on journalists and the news organizations they work for.[5] Resources in most newsrooms remained tight. Safety concerns complicated efforts to report stories across beats. Stress and burnout ran high. Yet, despite the many constraints journalists faced while reporting in a pandemic, the virus also propelled an array of innovative approaches to news gathering and publishing, resulting in some of the most significant technological advancements since news websites went online *en masse* in the late 1990s.

At least three aspects of the pandemic have contributed to innovation. First, the ongoing nature of the story has given technology teams at news organizations the time necessary to design, write and test software. Daily deadlines drive journalism, but technology takes weeks, months, or even longer to bring to fruition. That discrepancy has long thwarted efforts to innovate in newsrooms. Outside of election coverage, which benefits from months of planning, developers in newsrooms don't often have the opportunity to put sustained energy into products whose longevity justifies an intensive time commitment.

Second, a massive, ever-expanding dataset from hundreds of local health departments has provided a panoply of ways to analyze, visualize, simulate, and animate the path the virus has taken and the direction it might head next. Three entities—Johns Hopkins University, the *New York Times* and the Covid Tracking Project—greatly simplified the task of accessing and using pandemic-related data by tracking, verifying, and standardizing daily updates from nations, states, and local entities. Each dataset offered strengths. Johns Hopkins had more detail on global cases and deaths; the Covid Tracking Project covered testing and hospitalization data; and the *New York Times* focused on comprehensive case and death tallies.

Third, as a global story that has unfolded in every local community around the U.S., the pandemic has provided opportunities for journalists to collaborate across newsrooms, whether on reporting, software development, or something else. These three factors, and the pace of innovation leading into 2020, set the stage for seven technological innovations that have defined pandemic-era journalism.

The balance of this essay presents noteworthy examples of each kind of innovation. Making complex, especially unfamiliar, information understandable is always a challenge for journalists. The pandemic intensified the need to familiarize the public with a variety of terms, phrases, and concepts that were previously unknown to the majority of the public. That's where an increased reliance on visualizations became critical.

Visualizations Told the Story

In March 2020, most of us were unfamiliar with such phrases as "exponential curves," "social distancing" and "forced quarantines." *Washington Post* graphics reporter Harry Stevens sought to explain these concepts and demonstrate how to blunt the spread of the virus with a 1,000-word story interspersed with graphical simulations. The resulting article, "Why Outbreaks Like Coronavirus Spread Exponentially, and How to 'Flatten the Curve,'" became one of the most-read pieces of journalism in the *Post*'s history, garnered a gold medal in the Society of News Design's Best of Digital News Design 2020 competition, and changed how many thought about their roles in preventing infection.[6]

Published March 14, 2020, just three days after the World Health Organization declared the novel coronavirus a global pandemic, "How to 'Flatten the Curve'" has since been translated into Russian, Arabic, Japanese and 10 other languages.[7] Stevens began the article by first addressing the fear that loomed largest at the outset of the pandemic: Exponential spread would result in overwhelming numbers of infections that could crush healthcare infrastructures around the country in a matter of weeks. He then presented visual simulations of the spread of a fictitious disease, aptly named "simulitis."

In Stevens' model, "simulitis," like the coronavirus, passed from one person to the next via contact. To visualize transmission, Stevens put 200 small dots in motion within a rectangle. Each dot represented a person moving through a community. The animations (Stevens built four, each representing a different pandemic response) all start with one infected person—a burnt-orange dot among a sea of healthy, teal-colored circles—and depict how quickly infection rates rise, depending on mitigation measures.

In the first scenario, a free-for-all without lockdowns or social distancing measures, everyone gets sick, and quickly. The rate of infection accelerates as more dots turn from blue to orange—until they turn pink, representing recovery and immunity. The second simulation depicts a forced quarantine. At first, the seal is airtight, and infections in the simulation spread only within a portion of the population. Over time, though, the barriers recede, exposing the uninfected population to a delayed, but still all-encompassing, outbreak.

The next two simulations mimic the effects of social distancing. In the less restrictive version, some dots appear fixed in place. With less movement, the virus has fewer opportunities to spread, and about a quarter of the people—50 dots—never get sick. The final simulation represents more extensive social distances—very few dots move about freely—and in this version about 125 dots stay healthy.

Stevens's graphics and accompanying textual annotations simplified complex scientific processes, clarifying the nature of a threat most readers had never pondered. In awarding the project a gold medal, judges with the Society for News Design called Stevens's work "one of the best pieces of the last year." "People shared this," the judges said. "Readers were able to read and think about the real consequences of the charts."

The project skyrocketed in popularity across social media. The day after it was published, former president Barack Obama tweeted the article to his 130 million followers. "Watch this," Obama wrote. "It shows why we should all do the right thing and stay home to the fullest extent possible."[8]

In an interview with Alex Mahadevan, a senior multimedia reporter with the MediaWise project at the Poynter Institute, Stevens said the project felt "like catching lightning in a bottle."[9] "It's orders of magnitude more successful than anything I've ever made before," Stevens told Poynter.

The success of "How to Flatten the Curve" can be attributed in part to its simplicity. Stevens created models not unlike those health scientists use to project the course of a disease outbreak. But he drastically simplified the recipe, simplifying key variables to clarify the takeaway message. "Simulitis," unlike the coronavirus, was guaranteed to cause infection. Every dot that came in contact with another spread the disease. And mortality wasn't accounted for—given enough time, all patients would recover as the simulations ran. And a recovered patient was always immune from reinfection.

For some, the simplifications didn't add clarity but instead advanced an ideological viewpoint. Stevens sought to show that social distancing worked, and he arranged his model to illustrate that point. But this is the kind of decision-making that journalists make all the time. Every news story is an act of simplification, a series of decisions about how to frame a story, what to include, and what to leave out. But most stories don't garner the kind of attention that Stevens's work captured.

Interactive Dashboards and Trackers Filled Homepages

If a single graphic can tell part of a story, a lineup of interconnected charts, graphs, and maps can reveal the entire tale. That's the philosophy behind the elaborate pandemic dashboards and trackers developed by most national and regional news organizations.[10]

These pages—kaleidoscopes of visualizations carefully organized to highlight key data points, whether infection rates, death rates, vaccination rates, or other trendlines, relied on a mix of original reporting and health department data from local governments.

Unlike the bulk of graphics produced pre-pandemic, these dashboards relied on live data feeds. The numbers, and the resulting visualizations, changed in real time as new data came out. For a fast-changing event like the pandemic, such a dynamic approach is necessary to prevent out-of-date, possibly even dangerous, information from persisting.

Live data also gave audiences a reason to keep coming back. Seeing the latest developments in accessible visual formats satisfied a real need to stay informed.

Pandemic dashboards captured the daily dynamics of the virus's spread, its economic impact, and, eventually, the rollout of vaccines. These technology-driven reports both supplemented and informed traditional coverage, and they stood on their own as traffic-driving showpieces that brought immediacy, context, and meaning to a sprawling, complex, and, at times, contradictory story.

AI Became the New Assignment Editor

Throughout the pandemic, Bloomberg, the leading business and financial news company, pored over press releases, earnings statements and other corporate communications to find data points that might germinate into full-blown news stories. In many ways, the search for anomalies, surprises, and contradictions reflected the news-discovery process that journalists have employed for generations. This time, though, something was different. It was software—not reporters—hard at work sifting through piles of information to find the next important story.

Troves of data published around the clock for public consumption, by companies large and small, enabled reporters and editors at Bloomberg to deploy technology to detect the blips of information likely to become financial stories of national—or global—significance. These tools capitalized on developments in the burgeoning field of automated journalism to alert reporters and editors to story ideas, with speed and precision.

Chris Collins, a senior executive editor at Bloomberg, called the pandemic "the ultimate data story" in an interview with Polis, a media think-tank at the London School of Economics. Bloomberg's "news detection tool," Collins said, became an indispensable aide in breaking news, giving journalists an edge in reporting the pandemic's economic impact, the mitigation steps businesses were adopting, and the changes to corporate policy that could affect office culture long after the virus had waned.[11]

Technologies like Bloomberg's detection tool rely on several strains of artificial intelligence that have gained a foothold in disparate sectors, from finance and defense to sales and, of course, technology. The media industry has been relatively slow to adopt these tools of automation, but larger companies like Bloomberg have made strategic investments to bring technologies of the future into the present.

What makes these tools special isn't so much what they can do but rather the scale and speed at which they can operate. Natural language processing, for example, one critical subset of AI, enables software to categorize and codify a spoken or written statement to discern its meaning. That's a task reporters can perform with ease. With software-driven algorithms, though, newsrooms can analyze vast datasets nearly instantly, performing a tedious feat that journalists can't—or shouldn't—get bogged down with and freeing them to work on the high-level critical thinking and storytelling tasks that even the most cutting-edge technologies are far from accomplishing.

Print Newsrooms Went Beyond the Static Story with "Live" Coverage

Some of the innovations with the biggest impact on newsroom operations—and website traffic—involved simple technological tweaks to how newsrooms published pandemic stories.

Eschewing the typical homepage and article structure common to news websites, organizations like the *Wall Street Journal*, *Washington Post*, *Guardian*, and *New York Times* adopted pages of continuously updating "live coverage" inspired by the up-to-the-minute timeliness of cable news.

Live coverage pages followed a similar format: Bullets at the top provided summaries of the latest developments, headlines and excerpts gave more detail, and links to full-blown stories revealed additional context and reporting. The pages also emphasized the timeliness of coverage, with prominent tags denoting just how many hours—or minutes—ago the latest entry was published.

Organizations approached their live coverage with different editorial styles. *The Wall Street Journal*'s excerpts mirrored content from their stories, whereas *New York Times* editors wrote custom briefs. *The Guardian*, meanwhile, wrote standalone summaries without accompanying stories.

Technologically, the live coverage was a decidedly lo-fi innovation, calling on well-worn digital publishing techniques. The real breakthrough could be found in the editorial approach adopted. By providing curated thematic coverage accessible in short-form and bite-sized formats, news organizations that adopted live coverage made the pandemic story more accessible by providing flexible ways to engage, depending on a reader's time and interest.[12]

Embeddable "Interactives" Sparked Collaboration Across Newsrooms

In March 2020, when Covid-19 took hold in the U.S., data reporters in newsrooms around the country faced a similar problem. Communities needed up-to-date information about local case rates to understand risk levels. County-level health departments were publishing that data, but often with hard-to-decipher, difficult-to-access reports that hid trendlines and obscured threat levels. These shortcomings in how local governments publicized health data emphasized the unique role journalists can play in 21st-century society, where it isn't a lack of access to information that most vexes citizens but rather scarcity of *meaningful* information—the kind of knowledge that can inform decision-making and improve communities.

In the early days of the pandemic in the U.S., daily county-level updates on cases typically revolved around testing. Officials released data on the number of tests administered and the number of results that came back positive, along with basic demographic information. Those data points, combined with insights from epidemiologists and other experts, gave journalists a springboard to answer pressing contextual questions. *How quickly is the disease spreading? What's the positivity rate? Are local officials conducting enough testing? What groups seem to be most vulnerable?*

Answering these kinds of questions is the bread and butter of reporting. But the all-consuming nature of the pandemic—local crises playing out, simultaneously, in communities from coast to coast—presented a novel opportunity for cross-newsroom collaboration. Counties were publishing similar data, and reporters faced the same questions. Perhaps they could combine efforts to provide even better answers. That's the conclusion four data reporters working in four public-media newsrooms reached. A cross-newsroom collaboration between Lisa Pickoff-White, Alexandra Kanik, Emily Zentner, and Dana Amihere resulted in a dashboard that tracked coronavirus cases at the county level and incorporated risk-factor data for additional context.[13]

After connecting on social media, the four data reporters realized their shared goals presented a chance to work together to build a dashboard that would serve their respective communities. Working individually, such a project would take more time than was feasible, as the virus tore through communities and reshaped every aspect of coverage, stretching journalists even further than usual. Collectively, though, the ambitious interactive project came within reach.

The resulting dashboard used a series of charts to show the trajectory of the virus over time along four key metrics: total cases, newly reported cases, total deaths, and newly reported deaths. Population data was included to express the number of cases per capita, and they highlighted the seven-day average for newly reported cases to correct for the day-to-day reporting anomalies that typified reports on transmission.

Pickoff-White, Kanik, Zentner, and Amihere brought context to their dashboard via an additional layer of data tied to groups at specific risk, for example seniors and people with diabetes. Synthesizing county-level data from several sources, including the Institute for Health Metrics and the American Community Survey, the group included county-level risk assessments in their dashboard. Depending on comorbidity prevalence and fatality rates, they ranked counties in one of four tiers in terms of chronic respiratory disease, cardiovascular disease, and diabetes.

As their work developed, the group of data reporters saw ways other newsrooms could benefit from their efforts, multiplying the value of their collaboration. They made their code open source, allowing other developers to piggyback on their efforts. And they took steps to make the dashboards easy to adapt to any state or county in the country by changing just a few lines of code. By outlining clear steps for embedding the project on a website, the group further encouraged use of the tool they had developed.

Technology can often be a disruptive force in newsrooms, but Pickoff-White, Kanik, Zentner, and Amihere's efforts show it can also unlock opportunities for collaboration and the cross-pollination of ideas both within and across organizations. If that trend continues, more innovation is likely to follow suit.

Specialty Gear Helped Reporters Stay Safe While Getting the Story

For reporters and photojournalists working in the field, keeping a distance from sources was one of the most important ways to work safely. But good reporting often relies on proximity—not only being on location but being close enough to subjects to carry on a conversation and see subtle changes in their expressions.

Fortunately, a lineup of tools familiar to visual and multimedia journalists made it possible to capture vital details—all while staying safe. These included telephoto lenses to capture close-ups of subjects, even when physically distanced from them; boom poles to record audio from a distance of six or more feet; and video call options like Zoom and Skype to conduct interviews from anywhere.

These technical workarounds came with certain drawbacks, but journalists found ways to work within the constraints they faced. When they couldn't get close, they made distance part of the visual aesthetic. Working for the *New York Times*, Brittany Greeson, a Michigan-based freelance documentary photographer, produced a harrowing collection of images for a March 2020 story about the spread of the virus through Detroit.[14]

Captured from a safe distance across barren streets and parking lots, Greeson's stark images depicted foreboding scenes from the pandemic's early spread in the U.S. They are the outcome of a dogged determination to get the story no matter the means necessary. While technology helped stories get done which might otherwise have been lost, it was the journalists themselves who went the extra mile, innovating in the process.

Journalists Went Beyond the Page—and Screen— with Experimental New Ways to Reach Audiences

One promising path to innovation has entailed new channels journalists have developed to reach audiences, including smart speakers and chatbots—two platforms BBC News, a vital information source for audiences in the U.S. and around the globe, experimented with throughout the pandemic.

Mukul Devichan, an executive editor at BBC focused on voice and AI technologies, saw these alternative platforms as ways to bring authoritative answers to audiences' many questions about the latest contours of the pandemic, from lockdown restrictions to the positivity rates in local communities.[15]

Answers to specific queries, especially context-specific questions tied to time and location, could be difficult to find in the deluge of pandemic-related content published by news organizations or returned by search engines. By providing streamlined interfaces to ask questions and receive responses drawn from select sources, including dozens of local newsrooms and the United Kingdom's National Health Service, BBC developers were able to expand their coverage and push high-quality information beyond their websites and airwaves.

In one case, they made briefings available on demand via smart speaker systems like Amazon Echo and Google Home. BBC developers were able to tailor these reports based on listeners' locations, utilizing data embedded in their speakers. In another example, they released a chatbot via Facebook's Messenger tool, providing a virtual "concierge" able to parse questions and provide automated replies based not only on the current question but an ever-growing history of previous queries.

For news organizations, one key advantage of these kinds of "pull" approaches to publishing news (as opposed to the "push" approaches typified in newspapers, broadcasts and websites) is the opportunity to understand what topics audiences most want information on. That knowledge can inform future reporting decisions and approaches to coverage.

What Comes Next

The pandemic helped journalists realize more fully the promise of the web from the early 1990s—immediate information, multimedia packaging, limitless customizability, and new delivery models that prioritize audience needs over the physical limitations of newspapers or broadcasts.

On the whole, progress was uneven, and the strain on news organizations' finances—and on individual journalists' mental and physical health—has not yet been fully assessed or understood. Yet during the pandemic, incremental advancements repeatedly gave way to major strides forward, and scores of journalists found ways to innovate, despite hardships and constraints. The results were new ways of gathering, producing, and publishing news.

As the focus shifts from pandemic coverage and newsrooms step away from the all-hands-on-deck approach that led to the kind of sustained focus that cultivates technological innovation, whether advances in technology decelerate after the pandemic will emerge as a critical question.

For an industry that has seldom rushed headlong into technological advancements—and the attendant disruptions they bring to culture, process, and business models—the possibility that the eclipse of the pandemic will ultimately stifle newsroom innovation looms large, and a return to normalcy may tempt newsrooms to return to safer, more predictable ground. Many of the most influential projects discussed in this essay emerged early in the pandemic, suggesting at least a short-term retracement may be likely.

But the events of 2020 and 2021 also gave journalists an opportunity to permanently reorient the role of technology in the production and publication of news, making it less a force to grapple with and more a resource to harness. The shift toward embracing technology, spearheaded by journalists including Harry Stevens, Lisa Pickoff-White, Alexandra Kanik, Emily Zentner, Dana Amihere, and the many data and graphics reporters and editors around the country, may be the single most important innovation to emerge from the pandemic.

The industry has long talked of adapting to "digital-first," "web-first," and "mobile-first" models of journalism. Ostensibly about technology, this shorthand is also a tacit acknowledgment of the need to shift values toward new approaches to delivering news. For an industry that has long seen financial rewards first and foremost in old approaches, though, the transition has been choppy and sporadic.

Outside the world of journalism, technology keeps evolving, the rate of change only accelerating. Innovations on the horizon, especially those connected to automation and artificial intelligence, promise to revolutionize decision-making in every corner of society. Whether the news industry is ready to adopt—and adapt to—these advancements will become a deciding factor in the health and vitality of journalism after the pandemic. The innovations covered in this essay should be cause for great optimism. Yet unknown is whether this unique moment in history becomes, technologically speaking, a brief deviation from the past or a stepping-stone into the future.

Notes

1. In a 2017 report, the *New York Times*, a leader in visual journalism, determined it wasn't doing enough. "Too much of our daily report remains dominated by long strings of text," the report concluded, and said the *Times* needed "to become more visual." David Leonhardt, Jodi Rudoren, Jon Galinsky, Karron Skog, M. Lacey, T. Giratikanon, and T. Evans, "Journalism That Stands Apart," *New York Times*, January 17, 2017, https://www.nytimes.com/projects/2020-report/index.html, retrieved March 13, 2021.

2. See, for example, N. Newman, "Journalism, Media, and Technology Trends and Predictions 2021," Reuters Institute, January 7, 2021, https://reutersinstitute.politics.ox.ac.uk/sites/default/files/2021-01/Newman_Predictions_2021_FINAL.pdf, retrieved March 6, 2021.

3. In at least one example, a survey of female journalists found evidence of deepening gender inequality in newsrooms: International Federation of Journalists, "COVID-19 Has Increased Gender Inequalities in the Media, IFJ Survey Finds," IFJ.org, July 23, 2020,

https://www.ifj.org/media-centre/news/detail/category/press-releases/article/covid-19-has-increased-gender-inequalities-in-the-media-ifj-survey-finds.html, retrieved March 6, 2021.

    4. Writing in 2012 for Poynter.org, media business analyst Rick Edmonds highlighted the steep print losses and modest digital gains experienced across the newspaper industry. Five years later, he underscored just how much further digital revenue had to go to catch up to print. See R. Edmonds, "Newspapers Get $1 in New Digital Ad Revenue for Every $25 in Print Ad Revenue Lost," Poynter.org, September 10, 2012, https://www.poynter.org/reporting-editing/2012/newspapers-print-ad-losses-are-larger-than-digital-ad-gains-by-a-ratio-of-25-to-1, retrieved March 14, 2021; and R. Edmonds, "Digital May Be the Future, but Print Still Looms Large in the Present Fortunes of Newspapers," Poynter.org, July 21, 2017, https://www.poynter.org/business-work/2017/digital-may-be-the-future-but-print-still-looms-large-in-the-present-fortunes-of-newspapers/, retrieved March 14, 2021.

    5. M.F. Perreault and G.P. Perreault, "Journalists on COVID-19 Journalism: Communication Ecology of Pandemic Reporting," *American Behavioral Scientist*, February 5, 2021, https://doi.org/10.1177/0002764221992813, retrieved March 27, 2021.

    6. Society for News Design, "SND 42 Best of Digital News Design Live Results," SND.org, February 24, 2021, https://www.snd.org/2021/02/snd-42-best-of-digital-design-live-results/, retrieved March 27, 2021.

    7. H. Stevens, "Why Outbreaks Like Coronavirus Spread Exponentially, and How to 'Flatten the Curve,'" *Washington Post*, March 14, 2020, https://www.washingtonpost.com/graphics/2020/world/corona-simulator/, retrieved March 3, 2021.

    8. https://twitter.com/BarackObama/status/1239267360739074048.

    9. A. Mahadevan, "How a Blockbuster Washington Post Story Made 'Social Distancing' Easy to Understand," Poynter.org, March 18, 2020, https://www.poynter.org/reporting-editing/2020/how-a-blockbuster-washington-post-story-made-social-distancing-easy-to-understand/, retrieved March 3, 2021.

    10. See, for example, https://www.nytimes.com/interactive/2021/us/covid-cases.html; https://www.latimes.com/projects/california-coronavirus-cases-tracking-outbreak/; https://www.ft.com/content/a2901ce8-5eb7-4633-b89c-cbdf5b386938.

    11. C. Beckett, "The Ultimate Data Story: Driving a Global Newsroom with AI During the COVID Crisis," Polis, May 20, 2020, https://blogs.lse.ac.uk/polis/2020/05/20/the-ultimate-data-story-driving-a-global-newsroom-with-ai-during-the-covid-crisis/, retrieved April 3, 2021.

    12. In January 2021, Marc Lacey, the *New York Times*'s assistant managing editor for Live, said, "Live briefings have become the lifeblood of our coverage and collapse traditional reporting boundaries at The New York Times. They've worked especially well with small teams where rank is thrown out the window, and it's about who can step up."

    13. D. Amihere, A. Kanik, L. Pickoff-White, and E. Zentner, "COVID-19 Story Recipe: A Dashboard with At-Risk Health Indicators," Source, September 1, 2020, https://source.opennews.org/articles/covid-19-story-recipe-dashboard-risk-health/, retrieved April 4, 2021.

    14. M.M. Chapman, J. Bosman, and J. Eligon, "Coronavirus Sweeps Through Detroit, a City That Has Seen Crisis Before," *New York Times*, March 30, 2020, https://www.nytimes.com/2020/03/30/us/coronavirus-detroit.html, retrieved April 4, 2021.

    15. "BBC Launches Pop-Up Corona Bot Service to Answer Questions on Covid-19 Related Changes," BBC Media Centre, May 27, 2020, https://www.bbc.co.uk/mediacentre/latestnews/2020/corona-bot Retrieved April 4, 2021.

Diversity

Covid-19, George Floyd and Lessons Learned

Lillian R. Dunlap

A 2019 survey by the News Leaders Association showed less than 22 percent of all salaried newsroom positions were held by people of color. They conclude that "the racial diversity of newsrooms does not come close to the fast-growing diversity in the U.S. population as a whole."[1]

Mission Accomplished?

The Covid-19 pandemic of 2020 accomplished what diversity, equity, and inclusion coaching had sought for decades. It pushed journalists and journalism educators to broaden their definition of news to reflect seemingly hidden and essential truths. The more traditional ways of reporting proved less than adequate to describe the U.S. government's response to the virus or the systemic inequities along race, gender and socio-economic lines. Journalists met the challenge, and journalism may be better for it.

Post-pandemic American journalism has an opportunity to retain what we've learned from covering Covid-19 and to fully embrace the value of those multiple voices and perspectives drawn from lived experiences.

During the economic shutdown caused by the high rate of viral infection in the United States, most newsrooms were forced to operate with skeletal staffs. As we've read in other essays contained here, most journalists worked from home and face-to-face interviews were replaced by interviews via Skype and Zoom. Schools were closed, but essential workers were expected to show up for work. That group included first responders, healthcare workers, grocery store workers and others. And, as it turns out, that group of essential workers was composed disproportionately of people of color. Journalists came face to face with the intersectionality of race, economic suppression, and lack of access to healthcare as they began to analyze the high death rate among essential workers. Covid-19 killed more than half a million Americans, and a disproportionate number of those deaths were people more likely to have co-morbidities like high blood pressure and to not have healthcare. Suddenly, journalists were forced to report these numbers in context. Stories about a virus also became stories about inequity. Stories about the soaring number of people needing hospitalization also became stories about systemic racism.

In many ways, the experience of covering Covid-19 helped to prepare journalists to cover the Black Lives Matter–inspired protests that followed the killing of George Floyd, a Black man, by a White police officer in Minneapolis on May 25, 2020. Journalists showed a willingness to vigorously interrogate authority, scrutinize official reports and acknowledge the centrality of lived experiences in many, if not most, stories.

This essay looks at the state of diversity in the journalism industry and in the academy before the pandemic beginning March 2020, and how the profession and the academy have responded to the restrictions and opportunities during the pandemic. Then, by examining media response to the George Floyd murder, the hope is to project how the industry and the academy might benefit from lessons learned.

Standing for More Voices, More Truths

The experience of covering the pandemic has given journalists permission to rethink how we do several things:

- Define news
- Hold personal experiences
- Regard historical, cultural and societal contexts
- Use information gathered by non-journalists
- Evaluate traditional sources

Before Covid-19, diversity, equity, and inclusion (DEI) were the highest priority in neither the journalism industry nor the academy. Year after year, studies from the American Society of News Editors (ASNE), the News Leaders Association and Radio Television Digital News Association (RTDNA) report small percentages of people of color in newsrooms and even fewer in positions of leadership. A 2019 survey by the News Leaders Association showed less than 22 percent of all salaried newsroom positions were held by people of color. They conclude that "the racial diversity of newsrooms does not come close to the fast-growing diversity in the U.S. population as a whole."[2]

The 2020 RTDNA/Newhouse School at Syracuse University Survey showed people of color made up fewer than 24 percent of the total television news force. And when we look at positions of leadership, a full 82 percent of television news directors and 93 percent of general managers are White. The online journalism numbers are a bit better. They report that nearly 31 percent of salaried workers at online-only publications are people of color.[3]

Among U.S. colleges and universities, there has been increased, but still less than robust, attention to DEI in classrooms and in administrative decision making. College and university journalism programs that are accredited by the Accrediting Council on Education in Journalism and Mass Communications (ACEJMC) are required to pass eight standards, including "Diversity and Inclusiveness," which is Standard 4. The other standards are (revised and effective for 2022):

1. Mission, Governance and Administration
2. Curriculum and Instruction
3. Assessment of Learning Outcomes
4. Diversity and Inclusiveness
5. Faculty
6. Student Services
7. Resources, Facilities and Equipment
8. Professional and Public Service[4]

When it comes to the Diversity and Inclusiveness standard, the goal is for campuses not just to say they support the idea of diversity. The charge is to make it obvious by developing a diversity statement and describing specifically how their chosen goals will be accomplished.

There are only 117 ACEJMC accredited programs, most of which are in the United States. Even among those programs, many struggle to update the competency of faculty, and those faculty are sometimes unable to accomplish the inclusion of diversity into class syllabi and activities. As a diversity and inclusion consultant to media organizations and the academy, I've worked with many journalism faculties in the United States and others in South Africa and Europe. I can attest from personal experience that professors are often uncomfortable talking about issues of diversity; this is especially true for those faculty members who do not identify as members of underrepresented or underserved groups. In my work, I encourage deans and professors to examine every aspect of their teaching and environment for ways to include more diversity. We talk about ways to infuse principles of diversity into each section of every syllabus. In some instances, I have encouraged leaders at predominantly White campuses in the U.S. to consider forming partnerships with faculty at historically Black colleges and universities (HBCUs) and tribal colleges and universities (TCUs). And I often talk about opportunities to collaborate with programs run by the National Association of Black Journalists (NABJ), the National Association of Hispanic Journalists (NAHJ), the Asian American Journalists Association (AAJA), the Native American Journalists Association (NAJA), NLGJA: The Association of LGBTQ Journalists, and the South Asian Journalists Association (SAJA).

During the Pandemic

The effects of the pandemic were unevenly felt, and most newsrooms (and classrooms, for that matter) were unprepared to cover or even intelligently discuss them—or the cultural, racial divide that was about to occur in the same space where Covid-19 was taking hold. The near nationwide shutdown pushed everybody to adjust. Then, just as the country was getting used to having the entire family always at home and just as parents were getting accustomed to school delivered by Zoom, a police-related murder in Minneapolis rocked the world.

George Floyd, an unarmed and handcuffed Black man, was killed by a White Minneapolis Police officer in broad daylight on May 25, 2020. The story began when a store clerk called the police after suspecting that Floyd had paid for cigarettes with a fake twenty-dollar bill. In total, four officers arrived on the scene and questioned or restrained Floyd. The officers were Derek Chauvin, Thomas Lane, J. Kueng and Tou Thao. The questioning ended with Floyd's being pinned to the ground. Officer Chauvin had one knee on Floyd's body and one pressing on his neck. There were witnesses. Some watched in horror as Floyd complained about twenty times that he couldn't breathe and later called out to his deceased mother. Some of the witnesses pleaded for the officer to stop. But Officer Chauvin continued to kneel on Floyd's neck and body for nearly ten minutes.[5] Among the bystanders was seventeen-year-old Darnella Frazier. She captured the killing on video and posted it online. Frazier's presence of mind to start recording provided critical information. Her ability to keep recording changed the conversation about police brutality and systemic racism around the world. The response from readers and viewers was immediate. Regardless of race, humans had watched another human being treated like a subhuman object.

People poured into the streets, demanding an end to police brutality and systemic racism. They demanded justice for the killing of George

Floyd and others, including twenty-six-year-old Breonna Taylor, who had been shot earlier by Louisville, Kentucky, police. Tessa Duvall, a reporter at the Louisville *Courier Journal*, described Breonna as a person who helped to save other people's lives. An emergency room technician at two Louisville hospitals, Taylor was killed by plainclothes officers trying to serve a "no-knock" search warrant at her home on March 13, 2020.[6]

People protested against police brutality and systemic racism directed at people of color generally, and African Americans, specifically. The country is accustomed to seeing Black people protesting. This time, however, was different. After the Floyd murder and the shooting of Breonna Taylor, the protesters included thousands of young White people and people of all ethnicities, ages and incomes.

Inspired by the Black Lives Matter (BLM) movement, people marched in various places around the world, spanning forty different countries and nearly every U.S. state. This time, because of BLM's ability to get the word out, the protests went on for weeks. The *New York Times* described it as perhaps the biggest protest movement in United States history.[7] By the peak date of June 6, 2020, there had been more than 4,700 demonstrations, or an average of 140 per day, since May 26. Turnout ranged from dozens to tens of thousands in about 2,500 towns.[8] People decided to stand on the side of social justice. They voted with their feet. They wanted police brutality to end.

Traditionally, journalists would gather facts about any protests. Journalists would be keeping track of how much damage there was and how much it cost. But, this time, journalists had also seen the Frazier cell phone video of Floyd's murder. Journalists had witnessed a human being killed in the street by a cop. So, this brings up the question of a new approach. *Where will journalists stand?*

Where will we stand to tell the story? Are we observers of events? Are we gatherers of opinion of the witnesses of events? Are we part of the event's impact and thus reporting its effect through our own experience? Are we telling the story through the voices of those affected by the event, including ourselves?

Where did journalists stand to report the George Floyd murder? Did journalists simply play and react to the amateur-produced video? Do we stand with Black and Indigenous people and people of color as they press the idea of systemic racism, police brutality and the need for reform? Or do we stand with officials to describe what didn't, couldn't or needs to happen?

A Black man is killed by a White police officer, protesters take to the streets, police respond with military tactics, arrest people, and violence and destruction of property follow. This describes not just the protests of

2020, but of the 1960s. There are lessons to be learned. Back then, President Lyndon Johnson created the Kerner Commission to find the causes of the civil rights rebellions in major cities. The commission's now iconic conclusion was, "Our nation is moving toward two societies, one black, one white, separate and unequal." And there is still a need to look back at what Kerner said about the role of the press: "The press has too long basked in a white world, looking out of it, if at all, with white men's eyes and white perspective."[9]

The late award-winning *Newsday* journalist Les Payne, who was a founding member and former president of the National Association of Black Journalists (NABJ), spoke eloquently about the report during NABJ's observance of the 50th anniversary of Kerner. Payne offered that the sharp rebuke of the press "was as surprising to white Americans—including President Johnson—as it was encouraging to African Americans long under the jackboot."[10] The size and staying power of the Floyd protests show that people were demanding more from their federal government, more from local government, more from the police and more from media.

"The press has too long basked in a white world looking out of it, if at all, with white men's eyes and white perspective." Think about that for a moment. The phrase "If at all" is striking. It appears that the commission was questioning whether journalists were thinking at all or simply recording what they saw or reporting what they were given in press releases and official statements. Commissioners seemed to question whether journalists were able to understand what they were witnessing.

Journalists traditionally have leaned toward reporting about the result at the expense of the cause of particular events. We would be repeating the same failed response the commission wrote about if we forget to unpack the cause of the weeks of protests following the Floyd murder. It is always useful to gather official accounts of events from authorities. Police reports have been a mainstay of the scaffolding for our stories. But here's the Minneapolis Police Department's official report about the encounter with George Floyd:

Man Dies After Medical Incident During Police Interaction.
Two officers arrived and located the suspect, a male believed to be in his 40s, in his car. He was ordered to step from his car. After he got out, he physically resisted officers. Officers were able to get the suspect into handcuffs and noted he appeared to be suffering medical distress. Officers called for an ambulance. He was transported to Hennepin County Medical Center by ambulance where he died a short time later.[11]

CNN journalist Eric Levenson concedes that everything in the police post is, "technically speaking, true." But, he says, as a whole, the police post is deeply misleading and works to obscure the officers' role in Floyd's death. It notes that he was put in handcuffs and "suffering medical distress" in the same sentence, even though they occurred about 20 minutes apart. Most importantly, it ignores what police did in between those two events, says Levenson.[12]

Fortunately, Darnella Frazier's video got to the world first. There was no video in Louisville when Breonna Taylor was shot. But, this time, there was video. Frazier decided, at great personal cost, to stand with George Floyd. She said, "Even though this was a traumatic life-changing experience for me, I'm proud of myself. If it weren't for my video, the world wouldn't have known the truth."[13] She was right.

The video made the difference. Officer Derek Chauvin was convicted of second-degree unintentional murder, third-degree murder and second-degree manslaughter. He was sentenced to 22.5 years in prison.

A familiar chant of the protestors was, "No Justice, no peace; if we don't get no justice, you don't get no peace!" Their intention was to continue protesting until something happened. The conviction and sentencing of a White Minneapolis police officer for killing a Black man was an unprecedented "something."

Black Lives Matter was not a newcomer to protests. This group was founded in response to the 2012 killing of Trevon Martin. The Miami *Herald* revisited the case with this headline on March 1, 2017: "A teen was shot by a watchman 5 years ago. And the Trayvon Martin case became a cause."

Trayvon had been visiting his father and his father's girlfriend at her townhouse in Sanford, Florida. George Zimmerman, a watchman for the development, stopped and questioned Martin as he walked back from a convenience store with a bag of Skittles and a can of Arizona fruit juice cocktail in his hands. Zimmerman carried a loaded gun. They struggled. Trayvon was shot. George Zimmerman was acquitted of the charge of second-degree murder. His lawyers successfully argued that he had acted in self-defense.

The founders of Black Lives Matter, Alicia Garza, Patrisse Cullors and Opal Tometi, took up the cause of Trayvon Martin and focused their work on what they called "anti–Black violence." Black Lives Matter became a movement with a mission to "connect Black people from all over the world who have a shared desire for justice to act together in their communities."[14] In this way, BLM is like the National Association for the Advancement of Colored People (NAACP) and the National Action Network (NAN), led by the Rev. Al Sharpton. But BLM does not have chapters like these groups. Those protests around the world were organized independently by the people in those communities.

Covering both Covid-19 and protests against the virus of systemic racism proved a real challenge for media, especially as newsrooms were emptied of staff due to the virus and journalists were reporting from home or far away from the action in many instances. But a more challenging aspect may have been the need to cover social justice and systemic racism, not as history, but as current issues. BLM had been raising awareness since the Trayvon Martin case. Now, people in various parts of the world were united in their opposition to police brutality and systemic racism, and they were demanding to be heard.

Post-Pandemic Journalism

The numbers of journalists of color will still be small in local newsrooms after the pandemic. But there are reasons to expect that the current trend will continue and there will be more journalists of color in online and non-traditional media.

There will be more Black journalists reporting for outlets like TheGrio, an online publication owned by media mogul Byron Allen that produces stories that "affect and reflect Black America."[15] This is a mission similar to the one posted by the Black News Channel (BNC), which is headquartered in Florida and internationally distributed.

Leaders of the BNC say quite clearly that their programming is designed "by Black people for Black people" to achieve these goals:

- To give voice to an underserved community;
- To build bridges to connect the many diverse cultures in our nation;
- To facilitate a more informed national conversation about challenges facing our urban communities;
- To engage African American viewers in our nation's social, economic and political discussions and debates;
- To recruit and train aspiring African American journalists.[16]

With this list, BNC may have described a mission for all of journalism. The charge may be to report *from* currently underserved communities and use that information to include more voices in the larger conversations about events in our shared humanity.

Darnella Frazier was a witness to the Floyd murder. She is not a journalist, but the Pulitzer board awarded her a special citation, recognizing her courage and her truth telling: "For courageously recording the murder of George Floyd, a video that spurred protests against police brutality around the world, highlighting the crucial role of citizens in journalists' quest for truth and justice."[17]

Author and columnist Miki Kendall charges that a "special citation" was not enough for what Frazier had done. Frazier experienced the event as a teenager watching a man who may have looked like her father or uncle or cousin or brother die in the street. Kendall offers the idea of creating a new category or considering how the award could be made in an existing category instead of a "special citation."

Kendall insists that the list of Pulitzer Prize Award recipients reflects the systemic racism of the United States. Fully 84 percent of its recipients are White and mostly men. Until 2016, only 30 African Americans had ever won a Pulitzer Prize.

Kendall is the author of *Hood Feminism: Notes from the Women That a Movement Forgot*. She says the Pulitzer award misses the point when it comes to Darnella Frazier and may even be insulting:[18]

> Even the way the award is worded—the citation's failure to mention racism or trauma, for instance—devalues in some ways the impact of Frazier's choice to record and keep recording—even as you can hear in her voice on film how scared and appalled she was by what she was seeing.

Frazier knew that it was important for her to keep recording the brutal murder of George Floyd not because it was newsworthy, but because it was proof.

The Minneapolis *Star Tribune* received the Pulitzer for "Breaking News Reporting" "for its urgent, authoritative and nuanced coverage of the death of George Floyd at the hands of police in Minneapolis and of the reverberations that followed."[19]

Where the academy and the media may be able to stand post-pandemic will depend upon these things:

1. How well we acknowledge where the academy and the media have been standing historically;
2. How honestly we examine where we are standing; and
3. How we acknowledge the path and cost of change.

It may be time for journalists and journalism educators to decide if we will take the lessons learned from covering Covid-19 and the protests following the death of George Floyd to finally redefine news; if not, we risk missing the complexity of the real American story. With so many Americans sheltered in their homes during the pandemic's peak, Covid-19 coverage intersected on their screens with the racial protests following George Floyd's murder. The juxtaposition at a time when news media had the largest "captive audience" in a generation created an opportunity for journalists and audiences alike to learn about the deepest ruptures in our social, health, economic, and justice systems, while reinforcing the need for racial equity.

The Covid-19 pandemic created a new opportunity for diversity in journalistic storytelling and in academic classrooms. It shows us how changing where we stand can make a big difference in the story we see and tell. The conditions of the pandemic allowed us to see that only where diversity lives can there be excellent and effective journalism—journalism that answers more of the essential questions and includes a wide range of perspectives. Post-pandemic journalism offers professionals and academics the chance to stop standing with the authority and delivering stories through the lens of the privileged and to start seeking more voices and delivering more truths.

Notes

1. News Leaders Association, "Diversity." https://members.newsleaders.org/diversity.
2. "Digital-Only Platform Drives Race and Gender Inclusion Among Newsrooms in 2019 ASNE Newsroom Diversity Survey," Newsleaders, September 10, 2019, https://www.newsleaders.org/2019-diversity-survey-results.
3. "RTDNA/Newhouse School at Syracuse University Survey Newsroom Diversity," RTDNA, n.d., https://www.rtdna.org/uploads/files/2020%20Newsroom%20Research%20-%20Newsroom%20Diversity(1).pdf.
4. "ACEJMC Accreditation Standards," Accrediting Council on Education in Journalism and Mass Communications, n.d., http://www.acejmc.org/wp-content/uploads/2021/07/2021-June-RevisedStandardsFinal.pdf.
5. Evan Hill, Ainara Tiefenthäler, Christiaan Triebert, Drew Jordan, Haley Willis, and Robin Stein, "How George Floyd Was Killed in Police Custody," *New York Times*, May 31, 2020, https://www.nytimes.com/2020/05/31/us/george-floyd-investigation.html.
6. Tessa Duvall, "Fact Check 2.0: Separating the Truth from the Lies in the Breonna Taylor Police Shooting," *Louisville Courier Journal*, March 17, 2021.
7. Larry Buchanan, Quoctrung Bui and Jugai K. Patel, "Black Lives Matter May Be the Largest Movement in U.S. History," *New York Times*, July 3, 2020, https://www.nytimes.com/interactive/2020/07/03/us/george-floyd-protests-crowd-size.html.
8. Dana R. Fisher, "The Diversity of the Recent Black Lives Matter Protests Is a Good Sign for Racial Equity," July 8, 2020, https://www.brookings.edu/blog/how-we-rise/2020/07/08/the-diversity-of-the-recent-black-lives-matter-protests-is-a-good-sign-for-racial-equity/.
9. Les Payne, "NABJ Reflections on the 50th Anniversary of the Kerner Report," National Association of Black Journalists, n.d., https://www.nabj.org/page/LesPayneKerner.
10. Ibid.
11. Eric Levenson, "How Minneapolis Police First Described the Murder of George Floyd and What We Know Now," CNN, April 21, 2021, https://www.cnn.com/2021/04/21/us/minneapolis-police-george-floyd-death/index.html.
12. Ibid.
13. Joe Hernandez, "Read This Powerful Statement from Darnella Frazier, Who Filmed George Floyd's Murder," May 26, 2021, https://www.npr.org/2021/05/26/1000475344/read-this-powerful-statement-from-darnella-frazier-who-filmed-george-floyds-murd.
14. "What We Believe," Black Lives Matter, https://blacklivesmatter.com/what-we-believe/.
15. The Grio, https://thegrio.com/.
16. "Winners in Special Citations and Awards," Black News Channel, https://bnc.tv/14.

17. "Winners in Special Citations and Awards," Pulitzer Prizes, https://www.pulitzer.org/winners/darnella-frazier.
18. Miki Kendall, "Darnella Frazier's Pulitzer Citation Is Not Enough," June 12, 2021, https://www.cnn.com/2021/06/12/opinions/darnella-frazier-pulitzer-citation-isnt-enough-kendall/index.html.
19. "Staff of the Star Tribune, Minneapolis, Minn.," Pulitzer Prizes, n.d., https://www.pulitzer.org/winners/staff-star-tribune-minneapolis-minn.

Ethical Reporting in the Pandemic and Beyond

DENI ELLIOTT *and* ANDREA CHU

> "Journalism can never be silent: that is its greatest virtue and its greatest fault. It must speak and speak immediately, while the echoes of wonder, the claims of triumph, and the signs of horror are still in the air"
> —Henry Anatole Grunwald, then managing editor, *Time* magazine, 2001

The coronavirus pandemic challenged governments, citizens, corporations and social institutions to respond in unprecedented ways. News media were no exception. How well freelance journalists and legacy news organizations reported on the sudden global event depended on their flexibility to apply news judgment in ways different from before.

Prior to March 2020, ethical analysis of news coverage usually focused on a particular publication. Freezing a troubling moment in time and space provides the opportunity to circumnavigate it as though it were a sculpture. Ethics scholars and practitioners can examine and scrutinize the problem from all sides, pondering whether questionable intent masqueraded as news judgment. Story content and framing can be compared with what was believed at the time to be true. Ways that vulnerable people were harmed can be assessed. Ultimately, pre-Covid ethical analysis determined how journalists could have or should have avoided conflicts of interest, relayed inaccurate information or caused unnecessary harm to vulnerable others.

Covid-19 offered a simultaneous eruption of narratives rather than branching out from a single foundational story. The pandemic was a tsunami of illness and death; it was a shortage of life-saving supplies. It contained stories of medical workers' courage, helplessness and exhaustion and of the risk that grocery store clerks and other frontline workers were forced to face. It was the story of protective measures taken by some people and the magical thinking of others. It told stories of leaders who limited liberty to protect community and stories of leaders who declined to walk their limitations talk. It was the story of viral cacophony that resulted from political messages competing with data from scientists.

More than a year after the World Health Organization (WHO) declared the virus a pandemic, its source, as of this writing, remains undetermined. The future of the virus, variants and long-term efficacy of vaccines is unknown. In mid-2021, only one thing is certain: the pandemic story is continuing to explode in multiple directions.

Here we examine three ways that the pandemic has challenged journalists:

1. The virus has created **an ongoing narrative of uncertainty** for journalists who were more used to providing stand-alone, internally coherent stories.

2. The deluge of claims resulted in **journalistic framing that made truth hard to find**. That framing often left out important facts or focused on facts—such as illness and death census numbers—without explaining their importance, or folded misinformation and disinformation into the mix.

3. Governmental leaders used the virus to lob political attacks on opponents, tempting **a journalistic reflex to highlight the conflict between polarized perspectives and to create a false balance** between opposing claims regardless of underlying truth.

Along with meeting these challenges well, more or less, reporting in the time of Covid illustrated how fluid and responsive good journalism can be. Our review suggests that most legacy news organizations provided a palette of stories in the first year of the pandemic that included a variety of shades of ethicality. Our hope is that the best news coverage of Covid-19 will provide a model for how journalists and news organizations should cover globally evolving stories now and in the future.

We base our analysis on the unique, role-related responsibility of journalists and news organizations to provide citizens with information needed for self-governance.[1] Self-governance is construed here in its broadest conception to include personal choices such as whether to wear a mask and whether to get a Covid vaccine. It includes more traditional forms of citizen activism, such as deciding which candidate deserves one's vote. The pandemic required participation from every individual, family and community; apathy was not an option. The best stories were those that helped citizens understand the pandemic globally and its impact on them personally. The best stories gave audience members facts that led to educated action. We begin with the assumption that the pandemic, along with other worldwide concerns that loomed before us, created the need for journalists to apply new approaches to meet their role-related responsibilities.

Reporting on Uncertainty

Ongoing stories with complicated histories, a plethora of current narratives and no known outcome—such as war, terrorism, social disparity, climate change, and environmental sustainability—by their very nature have no clear margins. No one, journalist or scientist, knew what the virus would do next. Expert sources changed their messages as they synthesized new data. Reporting on uncertainty can leave citizens confused or it can help them feel empowered.

The Washington Post illustrated early and often how ethically ideal coverage focuses on helping citizens make meaning. Yet even this acclaimed news organization ignored its own complicity in creating confusion. In a *Post* story published May 28, 2021, about the origin of Covid-19, reporters wrote,

> The shifting terrain highlights how much of the early debate on the virus's origins was colored by America's tribal politics, as Trump and his supporters insisted on China's responsibility and many Democrats dismissed the idea out of hand—when the origins of the virus were in fact wrapped in uncertainty.
>
> The polarization, which left many feeling they had to embrace one theory or the other, was exacerbated by the tendency of some on the right to conflate the lab-leak theory with more easily dismissible ideas such as the notion that the coronavirus was part of a Chinese biological weapon.
>
> "Like everything else, it became politicized very early on," said Rep. Jamie B. Raskin (D–Md.), a member of the House select subcommittee on the coronavirus crisis.[2]

U.S. governmental leaders did, indeed, immediately politicize responses to the virus. But politicians could not have kept Covid in a "political opposition" frame without journalistic cooperation. "A Republican said this" balanced with "a Democrat said that" did not help citizens focus on what response to the virus was required of them personally.

As opposed to traditional journalism, which often means reporting from the perspective of a bystander with a large megaphone, reporting on uncertainty requires journalists to choose which voices to amplify and to look for stories beyond the performances designed to draw media attention.

In the early days of the pandemic, for example, CNN dutifully reported what U.S. government officials said—including public officials, scientists from the Centers for Disease Control and Prevention (CDC), the U.S. spokesperson on public health, and the U.S. surgeon general—without explaining contradictions or providing context for changing messages. Toward the end of February 2020, CNN reported that then CDC director Robert Redfield responded, "No," at a Foreign Affairs Committee meeting when asked by U.S. Representative Chrissy Houlahan, "Should you wear a mask if you are healthy?"[3]

The network repeated the March 1, 2020, tweet from U.S. Surgeon General Dr. Jerome Adams that read, "Seriously people—STOP BUYING MASKS! They are not effective in preventing general public from catching #Coronavirus, but if healthcare providers can't get them to care for sick patients, it puts them and our communities at risk."[4]

In a story on "myths and misunderstandings" on March 13, 2020, CNN reported that the mask-wearing prescription varied from country to country. "The CDC has said that Americans who are well do not need to wear face masks, while U.S. Surgeon General Jerome Adams warned that masks could actually increase the risk of infection if they aren't worn properly."[5]

By the beginning of April, the network quoted President Donald Trump, saying that while his administration recommended that Americans wear "non-medical cloth" masks, he had chosen not to follow that guideline. "I don't think I'm going to be doing it," he said. In the same story, CNN reported that Surgeon General Adams said that the mask-wearing recommendation was only a guideline that recommended the wearing of face masks in public spaces where social distancing guidelines were harder to maintain.[6]

In contrast to CNN's choice to ride the political and scientific seesaw of whether or not to mask, National Public Radio broadcast a story on April 10, 2020, that provided context for the controversy. In this report, audience members learned that Hong Kong and China had required masks since the end of January and that in some countries people could be arrested for not wearing masks. The NPR report also told listeners about cultural differences: Asian cultures had a long history of individuals' wearing face masks when ill to prevent spread to the community. The story explained that U.S. scientists had changed their recommendation from saving masks for healthcare workers to all people wearing masks when in public, once scientists learned that the virus was more contagious than initially thought and that it could be spread by people who were asymptomatic. NPR acknowledged that while U.S. scientists were urging masks as a way of decreasing spread, the World Health Organization was still balancing the dangerously low supply of masks worldwide against the likelihood of community spread in saying, "yes to masks for healthcare workers and people with symptoms, no for the general public."[7]

NPR addressed that contradictory information by including a CDC spokesperson who stressed the evolving nature of scientific understanding and said that while its guideline had changed due to increased transmission and studies that shows pre-symptomatic spread, the guideline might change again. Citizens were urged to cooperate with their officials. The story promoted the need for "consistent messages from many different levels of government." Sources said that "heads of government should lead by example, practicing what they preach." NPR did not tell audience members how to face the challenge but instead provided a broad foundation listeners could draw upon to make knowledgeable choices.[8]

Scientific Goals, Journalistic Goals and How to Achieve Citizen Understanding

Science differs from journalism in important ways, a salient point that Mark Jerome Walters's essay earlier in this collection explores. In the words of Aristotle, science focuses on what can be expected to hold always or for the most part. Journalism seeks the bizarre or unusual and then works to describe or explain it. Scientific truths, while accepted by most scientists at the time, are likely to evolve or become more nuanced as research continues and evidence is collected. Discoveries that serve as the basis for generalizable scientific knowledge, such as the communicability of a virus or the effectiveness of a vaccine, can predict future outcomes.

Statistics that have predictive power may not be able to explain what happened in a specific case. For example, analyzing factors like age and underlying health conditions may provide accurate predictions for the percentage of populations most likely to die after becoming infected with Covid-19. However, such scientific knowledge won't explain why a specific 90-year-old patient lived and a 30-year-old patient died.

Case analysis is the realm of journalism. Journalism seeks to describe and explain specific cases, without predicting what might happen in the future. Aside from forecasting the weather, journalism is not in the business of prediction. While audience members may project concerns for the future from journalistic reports, the account of a citizen's confrontation with a store clerk over mask wearing does not predict that more encounters will follow.

Predictability allows scientists to analyze risk for certain populations, but not necessarily for specific individuals. On the other hand, journalism tells community members what they can reasonably expect. If an individual learns that a bridge has been demolished to make way for new construction, they know that everyone inclined to cross the bridge will need to detour. The likelihood that a particular individual will be infected by Covid-19, however, is dependent on a variety of factors including individual age and health, as well as whether they are in the vicinity of someone spreading the infection. Explaining risk is not the goal of traditional newswriting.

To complicate matters further, people perceive statistical risk differently than they perceive the consequences of an observable fact like a demolished bridge. Individuals look to trusted sources to help them understand risk. They look to sources who make the most sense in the context of what they already believe to be true. According to crisis communications specialist Sharon Dunwoody, "Assuming that stories in *The Guardian* or on *Fox News* are trustworthy saves individuals the time needed to evaluate the credibility of each of the many sources that they encounter in the stories offered by those channels." However, what people understand will differ based on their sources of information. According to Dunwoody, while individuals may be exposed to a similar volume of messages about the pandemic, "Individuals may report relatively high levels of Covid-19 knowledge, but may, in fact, 'know' wildly dissimilar things."[9]

The varied responses by leadership within the U.S. and throughout the world made it difficult for individuals to know who or what to trust. According to Dunwoody, "While one country remains virtually locked down, another restricts only the elderly and infirm. While one city extends orders to stay home, another opens restaurants and hair salons. Country leaders uniformly express caution, but their messaging reveals wildly varying levels of coping with the pandemic."[10]

The truth—the truth that journalists needed to tell their audiences through most of the pandemic coverage—is that no one can predict the ultimate outcome in all contexts. According to philosopher Matti Hayry, "We simply do not know which choice will, in the end, be the best life saver, health promoter, or quality adjusted life year (QALY) producer overall. Nor do we know how to weigh and balance lives, health, and QALYs. Other values further complicate the matter. If the economy does not work, citizens will experience the adverse effects in their lives, possibly for years. And there are environmental, ecological, cultural, and political values which may be threatened by public policy choices."[11] Traditional journalism that presented quotes from governmental leaders and scientific experts as though those were certain and complete made even the most credible scientific sources, over time, seem as capricious as the virus and its variants. An alternative was to report what scientific experts had to say currently while including a boilerplate paragraph that emphasized the inability of scientists to be certain because of their ever-evolving findings, coupled with the need to prioritize public health in an atmosphere of uncertainty. Stories that reminded U.S. audiences that we have a long history of giving up some freedoms in exchange for public and personal safety might have provided context. Ultimately, wearing a mask and keeping social distance is no more restrictive than governmentally mandated motorcycle helmets and automobile seatbelts and child seats. Individual liberties sometimes take a backseat to public safety, such as the need to refrain from yelling "fire" in a crowded movie theater or wearing masks so that infected individuals do not threaten the health and safety of others by spreading Covid. When no one can provide definitive answers, some answers are still better than others.

Journalistic Framing and Truth-Telling

On March 18, 2021, Florida governor Ron DeSantis held a public health roundtable in which a controversial group of scientists claimed that masks were largely ineffective, should not be worn by children at school and that wearing masks could cause psychological harm. The panelists were best known for contradicting CDC guidelines and safety measures. The member most recognizable to a general audience was Dr. Scott Atlas, who, while serving on then-president Trump's coronavirus task force, spread discredited theories and encouraged citizens to "rise up" against coronavirus safety measures.[12] Some news organizations began their roundtable coverage by contrasting panelists' outlier positions with scientific consensus. Others did not.

A community news website, ClickOrlando.com, exposed the controversy at the top of their story. The headline read, "Florida Governor Gathers Panel of Experts to Validate COVID-19 Response: Gov. DeSantis Hosts Experts Known for Controversial Opinions on Coronavirus Response." The lede and nut graph read, "A year after the COVID-19 outbreak temporarily shuttered much of the economy and plunged the nation into debates over masks and lockdowns, Florida Gov. Ron DeSantis convened a hand-picked panel of health experts at the state Capitol on Thursday to help validate the actions he took against the pandemic. One by one, the experts provided vindication for DeSantis, whose insistence on lifting lockdowns, reopening schools and undermining mask mandates came under scrutiny as the public health crisis unfolded." After pointing out that DeSantis's handling of the pandemic will be a key issue in his re-election campaign, the story further described the panelists' outlier status: "The experts hailed from some of the world's most prestigious institutions but their views have been rebuked by many mainstream scientists."[13]

WINK-TV, a CBS affiliate in Fort Myers, described the panelists as "hand-picked" by the governor in the first paragraph and included the following in the third: "The experts he convened hailed from some of the world's most prestigious institutions but their views have been rebuked by many mainstream scientists, including U.S. infectious disease expert Dr. Anthony Fauci, who last year called the anti-lockdown, pro-herd immunity push 'nonsense.'"

On the other hand, Tampa Bay CBS-affiliated WTSP began its coverage of the March 18, 2021, roundtable this way:

> Florida Gov. Ron DeSantis held a public health roundtable in Tallahassee Thursday morning, where he invited a panel of scientists and researchers to weigh in on issues surrounding the Covid-19 pandemic.
> The governor was joined by former Trump White House coronavirus advisor Dr. Scott Atlas, epidemiologist Professor Sunetra Gupta, and scientific researchers Dr. Jay Bhattacharya and Dr. Martin Kulldorff at the Florida State Capitol.
> A big theme of the roundtable was fear—which that particular panel said was induced by both media and public health officials. The scientists largely rejected the steps taken by the U.S. to try to control the virus and expressed that more harm than necessary was caused by the public fear that developed around Covid-19.[14]

CDC recommendations for mask-wearing, social distancing and vaccinations were mentioned only in the last three sentences of the 712-word story.

The fact that the Florida governor convened a panel with speakers specifically engaged to validate his refusal to mandate masks or enforce vigorous shutdowns as did other states merited news coverage. What the discredited panelists said should not have been the focus for the story.

Legacy News Media Follows Social Media's Lead

Despite the governor's attempt to showcase the panelists as credible, within days, YouTube removed the discussion's recording for violating the social media's standards by communicating "COVID-19 medical misinformation." Following the lead of social media, after YouTube removed the governor's video from its platform, news organizations reported on the controversial perspective of the panelists.[15]

Before even declaring Covid-19 a pandemic, WHO director-general Dr. Tedros said that the world was fighting an "infodemic." On February 15, 2020, he said that fake news spreads faster and more easily than this virus and urged all countries and communicators to join together to fight the publication of false claims.[16] *The Lancet* highlighted the importance of factual reporting: "It is the rapid dissemination of trustworthy information—transparent identification of cases, data sharing, unhampered communication, and peer reviewed research—which is needed most during this period of uncertainty. There may be no way to prevent a COVID-19 pandemic in this globalized time, but verified information is the most effective prevention against the disease of panic."[17]

A year's experience with the pandemic and the accompanying "infodemic" shows that unverified claims were common and led to citizens' uncertainty about what to believe and how they could protect themselves, their loved ones and the community. However, it is important to note that the "infodemic" did not lead to widespread citizen panic in the U.S. or abroad.

In April 2021, the Poynter Institute's fact-checking arm, Politifact, detailed misinformation numbers as overwhelming as the number of Covid infections and deaths: "According to data shared by YouTube in March 2021, the company has removed more than 800,000 videos containing coronavirus misinformation since February of last year. Facebook reported in February [2021] that the company and its sister platform, Instagram, had removed more than 1 million pieces of COVID misinformation in the last three months of 2020. And last month [in March 2021], Twitter said it had removed more than 8,400 tweets and challenged 11.5 million accounts since the implementation of the COVID guidance."[18]

News organizations became more critical in how they reported claims from governmental officials, as social media set boundaries for what they would publish and attached flags to questionable material. It became clear that then-president Donald Trump was the major source of misinformation and disinformation.[19] The best attempt to combat the spread of coronavirus misinformation occurred when social media companies and traditional news outlets joined fact-checking programs to scrutinize their own stories pre-publication. For example, *USA Today*, Reuters, Associated Press, and Politifact joined Facebook's third-party fact-checking program, a system in which certified fact-checkers flag misinformation on the platform.[20] Covid-specific fact-checking sites sponsored by universities, news organizations and think tanks flowered to help news organizations and citizens better verify claims.[21]

News coverage of President Trump's messages about Covid-19 waned. For example, in March 2020, while six major networks showed President Trump's daily coronavirus briefings from the time that they began, within weeks, only Fox News consistently carried them in their entirety. CNN was the first to switch away moments into the daily briefing, which focused on self-congratulations, to return to its regular evening newscast, shortly followed by MSNBC. An MSNBC spokesperson said that it cut away because the information no longer helped promote the ongoing public health discussion. MSNBC political commentator Rachel Maddow was more pointed in her criticism of news coverage that focused on the president. Maddow said that if networks continued to broadcast the briefings, it was "going to cost lives."

Governments and Journalists Determine How Much Truth to Tell

Public officials shy away from truth-telling to protect their popularity among voters. Journalists publish as much truth as they can as quickly as they can. But when a governmental official pleads for information to be held to prevent public panic, even the most seasoned journalist will hesitate, despite the claim being made by the most self-serving politician.

It wasn't until September 2020 that U.S. citizens became aware that President Trump falsely claimed that Covid-19 was no more dangerous than the seasonal flu in his early messages and withheld information about dangers that he knew to be true. Trump cited "panic" as a reason for deceiving the American public. In a March 19, 2020, on-the-record interview for an upcoming book by journalist and author Bob Woodward, Trump told Woodward, "I wanted to always play it down. I still like playing it down... Because I don't want to create a panic."[22] In mid–March 2020, Trump told Woodward that he knew that Covid was deadly. Woodward faced criticism for not sharing the president's disclosure with the public or with journalists immediately.[23]

Esquire's Charles P. Pierce said, "Nearly 200,000 Americans have died because neither Donald Trump nor Bob Woodward wanted to risk anything substantial to keep the country informed." Journalist John Stanton tweeted, "There is no ethical or moral defense of Woodward's decision to not publish these tapes as soon as they were made."[24]

Others argued that as Woodward was no longer a working journalist, he did not have journalistic responsibility to report the contrast between Trump's private and public statements in a timely manner. Still others declared it a deadly conflict of interests in which Woodward put enhanced publicity for his book over public safety. Yet others thought Woodward's disclosure was unnecessary because the pertinent information was already available to journalists. The Poynter Institute's media scholar, Al Tompkins, for example, argued that Woodward's information was not vital given that there was an abundance of information at the time of the Woodward-Trump interviews that proved the deadly nature of the coronavirus. "Even in February, the evidence was clear that the coronavirus was deadly, that the threat was imminent and that the president was underplaying the danger."[25]

There were, indeed, indications early on that the White House knew of looming danger that was not being reported to the American people. In February 2020, the National Security Council ordered masks to be delivered to the White House to meet the needs for all White House employees. Masks arrived, but the message soon circulated that the president didn't want employees to wear them.

Plans were in progress for the U.S. Post Office to distribute 650 million masks—five face coverings for every household in the U.S.—in early April. That plan that was scrapped by the White House due to how it might look if the federal government issued masks to all Americans and how that distribution might reflect on President Trump's ability to control the pandemic.

As of this writing, another book on Trump's handling of the pandemic by *Washington Post* journalists has recently been published. As the authors are working journalists, they arguably had more responsibility than did Woodward to share new information with the public rather than to save juicy tidbits for their book publication. For example, if Yasmeen Abutaleb and Damian Paletta, authors of *Nightmare Scenario: Inside the Trump Administration's Response to the Pandemic That Changed History*, had known prior to the 2020 election that Trump had suggested sending passengers infected with Covid to the U.S. military compound at Guantanamo Bay,[26] that information might have made a difference to voters. In the days following the book's publication, interviews in which the journalist-authors addressed the timing of when they knew which information were not available.

In a democracy, disclosure should be the default. Suppressing information due to the potential for citizen panic is not rational during a global pandemic mediated in real time. Anyone with access to the Internet could follow pandemic reporting in any country, even if U.S. officials chose to play down the danger and U.S. news organizations chose to ignore all but the most dramatic international stories.

Missing from the controversy of the Trump/Woodward lack of disclosure was the idea that it is sometimes ethical for governmental officials and news organizations to withhold some truths.

Withholding information from the public is ethical only in cases that are public-serving rather than self-serving. Public officials who choose secrecy over transparency, because they are prioritizing popularity or other personal interests, have unethically set aside their responsibility to those they represent. Arguing that being re-elected is in the public interest creates an unwarranted and unknowable means to an end.

On the other hand, it is sometimes appropriate for public officials to withhold information to protect national security. In addition, citizens agree to governmental deception, at least indirectly, by living without protest in a society with unmarked police cars and radar monitoring to catch those speeding down the highway.

News organizations have correctly chosen to withhold information that puts innocent lives in danger when hostages are being held. They may cooperate with crisis managers during natural disasters by not broadcasting officials' belief that some evacuating citizens may not make it to safety before the levee breaks. Citizens, upon learning the full story after the fact, understand that prevention of panic and protection of lives is more important than news organizations telling in-the-moment truth. Withholding information likely to cause panic when a dam is on the brink of breach is justified because it is clear that harm is limited by not causing panic.

Research and lived experience in 2020 indicate that individuals are not likely to panic during long-term, evolving events. People tend to perceive themselves as "more immune to a risk than are others." Dunwoody reports that Americans reveal an optimism bias when it comes to Covid-19: "A recent survey supporting this 'me/them' differential pattern found that, while 62% of Americans thought the coronavirus will do a 'great deal' of harm to people in the country, only 25% felt that the virus would harm them personally."[27]

Some Stories Have Many Sides; Some Have One

In a situation in which the stakes are so much higher than a particular official's popularity, the best journalism avoids framing an issue as a contest between polarized, politicized views. This is particularly hard, as journalism has a longstanding tradition of telling citizens what governmental officials or experts are saying about important topics and of looking for the "other side" of the story. But when the issue is the pandemic, in which the only reasonable side of the story is how individuals and nations can best deal with the many facets of the problem, it is ethically problematic for journalists to create false balance between political perspectives or to create a false equivalency between facts and claims that are not evidence-based. Christiane Amanpour, multiple award winner and the recipient of more than a dozen honorary doctorates, has counseled that journalists should choose truth over neutrality: "It appeared much of the media got itself into knots trying to differentiate between balance, objectivity, neutrality, and crucially, truth. We cannot continue the old paradigm—let's say like over global warming, where 99.9 percent of the empirical scientific evidence is given equal play with the tiny minority of deniers."[28]

Scholars argue that devoting equal coverage in a news story to competing truth claims leads audiences to believe that an unlikely claim enjoys more support within the scientific community than it actually does.[29]

At the worst, this type of coverage hampers citizens' choices and can incite violence. As members of the public received mixed messaging on mask-wearing, some were led to believe that masks were, at best, ineffective. Other citizens were passionate about wearing them and insisting that all others do so as well. The resulting conflicts included unmasked individuals intentionally coughing on frontline workers in stores, screaming at or threatening business owners, and directly or indirectly causing harm and death.[30]

Ethically problematic reporting gave time and space to claims that turned out to be dangerously false without retracting or providing response to the initial publication. For example, a CNN editorial on March 7, 2020, argued that viral mutation is normal and not dangerous. "Is this something we need to worry about?" the authors ask. "No, and here's why. The first claim that the coronavirus is mutating is actually true, and it's fine!"[31] The recognition of dangerous Covid variants following that publication provides an opportunity to refer back to previous claims and explain why the new understanding is different.

The best reporting addresses known falsehoods. A different report from CNN on March 7, 2020, shows how that can be:

> President Donald Trump's top economic adviser, Larry Kudlow, falsely claimed on Friday that the coronavirus "is contained" in the U.S. Another senior Trump official, counselor to the President Kellyanne Conway, made a similar though slightly less definitive claim, saying that the virus "is being contained." **Facts First:** *Experts say the US has not come close to containing the coronavirus. They also say the small number of tests conducted in the United States so far has prevented the government from getting an accurate picture of how widespread the virus truly is.* "In the US it is the opposite of contained," said Harvard University epidemiology professor Marc Lipsitch, director of Harvard's Center for Communicable Disease Dynamics. "It is spreading so efficiently in so many places that it may be difficult to stop."[32]

Fox News was criticized for spreading misinformation, both through news and opinion programming. As media columnist Margaret Sullivan put it, "Americans who relied on Fox News, or similar right-wing sources, were duped as the coronavirus began its deadly spread."[33] Academic studies correlated citizen misunderstandings about Covid-19 with their media consumption. A joint peer-reviewed study conducted through the Annenberg Public Policy Center at the University of Pennsylvania and the University of Illinois at Urbana-Champaign, for example, showed, through "a nationally representative phone survey with 1,008 respondents," that people who got most of their information from mainstream print and broadcast outlets tended to have an accurate assessment of the severity of the pandemic and their risks of infection. But those who relied on conservative sources such as Fox News and Rush Limbaugh were more likely to believe in conspiracy theories or unfounded rumors, such as the belief that taking vitamin C could prevent infection, that the Chinese government had created the virus, and that the U.S. Centers for Disease Control and Prevention exaggerated the pandemic's threat "to damage the Trump presidency."[34]

The best reporting leans on the weight of evidence. Ideal weight-of-evidence reporting not only offers a clear explanation of what scientific experts say but also devotes text coverage and airtime to topics in proportion to their scientific validity. Journalists should look at where their sources come from, where the work was published, and whether the work is consistent with existing scientific claims. Balancing misinformation or disinformation with scientific claims only increases the chances that audience members will consider the mis- or disinformation as credible. Including disclaimers that a particular politician's claim is false only makes the news organization seem biased. The journalists' choice of frame should exclude mis- or disinformation unless that is a story in itself.

Most reporting during the pandemic was neither ideal nor unethical but was relatively unhelpful to citizens. For example, news organizations throughout the country published the daily county, state and national census of new infections and deaths. Comparative numbers per 100,000 people in geographically similar areas were rarely provided. Seldom did the methods that local health officials used to collect and record data, or comparisons with other methodologies, make it to print. Cases were often reported county-wide without attention to case clusters or to health officials' explanations for the rise or decline of cases or deaths.

Scientists throughout the world worked nonstop to better understand why some nation's infection rates soared while others remained low. These stories, while more difficult to report than the local daily litany of infections and deaths, helped audience members situate the deluge of numbers that were otherwise meaningless to report. A simple count of infections and deaths did not inform citizens about how economic disparity in health care systems played a part in those statistics. Who paid the costs for all of those sick people? Which sick people got top shelf care and which got comfort care only? To date, the answers in the U.S. largely remain unknown. A good comparative story on who pays for Covid-19 medical care ran on CNN.[35]

The pandemic presented an ideal opportunity for journalistic lessons in comparative approaches to democracy. For example, liberal democracies like the United States prioritize the rule of law, civil rights, transparency, and participatory governance. According to Hayry, "different democracies put different levels of emphasis on the common good and may assume a more lenient or stringent stand on restrictions of individual freedom."[36] American citizens might have been interested in knowing, for example, that other countries provided a contrast to the ideological and political polarization in the U.S., in the early days of the pandemic: "The Public Health Agency of Sweden and the Finnish Institute for Health and Welfare produced recommendations based mainly on epidemiological calculations, politicians made decisions according to the recommendations, and key ministers announced them to the general public as inevitable medical truths."[37] The way that the U.S. ran the pandemic was not the only way.

Some people may argue that creative reporting on uncertainty, fact-checking and telling untold stories take financial resources that a news organization may lack. Many of the changes suggested in this essay, such as ensuring that headlines and ledes focus on known facts rather than political conflict or false balance, cost nothing but a change in journalistic mindset. The pandemic and other evolving stories of global concern require new ways of reporting so that the world's citizens learn what we need to know for self-governance.

Notes

1. Tom Rosensteil and Bill Kovach, *The Elements of Journalism*, 3rd ed. (New York: Three Rivers Press, 2014).
2. Anne Linskey, Shane Harris and David Willman, "Renewed Focus on Wuhan Lab Scrambles the Politics of the Pandemic, *Washington Post*, May 28, 2021, https://www.washingtonpost.com/politics/wuhan-lab-theory-scrambles-politics/2021/05/27/55cbe448-bef6-11eb-83e3-0ca705a96ba4_story.html, retrieved May, 28, 2021.
3. Amanda Watts, "The CDC Director Just Answered a Bunch of Simple Questions About Coronavirus," CNN, February 27, 2020, https://www.cnn.com/asia/live-news/coronavirus-outbreak-02-27-20-intl-hnk/h_0a2607bada22056c9fd10010734a9e1e.
4. Leah Asmelash, "The Surgeon General Wants Americans to Stop Buying Face Masks," CNN, March 1, 2020, https://www.cnn.com/asia/live-news/coronavirus-outbreak-03-01-20-intl-hnk/h_c27f086d764c010b473ecf41dc2fd87c.
5. Harmeet Kaur, "Coronavirus Myths and Misinformation, Debunked," CNN, March 13, 2020, https://www.cnn.com/2020/03/04/health/debunking-coronavirus-myths-trnd/index.html.
6. Chandelis Duster, "This Is What the Surgeon General Had to Say About Mask Mandates," CNN, July 12, 2020, https://www.cnn.com/2020/07/12/politics/jerome-adams-surgeon-general-mask-mandate/index.html; Arman Azad and Susanna Cullinane, "US Surgeon General: Coronavirus Face Masks Promote Freedom," CNN, June 14, 2020, https://www.cnn.com/2020/06/14/health/us-surgeon-general-coronavirus-masks/index.html.

7. Huo Jingnan, "Why There Are So Many Different Guidelines for Face Masks for the Public," NPR, April 10, 2020, https://www.npr.org/sections/goatsandsoda/2020/04/10/829890635/why-there-so-many-different-guidelines-for-face-masks-for-the-public.
8. Ibid.
9. Sharon Dunwoody, "Science Journalism and Pandemic Uncertainty," *Media and Communication* 8, no. 2 (June 26, 2020): 471–474.
10. Ibid.
11. Matti Häyry, "The COVID-19 Pandemic: Healthcare Crisis Leadership as Ethics Communication," *Cambridge Quarterly of Healthcare Ethics*, May 22, 2020, https://www.cambridge.org/core/journals/cambridge-quarterly-of-healthcare-ethics/article/covid19-pandemic-healthcare-crisis-leadership-as-ethics-communication/CE6B85449991BF962CF232B2FC9CB9C1.
12. Kaitlan Collins, Jim Acosta, and Devan Cole, "Dr. Scott Atlas Resigns from Trump Administration," CNN, December 1, 2020, https://www.cnn.com/2020/11/30/politics/scott-atlas-resigns-trump-administration-coronavirus-task-force/index.html, retrieved May 5, 2021.
13. Jerry Askin, "Florida Governor Gathers Panel of Experts to Validate COVID-19 Response," ClickOrlando, March 18, 2021, https://www.clickorlando.com/news/local/2021/03/18/florida-governor-gathers-panel-of-experts-to-validate-covid-19-response/.
14. "Gov. DeSantis' Roundtable Panelists Reject Lockdowns and Mask-Wearing," 10 Tampa Bay, March 18, 2021, https://www.wtsp.com/article/news/regional/florida/desantis-public-health-roundtable-florida-state-capitol/67-e4b48bf0-7610-43e9-ba4d-eff89c5c4957.
15. Victoria Knight, "Censorship or Misinformation? DeSantis and YouTube Spar over COVID Roundtable Takedown," Politifact, April 21, 2021, https://www.politifact.com/article/2021/apr/21/censorship-or-misinformation-desantis-and-youtube-/.
16. United Nations, "'This is a time for facts, not fear,' Says WHO Chief as COVID-19 Virus Spreads," February 15, 2020, https://news.un.org/en/story/2020/02/1057481.
17. "COVID-19: Fighting Panic with Information," *The Lancet*, February 22, 2020, https://www.thelancet.com/journals/lancet/article/PIIS0140-6736(20)30379-2/fulltext.
18. Knight, "Censorship or Misinformation?"
19. David Bauder, "Networks Face Decision: How Long to Stick with Trump?" ABC News, March 23, 2020, https://abcnews.go.com/Entertainment/wireStory/networks-face-decision-long-stick-trump-69761779.
20. Clark Merrefield, "How Journalists Can Avoid Spreading Coronavirus Misinformation," *The Journalist's Resource*, February 15, 2021, https://journalistsresource.org/politics-and-government/coronavirus-misinformation-crowdsourcing-truth-mit-david-rand/.
21. "COVID-19 Misinformation Types Coding Schema & Dashboard," Covid19misinfo.org, n.d., https://covid19misinfo.org/covid-19-claim-types/.
22. Philip Rucker and Robert Costa, "Woodward Book: Trump Says He Knew Coronavirus Was 'Deadly' and Worse Than the Flu While Intentionally Misleading Americans," *Washington Post*, September 10, 2020, https://www.washingtonpost.com/politics/bob-woodward-rage-book-trump/2020/09/09/0368fe3c-efd2-11ea-b4bc-3a2098fc73d4_story.html.
23. Al Tompkins, "Was It Unethical for Bob Woodward to Withhold Trump's Coronavirus Interviews for Months?" Poynter, September 10, 2020, https://www.poynter.org/ethics-trust/2020/was-it-unethical-bob-woodward-to-withhold-trumps-coronavirus-interviews-for-months/.
24. Ibid.
25. Ibid.
26. William Hanage, "How Trump's Blunders Fueled Our Coronavirus Nightmare," *Washington Post*, June 25, 2021, https://www.washingtonpost.com/outlook/how-trumps-blunders-fueled-a-coronavirus-nightmare/2021/06/24/6cda4b44-d507-11eb-ae54-515e2f63d37d_story.html.
27. Dunwoody, "Science Journalism," 472.

28. Christiane Amanpour acceptance speech, Committee to Protect Journalists, November 22, 2016, https://cpj.org/awards/christiane-amanpour/.

29. Patrice Ann Kohl, Soo Yun Kim, Yilang Peng, Heather Akin, Eun Jeony Koh, Allison Howell, and Sharon Dunwoody, "The Influence of Weight-of-Evidence Strategies on Audience Perceptions of (Un)certainty When Media Cover Contested Science," *Public Understanding of Science* 25, no. 8 (2015): 976–991.

30. First Coast News Staff, "Woman in Viral Video Coughing on Cancer Patient in Jacksonville Pier 1 Store Arrested," July 31, 2020, https://www.firstcoastnews.com/article/news/crime/pier-1-cougher-arrested-for-assault-after-covid-contagion-video-went-viral/77-50f858fb-c103-455e-a3ee-0fa0822b0637, retrieved April 5, 2021.

31. Mary Petrone and Nathan Grubaugh, "Coronavirus Mutations: Much Ado About Nothing," March 7, 2020, https://www.cnn.com/2020/03/07/health/coronavirus-mutations-analysis/index.html.

32. Daniel Dale, "Fact Check: White House Falsely Claims the Coronavirus Has Been 'Contained' in the US," CNN, March 7, 2020, https://www.cnn.com/2020/03/07/politics/fact-check-white-house-coronavirus-contained/index.html.

33. Margaret Sullivan, "The Data Is In: Fox News May Have Kept Millions from Taking the Coronavirus Threat Seriously," Washington Post, June 28, 2020, https://www.washingtonpost.com/lifestyle/media/the-data-is-in-fox-news-may-have-kept-millions-from-taking-the-coronavirus-threat-seriously/2020/06/26/60d88aa2-b7c3-11ea-a8da-693df3d7674a_story.html.

34. Christopher Ingraham, "New research explores how conservative media misinformation may have intensified the severity of the pandemic," *Washington Post*, June 25, 2020, https://www.washingtonpost.com/business/2020/06/25/fox-news-hannity-coronavirus-misinformation/.

35. Ivana Kottasová, Tami Luhby, and Valentina Di Donato, "She Was Asked to Pay Thousands for Her Coronavirus Treatment, He Got a Free Ride. She's American. He's Italian," CNN, May 1, 2020, https://www.cnn.com/2020/05/01/health/health-care-europe-us-medical-bills-coronavirus-intl/index.html.

36. Häyry, "The COVID-19 Pandemic," 42.

37. Häyry, 46.

Teaching Journalism During (and After) the Pandemic

Tony Silvia *and* Janet K. Keeler

> "How do you teach student journalists the importance of reporting on their community when that community is closed off to them? After all, the community is where many journalistic careers begin"
> —Michael Sunderland, journalism education researcher

None of us could have known when we left our classrooms in March 2020 that it would be the last time we would see our students face to face for the balance of that year and well into the next. The rest of 2020 turned into a year of adaptation, innovation, and, to some extent, aggravation—not with our students or colleagues, but with the situation. Suddenly, upon returning from spring break, we didn't "return" at all. Instead, life became a steady, daily introduction to concepts like "the new normal" and "social distancing" and expanded rituals of hand-washing and sanitizing.

For journalism educators—and educators in general—the transition to virtual learning left many faculty and students on their own to find ways to "meet." Some institutions, such as Roger Williams University in Rhode Island, where our colleague Bernardo H. Motta (see his essay on community journalism earlier in this book) teaches, purchased premium access to Zoom for all faculty and provided workshops and information sessions to guide them through its use. Others counted on the ingenuity and resourcefulness of individual faculty members to navigate the virtual landscape alone or collaboratively. Students, many of whom were (and often are) ahead of their teachers in terms of technology, had to self-guide or sit through online tutorials to learn this way to learn. Like Google, Zoom became a verb, as in "to zoom."

Figuring out how to conduct classes was, in retrospect, the easier challenge for faculty to solve. Physical classrooms are shared spaces that build community—especially important in a discipline like journalism. In fact, the entire concept of "community" is integral to the field itself, a foundation for stories being discovered, explored, and ultimately written. Preserving community in the broader sense was among the most difficult challenges, and it wasn't only a problem for American journalism schools. As the name "pandemic" implies, it was a global problem, as recognized by educators in the United Kingdom, where one journalism instructor wrote:

> How do you teach student journalists the importance of reporting on their community when that community is closed off to them? After all, the community is where many journalistic careers begin with traditional patch reporting. Covid-19 changed the rules: Forced to share computers or work from their bedrooms, many students found common barriers to news gathering even more impenetrable. As journalism educators ... we had to re-imagine their lives under unusual constraints.[1]

Building community in the classroom is important and seemingly more difficult with remote classes. Students aren't sitting next to each other, engaging in conversation before and after class. Instructors have to employ digital tools to take the place of those interactions, and the substitutes could be small group discussion assignments or virtual break-out rooms. Add to that the need to find new ways for journalism students to practice the craft of interviewing. Events were often cancelled because of the pandemic, and students grew weary of virtual events. There weren't a lot of people on campus. If they were comfortable venturing out, they had to conduct interviews at a distance, wearing masks. In a normal semester, they meet students in other classes who become sources or provide tips for stories. That didn't happen as much. They had to work harder at finding sources to interview. In spring 2021, some students were comfortable covering outside events that included small groups where people were wearing masks. Though that offered some semblance of a return to normal, it also required teachers to keep track of who would be willing to cover an assignment in person and who would not. That required a second assignment to be created. Classes themselves were still being held virtually, for the most part.

The quandary of individualizing assignments doesn't begin to address the challenges *inside* the virtual classroom. Web cams on or web cams off? That was the question. Some faculty preferred to have students turn on their cameras because lecturing to initials in circles felt like talking to a wall. Others didn't want the cameras on because the students' backgrounds, plus the eating, drinking, and multi-tasking, could be distracting. It's best to come to terms with the fact that the synchronous virtual classroom is not like a traditional classroom. One lesson learned is that a good icebreaker at the beginning of class is discussing virtual class etiquette—a protocol that existed before the pandemic but became critical during it and will no doubt be sustained after it.

We also learned that technology issues couldn't be ignored. People got kicked out of the "classroom" if the platform's bandwidth couldn't handle over a certain number of students simultaneously. Or the instructor suddenly dropped out. Microphones were unknowingly muted. Individual Wi-Fi connections were not equal. Some were spotty, depending upon the area where the student lived or whether others in the same domicile were using the connection at the same time for data heavy purposes like video gaming or streaming. Screen sharing went awry. Technology is part of the contemporary student's DNA, but they tend to be adept at different platforms. Plugging into their knowledge and having them take the reins in the virtual classroom to teach us what they know was another community builder and confidence booster.

But just because students knew the technology didn't mean they liked it. Keeping schedules and delivery modes (hybrid, asynchronous or synchronous) straight was a challenge, as was staying on top of the changes for multiple classes. By fall semester 2020, many were Zoom-weary. For savvy teachers, however, the quick switch to online classes showed possibilities. Could we keep students more interested in a combination of course deliveries, post-pandemic? Does every topic need to be delivered face to face in a classroom just because that's what the course schedule says? The pandemic might have helped to carve out an innovative college classroom experience.

However, in the midst of the pandemic, with classes moving quickly online, instructors had to work harder just to "read the room," to look for signs that their lectures were connecting. The teacher-student connectivity, or lack thereof, might have shown up eventually in work turned in, but in the traditional classroom, the hope is always that it will be apparent through discussion. For some—students and faculty alike—it felt like the adage "building the plane while flying it" was playing out in the first full semester of all-online classes. What was working? What needed to be tweaked or eliminated? It was clear that some students were depressed and stressed by having four or five classes online, with each teacher handling the modality differently. It was easy to empathize with them because faculty were undergoing different, but similar, stress levels. Those were some of the challenges, but in the midst of reinventing instruction on the fly, there were faculty who saw significant advantages to this new way of envisioning journalism education.

Booking guest speakers through video conferencing platforms allowed people to join classes from remote locations, bringing professional expertise to our journalism classrooms that might never have been happened, given time and distance restrictions. Dr. Keeler, this essay's co-author, had speakers in her classes from Michigan, Washington, D.C., and California.[2] Even local speakers liked video conferencing because it took less of their time—no commute or paying for parking. She found that students were more engaged because they could ask questions through the chat window. Another of her innovations was holding virtual office hours and workshops which she created, sharing the link with students. By billing these sessions as "workshops," and making them specific to individual classes, and not so general, there was more participation. It became another way of building community. Students came to talk about story ideas and challenges, and they all went away more comfortable with the direction of their stories. They also gleaned sources, since their fellow students always seemed to know somebody who could be interviewed. But not all students attended these workshops, sometimes including those who could have benefited the most.

The pandemic tested the assumption by many higher education administrators that students prefer online course instruction over the traditional classroom. The studies in this area are inconclusive, with students citing numerous factors that influence their choice. One 2021 survey suggests a division between faculty and students over preference for online courses going forward. Nearly three-fourths (73 percent) of students surveyed said they would prefer to take some of their courses fully online; only 53 percent of faculty expressed an interest for continuing to teach online. Sixty-eight percent of students were also in favor of some combination of in-person and online courses. On the faculty side, 57 percent said they would prefer teaching hybrid courses post-pandemic—slightly more than those who preferred teaching fully online.[3]

Another survey cited mitigating factors like difficulty in finding a quiet place to study as affecting students' satisfaction with entirely online learning.[4] Still another found that the majority of the 5,000 college students surveyed said their experience with online classes during the pandemic was unsatisfactory, and 90 percent of the 5,0000 students, when asked, stated that they felt they should be paying less for online classes than traditional classroom instruction.[5]

Dr. Keeler's experience in her own classes reflects other social factors among her students:

> Students who aren't fond of online classes often say that they learn better in person. We need to know more about what they mean. Is it the human contact? Or is it that coming to campus and attending class puts structure in their lives? Or is it that some teachers aren't particularly good at online instruction? I know that students longed for normalcy in the fall 2020 semester but being on campus wasn't going to be normal either, sitting 6 feet away from fellow

students and everyone wearing masks. Also, online classes take more effort by students to keep up with schedules, readings and assignments without a reminder in the classroom.

Many in higher education suggest that its future survival may rely on so-called "hybrid" courses (part face to face and part online).[6] In journalism education, specifically, there are reasons to take advantage of the technology used in hybrid courses to help make journalism instruction more relevant, since the field itself is intricately linked to understanding technology and learning to use it effectively. In that sense, the pandemic may have, in hindsight, helped accelerate many students' learning curve on technology, born of the *necessity*, rather than the *choice*, to take online courses. Learning to use Zoom for their classes parallels the learning that professional journalists were simultaneously undertaking in order to complete their daily story assignments.

Perhaps one of the most important outcomes from the pandemic is that the field of journalism education began a process of self-evaluation, provoking a number of questions about why we teach the way we do and, most importantly, whether it is the only way or even the best way to teach our courses. Everything from course scheduling to lecture delivery was upended and maybe, in the long run, for the better. Questions arose such as: "Why meet twice a week because the schedule says so? What courses need to be face-to-face?" Dr. Keeler, as one example, relates, "I met once a week synchronously a dozen times for the semester and, combined with the workshops, that was enough. What was more important than them listening to me talk was getting experience in reporting, and this could be done on their own with guidance from me." Some students might even learn better by having the ability to go back and listen later to a lecture or class discussion.

Another flaw in how we have taught journalism for so long was exposed by a severe lack of proper classroom technology in many departments and schools of journalism across the U.S. A Koch Foundation survey found that even those students who were mostly satisfied by taking classes online suggested they could be improved by the use of better technology.[7] Ironically, given the accelerated demand for high-level technology in the field of journalism, in 2021, too many institutions have antiquated equipment, including low-quality cameras and poor sound systems. Those inadequacies became glaringly apparent during the pandemic and will have to be addressed if, after the pandemic, journalism education is to thrive—or even survive. Cutting edge technology, combined with instructors who know how to maximize its use, will be mandatory for delivering curricula either online or in a hybrid format.

Most of all, we will face challenges as journalism educators in redefining the entire concept of objectivity in a post-pandemic world. Perhaps it is a concept, both in practice and theory, that ought to have been challenged many times in journalism history—but it seldom is, unless we are forced to re-examine the premise that objectivity is always the most effective way to tell every story. Covid forced us as educators, as it forced practitioners, to ask ourselves questions *about ourselves*. It put before us a story that was as much about us and our families as it was about the community we cover. If professional journalists were feeling the inner conflict, so, too, were—and still are—journalism educators.

A collective named the Journalism Research Group, at England's Bournemouth University, observed early on that this was more than a pedagogic dilemma. Its origin goes deep into the roots of the discipline itself.

Journalists usually report *on* crisis, but the Covid-19 pandemic places journalists, like everyone else, *in* the crisis. When the BBC's health correspondent, Fergus Walsh, put on PPE to report from an intensive care unit (ICU) in London's University College Hospital,[8] his powerful report showed people the effects of coronavirus "from the frontline." He was reporting on a story that he was a part of, as we all were. This situation presents unique challenges for journalism that we as a small group of journalism educators have tussled with and reflected upon over the past few months. We are trying to teach undergraduate and postgraduate journalism students how to report on this crisis, how to be impartial observers, telling the stories of others, while living within it.

This raises an important, sustaining point for the future of journalism education. It is a layered yet essential discussion that must be had at multiple levels if the pandemic is to teach us how better to teach our students. As the authors of the above study reflect, "Covid-19 is redrawing the boundaries of the journalistic field. It has broken down objectivity, amplified subjectivity, and reminded students and professionals alike that, sometimes, we are all part of the story."[9]

At its most basic level, in addition to challenging the boundaries of good journalism or "best practices," as illustrated by other essays in this collection, students and faculty were challenged simply to *adapt*. At Arizona State University's Walter Cronkite School of Journalism, as at most journalism schools, projects were underway, assignments made, and a plan in process for a semester that no one could have predicted would be unlike every other in our academic lives. Former *New York Times* journalist Fernanda Santos, who teaches narrative and bilingual journalism at ASU, had a project in progress titled "What Do Dreamers Want in 2020?" that threatened to be shelved by the pandemic. Instead, she and her students were challenged to be flexible, to adapt and get the story done, but differently than originally planned.

Stay-at-home orders forced her to be flexible and teach her students to do the same. She began by asking herself,

How can I teach or what can I teach my students about reporting that can be done when they can't go out and interview people face to face? I started thinking about my own life and my own experience with my family in another country. I adapted a lot of the things that I already used to my classes or have suggested that my students use them. For example, Zoom interviews. You have the video recording, you have the audio recording. So if you're doing a video piece you can have the footage. If you're doing a digital story, you have the words that are there registered to make sure you got everything right.[10]

In the end, she sees a silver lining to the pandemic's impact on journalism instruction:

What journalism students are learning right now is a skill that's going to be helpful in the future, whether or not you're stuck at home," says Santos. "The fact that journalism students at Cronkite are now having the opportunity to use these skills in college means that when they are faced with a story that they cannot get to right away, they won't be paralyzed. I think that this is going to create a generation of journalism students who are more equipped to deal with all the different stories that we have to do these days.

In addition to exposing students to increased levels of adaptability, journalism education post-pandemic should seek to present a broader *context* to the base of knowledge students have when reporting on crises. At Georgetown University, a course was created titled "Covering a Pandemic." It consists of three modules, including writing a story about Covid that focuses on shared humanity, another on the mental health of journalists and how they cope with trauma, and the third a contextual module that "looks into the history of pandemics such as AIDS, Ebola, and the Spanish flu, as well as the Bubonic plague outbreaks in 1905 that resulted in increased discrimination against Asian Americans."[11]

Adjunct professor Britt Peterson created the course "in the hopes of educating students on the best practices of journalism and understanding news in the midst of the extraordinary circumstances that the corona virus has presented." Rather than seeing this approach as a temporary stopgap, Peterson views it as "a different type of course than the others that I have taught at Georgetown, but that is only appropriate because this is an entirely different kind of moment. We now have to think about journalism differently because it is a novel time in our history."[12] Peterson's ability to move quickly to design the new course is a lesson for all journalism educators. That she seized the opportunity to teach students how professionals react to news not only showed the mission of journalism in action but also gave students a purpose. The work they were doing was relevant to their own situations.

Because the pandemic was (and is, at this writing) such a unique experience in all our lives—for faculty, students, journalists, media organizations of every platform—it continues to present opportunities for creative responses to many of the challenges posed. Where many journalism curricula have remained stagnant since their inception, questioning their efficacy now and in the future is a vital role for journalism educators to undertake. One example of innovative instruction that could pave a road to the future came at Chicago's Columbia College. Faculty member Sharon Bloyd-Peshkin's timing was fortuitous when creating a course titled "Solutions Journalism." The course was based on four major points:

1. Focusing on a response to a known problem
2. Learning how that response came about
3. Documenting evidence of impact, reporting on any insights that were key in making the response a success that others might replicate
4. Understanding the limitations of the response and where there was room to improve.

Students work in groups of three or four and, according to Bloyd-Peshkin, "report and write about a problem they are concerned about, substantiating it with data and expert interviews, and ... all independently write one story about one response to their group's problem that includes interviews and evidence from people implementing the response, people benefitting from the response and knowledgeable people who can critique it from the outside."[13]

What made this course so different was that it was conceived pre-pandemic but had to acknowledge the ongoing disruption that lasted through the spring 2021 semester. It brought a dose of unfiltered reality both to the instructor and her students. "If my experience with emergency remote instruction in spring 2020 taught me anything," Bloyd-Peshkin says, "it was that the idealized syllabus of the past—the one created in a spirit of great optimism and enthusiasm—was not appropriate to this moment." Instead, "in the fall, my students would be struggling with the many impacts of the ongoing pandemic, the Black Lives Matter reckoning and a polarizing election season. Not only would their attention to academics be challenged; their needs would also be different and greater. This course could no longer be just about learning and creating. It had to acknowledge and address the disruption."[14]

Implicit in her experience is the question of how far and how long it is possible to shield journalism students from the "disruption" of an increasingly disruptive society and world. Further, is that our job as journalism educators? These are questions to ponder, discuss, and debate as we proceed in our traditional and virtual classrooms. While we bear responsibility for our students' physical and mental safety, we also must help them adapt to a new journalistic paradigm that we ourselves, in most instances, have never experienced. It is a complex problem that, in itself, is in search of a solution.

Notes

1. Michael Sunderland and Graham Majin, "Reflections on the Shifting Shape of Journalism Education in the COVID-19 Pandemic," *Digital Culture and Education*, June 22, 2020, https://www.digitalcultureandeducation.com/reflections-on-covid19/journalism-education, retrieved July 25, 2021.

2. Dr. Keeler's experiences, as expressed in this essay, are gleaned from her experience while teaching both online and hybrid courses in the spring and fall semesters of 2020 at the University of South Florida. Those courses included "Media Writing," "Beginning Reporting," "Senior Seminar," and "Food Writing."

3. Ria Kelly, "73 Percent of Students Prefer Some Courses Be Fully Online Post Pandemic," Campus Technology, May 13, 2021, https://campustechnology.com/articles/2021/05/13/73-percent-of-students-prefer-some-courses-be-fully-online-post-pandemic.aspx, retrieved July 26, 2021.

4. Melanie Hanson, "Online Education Statistics," Education Data, July 10, 2021, https://educationdata.org/online-education-statistics, retrieved July 25, 2021.

5. Matt Small, "Most College Students Unsatisfied with Online Learning," WTOP News, June 25, 2020, https://wtop.com/education/2020/06/survey-most-college-students-unsatisfied-with-online-learning/, retrieved July 24, 2021.

6. Adam Stone, "Making Hybrid Learning Happen in Higher Ed," Ed Tech, May 3, 2021, https://edtechmagazine.com/higher/article/2021/05/making-hybrid-learning-happen-higher-ed, retrieved July 27, 2021.

7. "Covid-19 on Campus: The Future of Learning." A College Pulse and Charles Koch Foundation Study, June 2020, https://marketplace.collegepulse.com/img/covid19oncampus_ckf_cp_final.pdf, retrieved July 27, 2021.

8. Nicki Stiastny and Adam Walker, "Coronavirus: Inside an ICU Fighting Covid-19," BBC News video, April 6, 2020, https://www.bbc.com/news/av/health-52190961.

9. Miriam Philips and David Brine, "Under Fire: Reflections on Changing Perceptions in Teaching Professional Journalism Standards," Digital Culture and Education, June 22, 2020, https://www.digitalcultureandeducation.com/reflections-on-covid19/journalism-education, retrieved July 20, 2021.

10. Stephany Rosales, "Covid-19 Pandemic Taught ASU Journalism Students Important Lesson: Flexibility," ASU News, May 22, 2020, https://news.asu.edu/20200522-solutions-asu-cronkite-school-fernanda-santos-teaching-adaptability-covid-19, retrieved July 24, 2021.

11. Shelby Roller, "Non-traditional Journalism Course Examines How to Cover Stories During a Pandemic," Georgetown College, May 22, 2020, https://college.georgetown.edu/news-story/non-traditional-journalism-course-examines-how-to-cover-stories-during-a-pandemic/, retrieved July 26, 2021.

12. *Ibid.*

13. Sharon Bloyd-Peshkin, "How Do You Adapt a Solutions Journalism Course for Online Teaching in These Uncertain Times?" Medium, August 7, 2020, https://thewholestory.solutionsjournalism.org/help-how-do-you-adapt-a-solutions-journalism-course-for-online-teaching-in-these-uncertain-times-8b1a738f2ca5, retrieved July 26, 2021.

14. *Ibid.*

Part IV

Revisiting News Practices Post-Pandemic
A Roundtable Discussion

"Journalism After the Pandemic" Roundtable

Introduction

Rather than writing a traditional conclusion, the contributors to this collection mutually decided that the best way to culminate the exploration of the topic would be to conduct a roundtable discussion summarizing and expanding upon the book's major points. The recorded conversation took place on June 22, 2021, and lasted an hour and ten minutes. The full transcript[1] was edited for length, redundancy, and clarity to what you see here. The goal is that you, the reader, will observe and experience a conversation among colleagues and, through that lens, take away more insight about the past, present, and future of journalism. The hope is that you may even come away with more questions to ask of yourself, your colleagues, and your students.

Speakers

Tony Silvia, Bernardo H. Motta, Lillian R. Dunlap, Jennifer Fleming, Deni Elliott, Mark Douglas Iusi, LaCrai D. Mitchell, Casey Frechette, Janet K. Keeler, and Mark Jerome Walters.

Tony Silvia: *How has reporting during the pandemic improved the practice of journalism, or has it?*

Mark Douglas Iusi: Well, I think it has improved reporting. I consider it a stress test, a stress test not only for the institutions, but for the reporters and the producers and the people who generate the content. And I think it forced everybody who's still in the profession to be better at it, by necessity.

LaCrai D. Mitchell: I think that in a lot of ways, it forced us to rethink what exactly reporting meant, right? You know, I think before the pandemic, I talked a little bit about how sometimes a pitch (for a story) would get ruled out, if we felt like we couldn't get to a place. The thinking was that you have to be there, you have to be in the setting to tell this story. And during the pandemic, we couldn't limit ourselves to sort of the traditional barriers that would sometimes get in the way of us telling a story. Instead, we had to really rethink and re-imagine and ask ourselves, "How can I still tell this story without being in that place? How can I still tell this story without getting this video that would add to it, you know, in a way that's still impactful?" So I think one of what I hope is one of the lasting impacts on journalism is that we keep having those re-imaginations of what storytelling can look like, even without physically being in places.

Tony Silvia: So the general question to the group is, will *we re-imagine journalism? Is this a permanent change? Or a permanent evolution? Or will we just go back to our old ways of reporting stories, whether they were good or not?*

Janet K. Keeler: Oh, feels like the changes are permanent *for now*. What I mean by for now is that I think that there a lot of journalists that figured out they can do their jobs without going into a newsroom every day. And they could do them just fine. And they liked that. I think they'll be eager to get back to talking to people in person, going to places and having that kind of interaction. I don't think they're eager to get back to the newsroom with endless meetings, and editors bugging them, and things like that. So I think that some of those changes are going to stay for the time being, especially for journalists in big cities, because they don't want that commute. They've realized now, "My God, it's like two to three hours a day" wasted in some sort of transportation issue when they could be doing other things. I'm not sure that it has totally anything to do with journalism, but it certainly does have something to do with being happy with your life. I do think that they're eager, at least the people I talked to, are eager to get back to journalism, where they're talking to people face to face, they're going on assignments, or they're hanging out, but there's some stories, they didn't really maybe need to do that.

Mark Jerome Walters: I think the pandemic has changed how journalists get their stories, but it hasn't improved journalism. Like any stress test, to borrow Mark [Iusi's] word, it has shown areas of weakness. It's produced something of a blueprint for needed changes. I don't know if this will stay in the printer tray or be acted on. But what I do know is that during the pandemic, for whatever the shortcomings of our profession, I've never been prouder to be a journalist.

Lillian R. Dunlap: I think many of the changes we've talked about in the book will stay just because the landscape has changed so much that there's more competition. For example, journalists now understand that they have to ask more questions. One example is the young woman who took the photo, who did the video of the George Floyd murder; there was a source of information that you wouldn't normally think about. But it also raised some more questions that you had to go follow some more interviews, you had to find and gather some more specific perspectives. And I, I'm really hopeful about this. I'm maybe naive about it. But I'm really hopeful that it is that impetus for journalists to say, you know, there are more questions to ask. There's context here that I really have to go after. And, in the meantime, some other entities have grown up during the pandemic that I think are going to stay and put pressure on journalists to hold on to some of those new approaches learned during Covid.

Deni Elliott: I'd like to think that good journalism will no longer be reporting a story, but rather looking for the stories that surround a particular event or issue. I think that some of the worst reporting we saw during the pandemic involved the politicization of the pandemic. Politicians are going to politicize stuff, but journalists don't have to repeat what they say and make that the story. And I think that journalists have shown that there are many stories out there surrounding an important global issue. And that there are many ways of telling the story. I'm thinking of the wonderful visuals that we got from the *New York Times*, *Washington Post* and some other places, and the really good comparative stories that some journalists did, not just reporting what's going on locally or nationally, but putting the local and national reporting into a global context. And I would like to think that that would continue.

Tony Silvia: One of the things that our colleague Mark Iusi has said is that the problem is not that we don't have enough reporters; we have too many repeaters. And that certainly was something that I think came to light during Covid. Yes, a lot of repetition, but not quite as much reporting. But that was a systemic problem before the pandemic. There's also an assumption that good reporting always has to include both sides to any story.

Deni Elliott: Well, I think that there's this traditional misunderstanding among people in the practice of journalism, as well as some outside of it, of the idea that there are two sides to a story, and I think that's just wrong. Some stories have one side, some stories have hundreds of sides. But if you, if journalists create this two-sided way of reporting to create some kind of false balance, then you lose the story.

Mark Jerome Walters: You not only lose the story, but sometimes you effectively create a false one. By missing the other sides of a story, you can turn what in reality is a debate into a seeming conflict.

Mark Douglas Iusi: If nothing else, this pandemic really highlighted that journalists need to understand about balance and false equivalence and what you just said, you don't need to balance a fact with something that is absolute fantasy, just because it's the opposite of what someone else said. I think that because of the flood of misinformation and, even worse, disinformation, a lot of journalism organizations really had to come to grips with that concept that they didn't have to report that false side or the ridiculous side or the Q-Anon conspiracy theories that had no basis or evidence. And I think that one of the things that came out of this pandemic is that we began sort of getting down to what we ought to be doing, and not getting bogged down in the false idea of fairness, when really, we're not being fair to anybody if we're obscuring and not getting to the truth.

Mark Jerome Walters: Yes, if there's one thing the pandemic has changed for good, it is that it has brought about the death of both-sides-ism.

Tony Silvia: Bernardo, along the lines of the changes we've seen, how has community journalism changed during the pandemic?

Bernardo H. Motta: A lot of the mainstream journalists and a lot of those in the community newsrooms and alternative newsrooms were able to actually get in the same places because of the pandemic. That's because many of the news conferences, many of the webinars, many of the training sessions for journalists and others moved online. They became a lot cheaper and a lot more accessible, many of them free, including bringing people from other countries. So you have all these people who never had a chance to actually meet and discuss journalism at this level, like what we're doing here. And now they're talking. Now they're talking about the different ways you approach journalism. So you're looking at people who never had this chance of sharing the spotlight now showing what they can do.

Tony Silvia: And in large part that had a lot to do with technology putting community and alternative journalists on a level playing field with so-called mainstream journalists. It seemed to me that anyone with a Zoom account—and anyone could get a Zoom account—potentially gained an access to an audience.

Casey Frechette: I think that one of the great opportunities and challenges in the pandemic technologically was the access to data that reporters and editors had. And the sheer amount of data, and the speed at which the data was changing, seems to be without precedent. And that data became the basis for any number of visualizations, interactive simulations, dashboards, the list goes on and on. And I think for many consumers, these visualizations became a gateway to the pandemic story. It's a split-second understanding of where we are in the current state of things.

But I think that there's a major potential pitfall here, and it speaks to the idea that the technology, the data, perhaps is neither good nor bad, or maybe it's a little bit of both. I think the particular challenge here is that there's often a misnomer that data is data, data is objective, data is good, data is going to give us something that we can really hang our hat on. And that's not always the case. So the data that journalists have been relying on, for the most part, has been data that's been released by county governments, local governments, and from countries, that in some cases, have been disorganized in how they've been tracking things. In some cases they may have been intentionally skewing numbers to create a certain understanding of what's happening in their respective areas. And I think that we've seen some really valiant efforts to filter out the noise and to create data that is valid and is meaningful, but not always. And the data, once it becomes visualized, once it's packaged in a really accessible, easy to understand way—and this is something that we've seen journalists excelling at in ways that governments don't; governments publish the data, but not in a way that's comprehensible, understandable. Journalists can make it understandable, but if we're not hypervigilant, we could inadvertently be amplifying something that's not true because of a problem earlier in the chain of how that data reached us.

Mark Douglas Iusi: I think there was a paradigm change during the pandemic when it came to the data element. I think in the past, journalists have more or less accepted government supplied data as gospel, as the truth, as factual and objective, like all the business data we get from the stock market, the economy, and so on. It seems to be pretty hard and true. Then comes the pandemic. And then comes the statistics and the numbers of how many infections and where are the infections? And what is the infection rate and how many people are dying in nursing homes? And at the beginning, I think journalists were simply repeating what they were hearing from the government sources that they were following. And somewhere in the middle of that, things started happening, like in New York with the governor and the nursing home deaths. And now we know that those statistics weren't all true and that data was really bad, apparently. Investigative journalists started challenging and questioning the data that they were receiving, and that was an important paradigm shift and an important turning point.

Tony Silvia: Journalists always face ethical issues, but I think the number and the severity of those issues were exacerbated at the pandemic's height, don't you think?

Mark Douglas Iusi: Oh, absolutely. And the funny thing is, you didn't have to be brilliant or a data scientist to figure this out. In Somalia and in Nigeria, the governments were boldfacedly lying about not having a Covid problem. The good journalists in those countries started interviewing grave diggers and ambulance drivers and getting data from the people who were actually collecting the real numbers. And so I think there was a lot of work around there and a lot of really good reporting, through creativity and innovation and just, you know, following your gut.

Tony Silvia: *When you're reporting a pandemic, can you do it at arm's length? I'm sure you can, but can you do it well, can you do it ethically? Can you do it representatively?*

Mark Jerome Walters: Doesn't that question apply to all reporting? No first person, no emotion. Just because the reporter hides those doesn't mean they're gone. I wonder how many journalists wrote "objective" stories about Covid when they themselves were infected? As humans, can we really ever deliver the "machine prose" of truly objective reporting? Maybe the pandemic helped to drive home this long-debated point.

Janet K. Keeler: Remember that those reporting on the pandemic were also suffering from the pandemic. It's not like a reporter out covering a fire, you know, it's happening *out there*; it's happening in your home, you're afraid of getting sick, maybe your company, your media company is not really providing you with the proper equipment to be out there anyway. Maybe you have someone in your family that's sick, there's all kinds of stuff that was happening to them, too. It makes it extraordinary in that sense. So I think that's something that we have to consider when we start kind of picking apart coverage. You know, people were in their bedrooms going, what the hell, I know, I'm working for a company that's not even helping me with my cell phone bill, or, you know, my Wi-Fi sucks. So, to me, it's remarkable how much work was done.

Tony Silvia: *I think journalism education is a big piece of this, not only in terms of its past and its present, but its future. If professional journalists were having problems covering the pandemic story, what about student journalists? What kinds of direction should we give them in terms of their preparation for covering any future pandemics?*

Jennifer Fleming: I think student journalists experienced a lot of the things professional journalists did, but they were essentially volunteers. Some are volunteering, some are minimum wage workers on their campus press. And they have little experience with journalism, in terms of training or just experience. I think overall, you lost a sense of community and continuity, but I think they also had increased opportunities to connect in terms of moving forward. Student journalists learned to look at their work within the context of freedom of expression and of the press, but also within the institutions that they're a part of, because in the end, they are students first and foremost, and there are regulations and rules that apply to them that wouldn't apply to professional journalists. In terms of our program, there were protests in our own city. And of course, as a journalist, as a student journalist, you go to the protest. Well, stop the presses! Overall I think the pandemic pushed student journalism in new directions.

LaCrai D. Mitchell: One of the things that I thought was particularly interesting was you talked about how students found themselves facing this inner conflict of, "Do I go out and cover what's happening in my community, or at this protest? Even if our rules at the student newspaper say no, right now? Do I just take off my media badge and go out there? Because this is a once in a lifetime moment, and I have to be there." And I wonder if, based off of the observations that you had during your research, what does that mean for future big stories and how students respond to the institutional rules in place? Do institutions have to start considering in moments like that the rulebook has to change?

Jennifer Fleming: Again, you have that conflict with "this is a big story, we have to report it." I think that looking ahead there will be an element of news literacy as part of student journalism training. We may take the approach that, "Okay, if there is a rule in place, but we're not going to stop you from attending anything; you are free." However, the editor will choose whether to publish that after the fact. So I think that this has given us a way to really look at our own policies and practices. Collegiate journalism doesn't have the support that major news organizations do. For example, if you're going to cover a protest for the *LA Times*, you have security, there is a chain of command, and we do not have that infrastructure at all, but as a private citizen or a citizen journalist, you can still exercise all these rights, just not in an official capacity.

Tony Silvia: If we look at the ultimate experiential education for journalism students, this might have been it, right?

Jennifer Fleming: Yeah, I think so, absolutely. I think experiential learning is a big part of journalism. But again, when you get into dangerous situations, that changes the conversation. We had a student who was arrested and spent the night in jail, and that was a wake-up call for him. His camera and equipment were taken by authorities, and numerous journalists were also arrested or roughed up at this particular event in LA. It got real, all of a sudden, because things were no longer abstract. These are very serious issues.

Tony Silvia: It seems to me that that role for an educator really got much more real when advising students how to cover Covid or protests related to George Floyd or Black Lives Matter, right?

Bernardo H. Motta: There are a few things that we can learn not just from the pandemic and protests, but also in different ways of reporting. The protests, for example, exactly, because our newsrooms on our university, for example, have that kind of infrastructure to protect our students from being arrested or suffering violence. How do we tell better stories and not treat people like just events? You're taking those people's stories, sometimes very hurtful stories, very traumatic moments, and trying to encapsulate that in one short story after only a couple of hours or even sometimes a couple of minutes that you spend with them. So it became a really good opportunity for us to actually go over all of this and give our students a level of trauma training to help inform their reporting.

Tony Silvia: Lillian, diversity is something that you're an expert in and have spoken about over the many years that we've known each other. What was the impact of the pandemic on diversity in our newsrooms?

Lillian R. Dunlap: I think in terms of the reporting, and storytelling, a lot has been gained. I think that just having to cover, for example, the issue of social justice, and the protests, the marching, covering the killing of George Floyd, and so forth, has pushed reporters. I hope to the extent that we stay pushed, we'll ask different and more questions to broaden our understanding of what the story is—that any story, whether the story of the pandemic or the story of racial justice and inequity—is really multiple stories. When it comes to our newsrooms, I'm less optimistic about that, about beefing up our journalists of color in the newsroom. We've sort of had crises before and then, when the crisis died down, the result looked about the same. But my optimism comes with other media that are cropping up to fill in some holes; now we have Grio, now we have Roots, and we'll have other journalistic concerns that are going to crop up that will be focused on diversity. So the conversation will continue to be enriched by the contributions of the focus and skills of those journalists. In both broadcast and print, old terms, and digital too, we have year after year done these surveys and studies about how many people of color or how many women there are in newsrooms and, of course, it's always discouraging. Even when there is progress, it's so small that it barely moves the needle. And I don't think anybody, or a lot of people, will stop caring about that, but I also think what people will start caring about is where can they get the information that they really need and focus less on who's actually in the newsroom. That's good, but it can also be bad for diversity.

Tony Silvia: I'm reminded of Workforce 2000, a diversity initiative undertaken by the American Society of Newspaper Editors. The goal was that we would have people of color represented in our nation's newsrooms to the same percentage they are in the general population. And when 2000 came, it was very discouraging. It's been 21 years and the needle hasn't moved that much.

Lillian R. Dunlap: No, it hasn't. But I'm hopeful that the pandemic has really forced journalists to come up with more tools and ask more questions. Many of the reporters covering both the pandemic and the racial justice protests were young, White people. We've learned that Covid disproportionately impacted communities of color and that, up till George Floyd, those marching in the street were overwhelmingly Black. Now journalists are asking themselves, "Who are those other people? And how do we cover them? And why isn't their input in the story? Why has it been missing in the reporting that we've done up until this time?"

Mark Douglas Iusi: Lillian, I think you make a good point there. If I were a news manager today, of course, I would be vigilant and concerned about the makeup and the demographics of the people that work in my newsroom, those who report the news and produce the news and manage the news. But I think it's even more important that we recognize and gauge the voices and the diversity of the people that appear in our newscasts. And in our stories. Regardless of the color of the person holding the microphone, what's the makeup of the person answering the questions, and are those people being represented, not just fairly, but adequately and accurately?

Tony Silvia: And I think from an audience perspective there were so many more people who might not ordinarily watch that much media, right? And while they're watching for Covid coverage, for information that is important to them, they couldn't help but see the racial reckoning piece of this because it was melded right in with the pandemic coverage. So now you have people who are being exposed to ideas that they'd never been exposed to before or possibly cared about or didn't know they cared about, but they couldn't avoid it. The George Floyd story was running parallel to the pandemic story and suddenly White audiences couldn't run from that story because everywhere they turned, they were inevitably going to see it. And they were going to have to do their own reckoning with it. So maybe, potentially, that's a positive outcome.

Lillian R. Dunlap: I would say, potentially, journalists and journalism educators like us are listening, and understanding the implications for us to prepare people to continue to do this work in the way that we've described as being a step forward. We're going to have to really listen and take this to heart. Because really the audience, yes they were watching, but they're watching with their same eyes and ears, many of them. They're going to need reinforcement here. They're going to need some backfill, some education, some assurance that this is real. It's not something that is one-off and we care because we cared about the pandemic. This is the way our lives are going to go forward.

Tony Silvia: *There is one question I think is really central that we haven't touched on. That is part of what we we've talked about, over the last year, year and a half, together and with others of our colleagues and some students. Are journalists better prepared to cover the next pandemic, if there is one, than we were in covering Covid? None of us want that to happen. If it does are we better prepared and equipped to do a better job?*

Mark Douglas Iusi: Everybody who was out there reporting and trying to do the work learned a certain amount of self-sufficiency and the confidence in themselves that they didn't need an entire institution behind them to get the job done. I mean, there were network anchors doing live reports on their own TV shows from home with their kids in their laps just out of camera range. There were things that people did, they didn't think would be possible. It was like covering a hurricane that is blowing down your house, along with everybody else's, and still continuing to do that. So I think, people became more self reliant. I think they became more creative. I think they used technology but didn't necessarily depend on it. I think people who survived this professionally and succeeded had to become better.

Janet K. Keeler: I think it also showed some of the holes in the support. Like Mark said, there were obviously a lot of people doing broadcasts from their living rooms and stuff, but then there were also people that were in danger. And I think it also showed that not everybody's got your back, because of money problems, because of being unprepared. When you're talking about the *New York Times*, compared to the *Sarasota Herald Tribune*, it's a world of difference. There was a lot of inequity there on what was going to be available to you for support.

Deni Elliott: Janet makes a really good point. I think that particularly in American journalism, we've learned it's one thing to read about the dangers that international journalists run into. It's something else for journalists to realize the dangers that every one of them run into, by doing the important stories. I'd like to think that consuming news during the pandemic made citizens more savvy about the information that is being offered. I'm not sure that's the case. But I am sure that journalists are more savvy. I think that with social media sometimes spreading misinformation, journalists realized that they had to stop the floodgates. And I think legacy news media figuring out how to report around this information while in the middle of it all taught us a lot.

Casey Frechette: In terms of whether we're better prepared next time,

I believe a lot of that's going to come down to what the recovery looks like. And I think part of that is addressing inequities in resources that only got worse as the pandemic progressed. Also looking toward what new support systems can be brought into play and how journalists can be better protected not only in physical environments but also online, where it's becoming increasingly hostile and dangerous to be a journalist. There's further reckoning needed on these fronts as well. And unless something happens in a systematic way, or a systemic way, I would be a little concerned about journalism's ability on the whole to take on a challenge and a story on the magnitude of the pandemic that we've just gone through.

Mark Douglas Iusi: I don't think journalism should be a combat sport, but it's become much more of one in the last four years and in particular most recently with government leaders striking back, making threats—either threats or just snide remarks—but sometimes actual death threats against journalists and imprisoning them and actually carrying out those things. What we've seen here is a real growth in aggressiveness toward the press in our efforts to ferret out the truth and striking back at us. And also, I think, the next wave is press, the members of these institutions, protecting each other, covering each other's backs. It has become a much more aggressive atmosphere. And that's something that journalists are going to have to reckon with. We have to prepare for that and have strategies for fighting back without physically fighting back, but by being ethical and proper and principled in what we do.

Mark Jerome Walters: The majority of people, once out of school, get most of their medical and other scientific information from the media. The pandemic really showed the critical role of journalists in the information chain. Sometimes as journalists we find ourselves in the role of passively disseminating critical health information. I think the pandemic has reinforced for CDC and other public health organizations that it is in their own best interest to work with journalists more effectively, to teach them and help them become better reporters on the health front. In other words, to help them better prepare for the next big public health crisis.

Jennifer Fleming: I believe we are better prepared. What does that mean? I mean, we all know what it's like to live through a pandemic, personally and professionally, but is journalism as a whole better prepared? I think this story proved how global our world really is. Yet no one was paying attention to the rumblings of Covid outbreaks worldwide at the beginning, or very few news outlets were. Where is the main story? What are some science stories from overseas to demonstrate the truly interconnected nature of society? As we've just been talking about online harassment and bullying, it's not exclusive to journalists. It's a huge problem. We're seeing more and more in-depth articles about the issue as a whole, maybe because now journalists are a part of that as well. In terms of journalism, education, how do you deal with that? How do you deal in a free speech environment? With people exercising free speech? Even if it's ugly speech? I don't know the answer. But civility is something I think that people are talking about across industries because of the frenetic nature of certain social media platforms, made even more frenetic during the pandemic. So we're better prepared, but what will we remember of what we learned? I'm not sure. We all know how to adapt to a pandemic. But again, will we be in a position to help prevent one?

Lillian R. Dunlap: I'm listening to Jennifer, a nagging thought just came to mind. One of the best things that the pandemic has taught us is the importance of understanding belief, and how that differs from person to person. It has taught us how belief is affected by fact. And how that becomes a part of the story, whether you want it to or not. Not only the beliefs of the people that you're talking to, but your own, and how all of those need to be examined, accounted for, you know, and checked, so that you can walk away with an understanding of really what happened. You can't even do that if you're not taking into account how people behave. I'm not pointing any fingers because we all have those beliefs to acknowledge and go past. But if we don't even understand that they're there, and how impactful they are on the ways that people act and react, then we'll miss the story and miss the opportunity of communicating. And if there's ever another pandemic, that's an opportunity we can't afford to miss.

Note

1. Transcribed using Otter (https://otter.ai).

Suggestions for Further Reading

Allen, Mike. "Fauci Says People Are 'Misinterpreting' the New CDC Mask Guidance." *Axios*, May 19, 2021.
Allsop, Jon. "The Media Industry's Preexisting Conditions." *Columbia Journalism Review*, May 18, 2020.
———. "Unmasking Certainty." *Columbia Journalism Review*, summer 2020.
Anthes, Emily. "The Delta Variant: What Scientists Know." *New York Times*, June 22, 2021.
Armstrong, D. "Data Heroes of Covid Tracking Project Are Still Filling U.S. Government Void." *Bloomberg*, November 20, 2020. https://www.bloomberg.com/news/features/2020-11-20/covid-tracking-project-volunteers-step-up-as-u-s-fails-during-pandemic.
Becket, Charlie. "The Future of Journalism Post COVID-19: Technology, Diversity, and Collaboration." London School of Economics and Political Science, June 12, 2020. https://blogs.lse.ac.uk/polis/2020/06/12/the-future-of-journalism-post-covid19-technology-diversity-and-collaboration/.
Bell, E., and J. Posetti. "Pandemic Project Asks What Is Needed to Keep Journalism Viable." *NiemanReports*, May 13, 2020. https://niemanreports.org/articles/what-is-needed-to-keep-journalism-viable/.
Bieler, Des. "Oklahoma State's Mike Gundy Says His Team Needs to Play for Benefit of State Economy." *Washington Post*, April 7, 2020.
Bird, Mike. "The False Choice Between Lockdowns and the Economy." *Wall Street Journal*, April 6, 2020.
Crowley, J. "'Adapt or die': Newsrooms amid COVID-19 Pandemic." *WAN-IFRA*, April 29, 2020. https://wan-ifra.org/2020/04/adapt-or-die-newsrooms-amid-covid-19-pandemic/.
Dahlstrom, Michael F. "Using Narratives and Storytelling to Communicate Science with Nonexpert Audiences." *Proceedings of the National Academy of Sciences* 111, supplement 4 (2014): 13,614–20.
Daley, Beth. "#covid-19: Social Media Both a Blessing and a Curse During the Coronavirus Pandemic." *The Conversation*, March 22, 2020. https://theconversation.com/covid19-social-media-both-a-blessing-and-a-curse-during-coronavirus-pandemic-133596.
Darrach, A. "What Has Journalism Learned from the Pandemic?" *Columbia Journalism Review*, winter 2020. https://www.cjr.org/special_report/what-has-journalism-learned-from-the-pandemic.php.
Drexler, Peggy. "What's Behind the Trauma of Taking Off Masks." *CNN*, May 5, 2021. https://www.cnn.com/2021/05/04/opinions/americans-confused-and-comforted-by-masks-drexler/index.html.
Ecker, Ullrich K.H., Stephan Lewandowsky, Briony Swire, and Darren Chang. "Correcting False Information in Memory: Manipulating the Strength of Misinformation Encoding and Its Retraction." *Psychonomic Bulletin and Review* 18, no. 3 (June 1, 2011): 570–78.

Elfrink, Tim, Ben Guarino, and Chris Mooney. "CDC Reverses Itself and Says Guidelines It Posted on Coronavirus Airborne Transmission Were Wrong." *Washington Post*, September 21, 2020.

Fazio, Marie. "How Mask Guidelines Have Evolved." *The New York Times*, April 27, 2021.

Foss, Katherine A. *Constructing the Outbreak: Epidemics in Media and Collective Memory*. University of Massachusetts Press, 2020.

Fox, Maggie. "What's the Science Behind CDC's Decision to Say Fully Vaccinated People Don't Need Masks?" *CNN*, May 14, 2021.

Fox News. "Lt Gov Dan Patrick." *YouTube*, March 23, 2020.

Gatling, Alex. "Bias in Reporting on the Covid-19 Pandemic." *North Star Editions*, August 2021.

IFJ (International Federation of Journalists). "Exposed: The Crisis Facing Journalism in the Face of COVID-10." April 30, 2020. https://www.ifj.org/media-centre/news/detail/category/press-releases/article/exposed-the-crisis-facing-journalism-in-the-face-of-covid-19.hml.

Ingram, M. "Coronavirus Patterns Make Local News Even More Important." *Columbia Journalism Review*, May 21, 2020. https://www.cjr.org/the_media_today/coronavirus-patterns-make-local-news-more-important-than-ever.php.

Jenkins, Sally. "Some May Have to Die to Save the Economy? How About Offering Testing and Basic Protections?" *Washington Post*, April 18, 2020.

Kamb, Ava. "The False Choice Between Public Health and Civil Liberties." *Voices in Bioethics* 6 (2020).

Kennedy, Dan. "The Johnson and Johnson Vaccine Announcement and the Limits of Journalism." 2021.

Kirby, Brendan. "23 Alabama Deaths Reported After Shots—but Health Experts Warn Against Making Link." *Fox10 News*, April 9, 2021. https://tn-archive.fox10tv.com/news/coronavirus/23-alabama-deaths-reported-after-shots-but-health-experts-warn-against-making-link/article_f7e52cac-997c-11eb-bce4-d7128e32a1b5.html.

Konnikova, Maria. "How Headlines Change the Way We Think." *New Yorker*, December 17, 2014.

Levina, Marina. *Pandemics and the Media*. New York: Peter Lang International, 2014.

Lewis, Seth C. "The Objects and Objectives of Journalism Research During the Coronavirus Pandemic and Beyond." *Digital Journalism* 8, no. 5 (May 27, 2020): 681–89.

Loane, Sara. "The Challenges of Covering Coronavirus: How We Can Help." Thomson Foundation, 2020. https://www.thomsonfoundation.org/latest/the-challenges-of-covering-coronavirus-how-we-can-help/.

Mair, John, Tor Clark, and Neil Fowler, eds. *Populism, Pandemic, and the Media: Journalism in the Age of Covid, Trump, Brexit, and Johnson*. Suffolk, UK: Abramis Academic, 2021.

McPhillips, Deidre, and Maggie Fox. "Risk of Dying from Covid-19 40 Times the Risk of Rare Blood Clot After Receiving J&J Vaccine." *Local 3 News*, May 12, 2021. https://www.local3news.com/local-news/vaccine-tracker/risk-of-dying-from-covid-19-is-40-times-the-risk-of-rare-blood-clot/article_6f9f14da-4bd3-580e-aba8-ab972e92b396.html.

National Academies Press. "Institute of Medicine (US) Forum on Medical and Public Health Preparedness for Catastrophic Events. The 2009 H1n1 Influenza Vaccination Campaign: Summary of a Workshop Series." 2010.

Newman, Nick. "Journalism, Media, and Technology Trends, and Predictions 2021." Reuters Institute, January 27, 2021. https://reutersinstitute.politics.ox.ac.uk/journalism-media-and-technology-trends-and-predictions-2021.

Oliver, David. "David Oliver: The False Dichotomies in Pandemic Commentary." *The BMJ* 372 (2021): m4937.

Papa, Arienne. "Reporting on Covid-19: Challenges and Strategies." New York Academy of Sciences, July 14, 2020. https://www.nyas.org/ebriefings/2020/reporting-on-covid-19-challenges-and-strategies/.

Perreault, Mildred F., and Gregory P. Perreault. "Journalists on Covid-19 Journalism: Communication Ecology of Pandemic Reporting." *American Behavioral Scientist* 65, no. 7 (2021): 976–91.

Pollock, John C., and Douglas A. Vacoch, eds. *Covid-19 in International Media: Global Pandemic Perspectives.* New York: Routledge, 2021.
Posetti, Julie, Emily Bell, and Pete Brown. "Journalism and The Pandemic: A Global Snapshot of Impacts." International Center for Journalists, April 2020. https://www.icfj.org/sites/default/files/2020-10/Journalism%20and%20the%20Pandemic%20Project%20Report%201%202020_FINAL.pdf.
Radcliffe, Damian. "The Impact of Covid-19 on Journalism in Emerging Economies and the Global South." Thomson-Reuters Foundation, 2020. https://www.trust.org/i/?id=45123257-a52d-4060-b0da-dad111b0c52d.
Solutions Journalism Network. Articles tagged "coronavirus." The Whole Story, 2020. https://thewholestory.solutionsjournalism.org/tagged/coronavirus.
Sonmez, Felicia. "Texas Lt. Gov. Dan Patrick Comes Under Fire for Saying Seniors Should 'Take a Chance' on Their Own Lives for Sake of Grandchildren During Coronavirus Crisis." *Washington Post,* March 24, 2020.
Stewart, J. "COVID-19 Guide for Visual Journalists." The Everyday Projects, November 12, 2020. https://www.everydayprojects.org/covid19-guide-for-visual-journalists.
Streisguth, Thomas. "Reporting: Pandemic 1918–1920." November 2, 2020. Archive LLC.
Tameez, H. "Newsrooms Can Prosper with Remote Work—but They Have to Make the Right Adjustments First." NiemanLab, August 3, 2020. https://www.niemanlab.org/2020/08/newsrooms-can-prosper-with-remote-work-but-they-have-to-make-the-right-adjustments-first/.
University of Michigan Office for Health Equity and Inclusion. *Covid-19 Vaccine Communication Handbook.* University of Michigan, 2021.
Wen, Leana S. "Opinion: The CDC's Mask Guidance Is a Mess. Biden Needs to Clean It Up." *Washington Post,* May 17, 2021.
Wright, Lawrence. *The Plague Year: America in the Time of Covid.* New York: Knopf, 2021.
Yong, Ed. "Why the Coronavius Is So Confusing." *Atlantic,* April 29, 2020.
Zillmann, Dolf, and Hans-Bernd Brosius. *Exemplification in Communication: The Influence of Case Reports on the Perception of Issues.* Mahwah, NJ: Lawrence Erlbaum, 2000.

About the Contributors

Andrea **Chu** is a digital journalist from Sarasota, Florida, who works for a news station in the Tampa Bay area. She is pursuing a master's degree in digital journalism and design at the University of South Florida's St. Petersburg campus.

Lillian R. **Dunlap** is the executive director of Your Real Stories Productions and is the principal/CEO of Communication Research Enterprises, LLC, specializing in strategic consulting in diversity and global mindset initiatives. Previously, she was a member of the diversity and leadership faculty at the Poynter Institute.

Deni **Elliott** is a globally recognized media ethics expert. She is the Eleanor Poynter Jamison Chair in media ethics and press policy at the University of South Florida's St. Petersburg campus and a professor of journalism and digital communication. She is also the co-chief project officer of the National Ethics Project, and the author of more than 200 articles and book chapters, as well as the book *Ethics for the Digital Era* (2018).

Jennifer **Fleming** is chair of the Department of Journalism and Public Relations at California State University, Long Beach. Her research focuses on journalism education, media literacy, and news literacy, on which she has written articles and presented at academic conferences. She has worked at CTV as a writer and producer to *CTV National News with Lloyd Robertson* and *Canada AM*.

Casey **Frechette** is an associate professor and chair of the journalism and digital communication department at the University of South Florida's St. Petersburg campus. He teaches digital media and researches the role of technology in learning. He was an interactive learning producer with the Poynter Institute's News University, where he worked with faculty and industry leaders to design and build custom training experiences for a community of 200,000 learners.

Mark Douglas **Iusi** is an award-winning journalist whose investigative reports and series have triggered judicial reforms, revealed government waste and exposed consumer fraud. His work has received three Emmy awards and has been published in professional journals for ethics and investigative journalism. He has written more than 350 newspaper stories for the *Tampa Tribune*, where a number of his still photos have also appeared.

Janet K. **Keeler** is a senior editor at the Penny Hoarder and has spent 35 years in print journalism, including 22 years at the *Tampa Bay Times*, where she served as the paper's food and travel editor for much of her tenure. She is also an adjunct professor at the University of South Florida's St. Petersburg campus, where she was the creative force behind the school's Food Writing and Photography Program.

LaCrai D. **Mitchell** is an associate producer for the CBS news program *60 Minutes*, working in its political reporting unit. Prior to her time at *60 Minutes*, she was an embedded reporter filing stories for all CBS News platforms about the Biden and Trump campaigns during the 2020 presidential election. She has written extensively about her experiences on the campaign trail.

Bernardo H. **Motta** is an assistant professor of journalism at Roger Williams University and specializes in environmental, community and ethnic journalism practice and education. His research focuses on how community-based journalism can address errors committed by historical newspapers when reporting on ethnic and disenfranchised communities. He is a coeditor of *Engaging with Environmental Justice* (2011).

Teresa **Puente** has spent her career reporting on immigration and Latino issues in the United States and Mexico. She has worked with the *Chicago Tribune*, the *Chicago Sun-Times*, the *Press Telegram* in Long Beach and the *Orange County Register*. Her work has been published widely, including in *Time*, *The Guardian*, *The Hill* and *Latino* magazine. She is an adjunct professor of journalism at California State University, Long Beach.

Tony **Silvia** is an emeritus professor of journalism and digital communication at the University of South Florida's St. Petersburg campus. A faculty fellow of the National Academy of Television Arts and Sciences, he has produced a series of media-issues programs for PBS, worked as a correspondent for CNN, and garnered three Emmy Award nominations and an Associated Press Award for best documentary. He is the author or editor of eight books, including *Dyslexia and the Journalist* (2021).

Mark Jerome **Walters** is a professional journalist and veterinarian who teaches narrative journalism and reporting, with a focus on science and medicine, in the Department of Journalism and Digital Communication at the University of South Florida. He holds a master's in journalism from the Columbia University School of Journalism and a DVM from Tufts University School of Veterinary Medicine. He is the author of five books.

Elliott **Wiser** lectures at the Poynter Institute and spent 38 years in the media industry, including as the president and general manager of WTSP-TV, news director at WTVR-TV, and producer and reporter at CNN Headline News. He has 12 years of experience as an award-winning television anchor and business reporter. He was a contributing author to Ann Utterback's *Broadcasting Through Crisis*.

Index

Adams, Jerome M. 107, 175, 186
Allsop, Jon 99, 108, 115–118
alternative media 96
anecdote 18, 67, 103, 105, 113–114
anecdotes *see* anecdote
Asian American Journalists Association 98, 164
Associated Press 11, 87, 180, 218
The *Atlantic* 107, 116, 148, 215

balance (in reporting) 15, 77, 94, 114, 120, 173, 178, 183, 186, 204
barriers to professional development 93, 190, 202
Biden, Joseph (U.S. president) 25–26, 33–37, 48
Black Lives Matter 45, 84, 97, 162, 165, 167, 170, 186, 207
Black Press 95–96
Bradenton Herald 27, 29
Brown, Neil 143–146
Burbank, Joe 27

California State University 76–77, 86
Callihan, Ryan 27
Campaign reporting 32–47, 64, 218
campus news sources 77
CBS News 32, 35–36, 44, 218
CDC 105, 107–109, 112, 115–116, 121, 129, 175–76, 178–179, 186, 211, 214
CNN 13, 51–52, 70–72, 108–109, 112, 116, 120, 166, 170, 174–175, 180, 184–188, 213–214
collegiate journalism 76–78, 83, 85–86, 207
Columbia Journalism Review 34, 98–99, 108, 115–117, 147, 213–214
community centered journalism 88, 94, 96, 87, 189, 204
Coronavirus 125, 195
covering protests 31

deception 111
Deggans, Eric 23
DeSantis, Ron 52, 64, 67, 74, 178–179
Detroit News 26

DiCarlo, Patricia 52
digital news 143, 145–146, 151, 160, 162
diversity 2, 23, 83–84, 92, 99, 161–164, 170, 208–209, 213

echo chamber (effect) 119
ethical decision making 15, 69, 149, 172, 174, 181–187, 2025–206, 211
ethics 1–2, 15, 25, 31, 84, 94, 99, 111, 116, 172, 187, 214, 217

Facebook 40, 44, 90, 92, 118, 125–126, 128, 132, 149, 158, 180
Fagan, Kevin 19
false choices 105, 110–111, 114
Fauci, Anthony 109, 116, 213
false dilemmas 110
Floyd, George 18, 21, 41–42, 48, 83, 87, 161–162, 164–170, 203, 207–209
Forbes 86, 106, 142, 147
foundational changes 172
Fox News 13, 116, 120, 122–123, 177, 180, 184–185, 188, 214
framing 131, 133, 172–173, 178, 183

Georgia 33, 38, 46
Government 17, 44, 52–58, 61–68, 71, 88, 92, 104–105, 107, 113, 124, 126, 146, 149, 153, 155, 161, 166, 172–174, 176, 178, 180–187, 205–206, 211, 213
grassroots journalism 39, 91
Gupta, Sanjay 109

Haelle, Tara 106
Harvard University 119, 128, 184
humanistic journalism 94

inclusion 161–163, 170
infodemic 124, 127–128, 133, 179–180
Instagram 80, 82, 126, 128, 180
investigative journalism 50, 52, 55, 59–62, 68, 70–75, 97, 217
isolation 11, 18, 23, 52, 57

journalism education 83, 189, 193, 195, 197, 206

219

220 Index

Korlhan, Antisa 51, 53, 56, 71–72, 75
Kumar, Anita 25

Leen, Jeff 56
Lewis, Seth C. 104, 116, 214
loss of newsroom jobs 21

McClatchy News Service 25
McGivern, Kylie 57, 67, 72, 75
Medill Media Industry Survey 146
mental health (related to the pandemic) 14, 18, 20, 76–78, 80–81, 85–86, 89, 195
Miami Herald 20, 29, 167
misinformation 22, 69,–70, 113, 117–119, 121, 123–128, 131–132, 173, 180, 184–185, 187–188, 204, 213
MSNBC 13, 73, 120, 180–181
Murrow, Edward R. Program for Journalists 50

n=1 *see* anecdote
narratives 15, 112, 117, 172, 174, 213
National Association of Black Journalists 22, 98, 164, 166, 170
National Association of Hispanic Journalists 98, 164
Netflix 13
New York Times 58–60, 105, 109, 111, 150, 154–155, 165 194
news judgment 86, 129, 172
newspaper industry challenges 8, 12, 17, 31
Nieman Journalism Lab 68, 75, 87, 99, 147, 213, 215
NLGJA: The Association of LGBTQ Journalists 164
North Carolina 30, 36–37, 43, 49
Northwestern University 126
NPR 23, 127, 131, 175–176

Orlando Sentinel 27–28

Pew research studies 12–13, 16, 22, 26, 31, 43, 125–126, 132, 137, 147
Politico 25
post pandemic journalism 14–15, 28, 30- 31, 47, 99, 139–147, 161, 168, 170, 191–195, 197, 200–212
Poynter Institute 11, 17, 19, 61, 73, 140, 143, 152, 180–181, 217–218
press freedom 28, 62, 64, 72–74, 93
public health 43, 57, 63–64, 87, 104–131, 178–181, 16, 211, 214

quotes 1, 177

racial inequities 22, 43
Radio Television Digital News Association (RTNDA) 143, 162
Reiley, Laura 23
remote interviews 47

reporter *see* journalists
Reporters Without Borders 55
Republican National Convention (2020) 44–45
responsibility (of the press) 12
Ressa, Mari 54
Reuters Institute 159, 214
Rutgers University 99

safety 9, 18, 20, 46–47, 56, 69, 78, 84, 122, 128, 159, 178, 181, 183, 196
San Francisco Chronicle 19
scientists 103–104, 106–109, 114, 116, 122, 149, 152, 173, 175–179, 183, 213
Snapchat 118, 126
social justice 77, 82, 168
social media 10, 22, 28–29, 41, 59, 84, 90–91, 119–132, 137, 143, 149, 180, 212–213
solutions journalism 90–91, 93, 97–98, 197. 215
South Carolina 32–37, 46
Spanish language journalism 81, 99, 195
student media 76–86
Super Tuesday 34-3, 39–40, 46, 48
systemic racism 99, 164–165, 167, 169

Tampa Bay Times 20–21, 31, 89, 140, 143–144
Tinder 128
Tompkins, Al 17, 19, 31, 61, 73, 181, 17
Trump, Donald 60–61, 127, 180–181
"Trump Bump" 60
Twitter 48, 59, 108, 118, 122–123, 125, 127–128, 160, 180

uncertainty 37, 49, 80, 105, 107–108, 110, 114, 120, 173–174, 178, 180, 186–187
University of Illinois 50, 58, 72, 99, 185

vaccine 1, 63–64, 68, 74, 104–105, 112–114, 117, 126, 128–129, 137, 153, 173, 176, 214–215
viability and sustainability of the press 194
virtual interviews 25, 40, 43
voters 33–38, 40, 43, 46, 48

Wall Street Journal 16, 111, 116, 120, 154–155, 213
Washington Post 6, 8, 10, 11, 17, 18, 19, 56
White House press corps 25
WHO (World Health Organization) 52, 54, 60, 124, 126, 128–130, 151, 173, 175
Wikipedia 126
working from home 27
World Partnerships 51, 54
Wright, Colleen 20

YouTube 48, 116, 128–129, 179–180, 187, 214

Zoom 10–11, 13–14, 16, 23, 29, 39, 56, 66, 72, 78–80, 82, 85m 138, 157, 189, 193, 195, 204